State Building and International Intervention in Bosnia

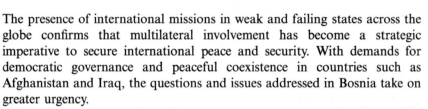

The presence of international missions in weak and failing states across the globe confirms that multilateral involvement has become a strategic imperative to secure international peace and security. With demands for democratic governance and peaceful coexistence in countries such as Afghanistan and Iraq, the questions and issues addressed in Bosnia take on greater urgency.

Focusing on Bosnia after the Dayton Peace Agreement (DPA) in 1995, this book examines the role of the international community in state building and intervention. It makes two arguments that challenge conventional, power-sharing approaches to conflict management based on group representation and elite collusion. First, the author explores the idea that effective intervention requires moving beyond the dichotomy between international imposition of state building measures and local self-government. When compromise among the former warring parties proves impossible and domestic institutions cannot autonomously guarantee efficient policy-making, the presence of international staff in domestic institutions can guarantee further democratisation and local ownership of the peace process. Second, this book argues that the long-term transformation of conflict requires the active involvement and empowerment of domestic civil society groups. Instead of considering domestic society as a desolate blank slate, international intervention needs to build on local resources and assets, which are available even in the aftermath of a devastating war.

Based on extensive field research, this book will be of interest to students, scholars and policy-makers struggling to understand and improve upon the dynamics of international intervention, and to those with a specific interest in the Balkans.

Roberto Belloni is Lecturer in International Politics at the School of Politics, International Studies and Philosophy at Queen's University Belfast, UK.

Security and Governance series

Edited by Fiona B. Adamson, School of Oriental and African Studies, University of London
Roland Paris, University of Ottawa
Stefan Wolff, University of Nottingham

This series reflects the broadening conceptions of security and the growing nexus between the study of governance issues and security issues. The topics covered in the series range from issues relating to the management of terrorism and political violence, non-state actors, transnational security threats, migration, borders, and "homeland security" to questions surrounding weak and failing states, post-conflict reconstruction, the evolution of regional and international security institutions, energy and environmental security, and the proliferation of WMD. Particular emphasis is placed on publishing theoretically-informed scholarship that elucidates the governance mechanisms, actors and processes available for managing issues in the new security environment.

Rethinking Japanese Security
Peter J. Katzenstein

State building and International Intervention in Bosnia
Roberto Belloni

The UN Security Council and the Politics of International Authority
Edited by Bruce Cronin and Ian Hurd

State Building and International Intervention in Bosnia

Roberto Belloni

Routledge
Taylor & Francis Group

LONDON AND NEW YORK

First published 2007 by Routledge
2 Park Square Milton Park Abingdon Oxon OX14 4RN

Simultaneously published in the USA and Canada
by Routledge
270 Madison Avenue, New York, NY 10016

Routledge is an imprint of the Taylor & Francis Group, an informa business.

© 2007 Roberto Belloni

Typeset in Times New Roman by
Taylor & Francis Books
Printed and bound in Great Britain by
Biddles Ltd, King's Lynn

British Library Cataloguing in Publication Data
A catalogue record for this book is available from the British Library

Library of Congress Cataloging in Publication Data
A catalog record for this book has been requested

ISBN 10: 0-415-44925-1 (hbk)
ISBN 10: 0-203-93800-3 (ebk)

ISBN 13: 978-0-415-44925-0 (hbk)
ISBN 13: 978-0-203-93800-3 (ebk)

To
Dino Tomasini
(1912-2003)
and
Ida Lolli
(1920-1999)

Contents

Acknowledgments   ix

List of abbreviations   xi

1   Introduction   1

2   Bosnia and international intervention   14

The Dayton deal: between partition and reintegration   15
International aspects of the Dayton Agreement   20
The intervention template   25
The intervention debate   28
Conclusion   42

3   Democracy from scratch   43

Institutional promises   44
Institutional problems   50
Proposals for change   54
The constituent peoples' case   58
Implementation and impact   61
Conclusion   71

4   Elections and electoral engineering   73

Consociational democracy and early elections   74
The rise of electoral engineering   78
The 2000 elections   80
The permanent election law and the 2002 elections   87
Conclusion   95

5   The limits and virtues of civil society   96

The political economy of peace   97
Growth and the ethnicisation of the economy   102
The rise of NGO development   109
Civil society that works   118
Conclusion   121

6   The antinomies of refugee return   123

    Displacement and the problem of minority return   125
    Forced repatriation and the creation of 'displaced warriors'   131
    Breaking the population logjam   136
    Impact and sustainability   144
    Conclusion   149

7   From NATO to the EU   151

    Future prospects I: European horizons   151
    Future prospects II: towards a 'post-settlement settlement'   160
    Conclusion   172

8   Conclusion   173

    The limits of international intervention   174
    Taking stock of positive lessons   181

    Notes   186
    Bibliography   192
    Index   209

Acknowledgments

Many friends and colleagues helped me improve my thinking along the long, tortuous path to the publication of this book. I was fortunate to receive expert guidance and support from Jack Donnelly, Tom Farer and Paul Viotti during my years at the Graduate School of International Studies at the University of Denver. Julie Mertus and Tim Sisk were remarkably encouraging when I thought I would not be able to complete this project. A research fellowship from Harvard's Belfer Center for Science and International Affairs between 2002 and 2004 gave me the opportunity to write a first draft of this book. Harvard provided me with both financial assistance and a stimulating home to test some of my ideas. My work benefited in particular from helpful critiques from participants in the BCSIA International Security Program brown bag seminar and the World Peace Foundation Program on Intrastate Conflict seminars.

The manuscript was revised and completed at the School of Politics, International Studies and Philosophy at Queen's University Belfast. Thanks to the Head of School Shane O'Neill for making the department an ideal research environment and to Adrian Guelke and Rick Wilford for their help. A small grant from the School allowed me to travel to Bosnia again in the summer of 2005 to undertake further research. Lively exchanges with students on the MA class in National and Ethnic Conflict Management pushed me to clarify my thoughts and made me appreciate the importance of linking teaching and research.

I received comments on some of my previous papers on Bosnia and on various chapters of this book from Florian Bieber, David Chandler, Bruno Coppieters, Chip Gagnon, Sarah Kenyon-Lischer, Neophytos Loizides, Tony Lott, Ben Reilly, Tim Sisk, Arnaud Vaulerin and Toby Vogel. An anonymous reader from Routledge went well beyond the normal duty of a reviewer by providing me with in-depth and very useful criticism. I thank you all. I am also grateful to Heidi Bagtazo for taking a chance on a first-time author, to Amelia McLaurin for guiding me through the intricacies of publishing a book, and to Laurence Cooley for his editorial assistance. Needless to say, I am solely responsible for any remaining errors.

Every time I travelled to Bosnia for my fieldwork I met competent and warm people who were always willing to help me. Many thanks to all of those Bosnians and international officials alike who took the time to talk to yet another foreign researcher. Massimo Moratti was especially supportive both in sharing his expert views on international intervention and by making me feel at home in Sarajevo.

Parts of this book have appeared previously in different forms. Sections of Chapter 5 are reproduced with permission from Roberto Belloni, 'Civil Society and Peacebuilding in Bosnia-Herzegovina', copyright © International Peace Research Institute (Oslo) PRIO, 2001, by permission of Sage Publications Ltd. I am grateful also to Taylor and Francis publishers for permission to reproduce in Chapter 4 parts of 'Peacebuilding and Consociational Electoral Engineering in Bosnia-Herzegovina', *International Peacekeeping*, 11 (2): 2004 and in Chapter 6 parts of 'Peacebuilding at the Local Level: Refugee Return to Prijedor', *International Peacekeeping*, 12 (3): 2005.

Finally, and most importantly, I am grateful for the support of my loved ones. Silvia Casini coped cheerfully with my mood swings and made me understand that there is more to life than work. Both my parents and my grandparents never quite understood why I left Italy to embark on an academic career abroad, but always assisted me in more ways that I can describe. My grandfather Dino was especially puzzled by my frequent trips to Bosnia. Unlike me, he never had the luxury of visiting the former Yugoslavia in civilian boots. In the early 1940s he was sent across the Adriatic to fight on behalf of an Italian regime he despised. With a clever stratagem he was able to return to Bologna to marry my grandmother Ida. One year later my mother was born. My grandparents' strength, faith and resilience allowed them to survive the hardships of wartime and the persisting poverty of a countryside untouched by the Italian post-war economic boom. I dedicate this book to them, in loving memory.

List of abbreviations

AEO	Association of Election Officials of BiH
AFP	Agence France Press
AI	Amnesty International
AV	Alternative Voting
BCR	Balkan Crisis Report
BiH	Bosnia and Herzegovina
CoE	Council of Europe
CRPC	Commission on Real Property Claims
DPA	Dayton Peace Agreement
DPs	Displaced Persons
EC	European Community
ECHR	European Court of Human Rights
ESI	European Stability Initiative
EU	European Union
FDI	Foreign Direct Investment
FRY	Federal Republic of Yugoslavia
GDP	Gross Domestic Product
GFAP	General Framework Agreement for Peace (The Dayton Accords)
HDZ	Croat Democratic Union
HVO	Bosnian Croat Army
ICC	International Criminal Court
ICFY	International Conference on the Former Yugoslavia
ICTY	International Criminal Tribunal for the former Yugoslavia
IEBL	Inter-Entity Boundary Line
IFOR	Implementation Force
ICB	International Commission on the Balkans
IMF	International Monetary Fund
IBL	Institutionalisation Before Liberalisation
KM	*Convertibilna Marka*
MMCs	Multi-Member Constituencies
MZ	*Mjesna Zajednica* (administrative unit at the neighbourhood level)
NATO	North Atlantic Treaty Organisation
NGOs	Non-Governmental Organisations
NHI	New Croatian Initiative
OHR	Office of the High Representative
OSCE	Organisation for Security and Cooperation in Europe
PDP	Party of Democratic Progress

PIC	Peace Implementation Council
PICSB	Peace Implementation Council Steering Board
PLIP	Property Law Implementation Plan
PR	Proportional Representation
RRTF	Regional Return Task Force
RS	Republika Srpska
SAA	Stabilisation and Association Agreement
SAP	Stabilisation and Association Process
SBiH	Party for Bosnia
SCC	Serb Civic Council
SDA	Party for Democratic Action
SDP	Social Democratic Party
SDS	Serb Democratic Party
SFOR	Stabilisation Force
SNS	Serb People Alliance
SNSD	Party of Independent Social Democrats
SPRS	Socialist Party of Republika Srpska
SRS	Serb Radical Party
UNDP	United Nations Development Prógramme
UNHCR	United Nations High Commissioner for Refugees
UNGA	United Nations General Assembly
USAID	United States Agency for International Development
VAT	Value Added Tax
VOPP	Vance-Owen Peace Plan

1 Introduction

The Bosnian peace process has transformed a bloody conflict into a cold peace, creating the conditions for the attenuation of historical ethnic and national rivalries. Yet, political antagonism between Muslims (often identified with the religiously neutral term Bosniak), Serbs and Croats remains severe. Bosniaks continue to see the strengthening of the central Bosnian state as their main political goal. Many Serbs and Croats prefer wide local autonomies and the development of further ties with neighbouring Serbia and Croatia respectively. The 1995 Dayton Peace Agreement (DPA) aimed to manage such tensions by preserving the territorial integrity of the state while endorsing the internal separation of the three main groups into two semi-independent entities: the Bosniak-Croat Federation and the Serb Republic (Republika Srpska – RS). It was a settlement designed to end three and a half years of the most brutal conflict on European soil since the end of World War II.

A massive international military and civilian presence was deployed to secure the peace. From early 1996, Bosnia has been the theatre of one of the most complex and large-scale peace operations ever undertaken. At the outset, the primary aim of international intervention was to avoid the outbreak of a new war. To this end, international agencies endorsed the need to separate the parties physically in ethnically homogeneous enclaves and limit the frequency of contact among them. They endorsed the view that Bosnians of different ethnic and national groups should be kept entirely separate and each group left to govern autonomously its own political, social and economic life. This minimalist goal soon proved unsustainable, forcing international agencies to get involved increasingly in Bosnian affairs to remove obstructive politicians, arrest indicted war criminals, defend individual human rights, support civil society and promote economic development and regional cooperation. These broader goals required an intrusive and assertive international presence. Since late 1997, international intervention gradually evolved from a strategy of providing assistance to the local parties to a de facto protectorate.

However, despite considerable international involvement and investment, the continuing divisions between the three main national communities still threaten the peace process. While armed confrontation is not a realistic possibility more than a decade since the end of the war, Bosnia's three main communities are profoundly divided and consider their mutual relations in zero-sum terms. Each community has been developing its own particular national markers (i.e. language) and denies the interdependence that characterised most of recent Bosnian history. Part of the Bosniak leadership has been flirting with the Islamic revival stimulated by the war – despite their stated commitment to the preservation of a multinational state. Radical, Wahabist Islamists are also growing increasingly bold, worrying both secular Bosnians and adherents of traditional Balkan Islam (Heći-mović 2006). Bosniaks, Serbs, and Croats alike still take the following view: dominate or be dominated, impose one's will or withdraw. Bosniaks' willingness to develop the state-wide institutions further make both Serbs and Croats fear the possibility of being dominated via institutional means.

Despite the international commitment to building and strengthening a multi-ethnic polity, the three main communities remain physically seperate in most areas. The political process has produced only modest gains for the (comparatively) moderate representatives of the three communities. The Party of Independent Social Democrats (SNSD) and the Party of Democratic Progress (PDP) in the RS have made important gains at several electoral exercises but did not succeed in marginalising extreme nationalists. At the October 2006 elections, the SNSD was able to affirm itself as the most important RS party – but only after its leadership campaigned on a nationalist agenda of separation from Bosnia's common institutions in Sarajevo. In the Federation, a Coalition for Change, including several moderate Bosniak and Croat moderate parties, was able to win the elections and rule between 2000 and 2002, but quickly lost the confidence of the electorate because of an overall weak and indecisive performance in office. At the October 2006 elections, the moderate Party for Bosnia (SBiH) achieved an important electoral success, thanks primarily to a sharp increase in its nationalist rhetoric. The SNSD in the RS and the SBiH in the Federation are mirror images of each other – political parties that moved across the ideological spectrum to become perhaps as nationalist as those radical parties that waged the 1992–95 war.

The way in which the peace process has developed, with both advances and setbacks, has raised a number of debates. To begin with, international commentators wonder whether or not Bosnia can survive as a multinational state. Can Bosnia's three main communities, deeply divided by profound mutual distrust, manage their differences peacefully and continue to live in the same geographical and political space? Or should political boundaries be re-drawn to create new nation-states, each with a clear ethnic majority? Whether the state should fit the people, or the people should fit the state, is a question that has divided liberals for a long time. While Lord Acton believed that the coexistence of several national groups in the same state is the best guarantee of its freedom, John Stuart Mill argued that a necessary condition for preserving and developing free institutions is that the boundaries of government should coincide with those of nationalities. Similarly to Mill's view, some analysts, whom we can identify as 'historical determinists', argue that the internationally led enterprise of supporting a state with limited legitimacy among its citizens is doomed to fail. The long-term political future of Bosnia, they argue, lies in the inevitable creation of ethnically homogeneous nation-states (Hayden 1999; Stokes 2003; Kaufmann 1999; Waters 2004). Others have pointed out how the continuing uncertainties about Bosnia's future are due not to the obvious fact that multi-national states are hard to preserve in the aftermath of a bloody conflict, but rather that the preservation of national diversity requires a more assertive international role (Caplan 2005; Cousens and Cater 2001; Donais 2005; Paris 2004).

Theoretical discussions on multi-ethnicity have led to a debate about which institutional arrangement can best accommodate the different needs of the three main Bosnian communities. Is consociationalism, a form of power-sharing widely adopted in conflict areas, the most appropriate institutional design to further the Bosnian peace process? The DPA is a prototypical consociational agreement, since it requires political elites to share power, in addition to prescribing proportionality in government and guaranteeing mutual veto rights and communal autonomy (Bieber 2006a; Bose 2006). Critics of consociationalism, however, question whether making ethnic differences integral to institutional design and relying on national elites' willingness for cooperation is an appropriate long-term strategy (Belloni and Deane 2005; Roeder and Rotchild 2005). Critics have also argued that the implementation of consociational principles is responsible for at least some of the setbacks in the peace process, in particular continuing segregation among the different communities.

The next main debate, closely linked with the first one, concerns the role of international intervention in preserving multi-ethnicity, building viable and legitimate state institutions, and, more broadly, furthering and sustaining the peace process. How can international organisations best contribute to the implementation of the DPA and the deepening and strengthening of peace? How to ensure that local mechanisms are in place gradually to hand over governing responsibilities to local institutions? Again, slow progress has led some observers to criticise the work of international interveners. 'Strong interventionists' argue that the establishment of a full-blown international protectorate and the presence of an assertive international force to protect liberal and multi-ethnic values at an early stage of the peace process could have brought about important beneficial results (see Donais 2005 and various reports from the influential think-tank, International Crisis Group).

'Autonomists' have taken the opposite stand, highlighting how post-Dayton international interventionism achieved some success but at grave cost. International agencies often imposed decisions on recalcitrant local parties, overturned policies taken by democratically elected politicians; removed elected officials (including serving presidents and prime ministers) and generally undermined the domestic capacity to formulate and implement public policy. While it is undeniable that the work of international organisations served a useful purpose primarily in preventing a return of armed hostilities, 'autonomists' argue that Bosnia as a whole should be given full ownership and control over its own political destiny (Bose 2002; Chandler 1999; Ivanić 2005; Knaus and Martin 2003). The autonomist position is useful in terms of underscoring the limits of international intervention, but less so in identifying a workable alternative. Although the need for greater local autonomy and democracy has intuitive appeal, it is not a blueprint for what should replace international assertiveness. Rather, to the extent that a possibly premature departure of international organisations is likely to lead to the further entrenchment of nationally homogeneous statelets, the autonomists' view is consistent with that of historical determinists, and might lead to the ethnic partition of the country.

Assessing the political future of Bosnia is inextricably intertwined with evaluating the progress made since the signing of the DPA in late 1995. As this book will show, despite persisting sectarianism, there have been major changes – many of them attributable to international intervention. More than a million displaced people were able to return home after the end of the war; many indicted war criminals have been arrested and tried; the state has grown considerably in both strength (the capacity to plan and execute policies and enforce decisions) and scope (the number of functions and goals taken on by the government); and Bosnia has begun the first steps towards membership in the European Union – an achievement that looks even more impressive when considered in the light of the situation of the country at the end of the war in 1995. Yet, many Bosnian citizens still see their state as alien and unrepresentative. Bosnia suffers from a 'stateness problem' (Linz and Stepan 1996: 16), whereby profound disagreements about the territorial boundaries of the political community and who has a right to citizenship remain. Tellingly, national symbols remain contested. Bosnia's national anthem, for example, is purely instrumental, since the three main communities could not agree on the lyrics. Even in this watered-down form, only the Bosniaks find the anthem reflects their patriotic attachments. Ninety-three per cent of Serbs prefer the Serb national anthem *Bože pravde* (God of Justice) while 76 per cent of Croats fell that the Croat national anthem *Lijepa naša domovino* (My Beautiful Homeland) best captures their national identity.[1]

Overall, the Bosnian experience raises important question about the ability of international intervention to transform weak and failing states into autonomous and self-governing political entities. How can international involvement influence local political and social processes in the direction of inter-ethnic cooperation and compromise? What, if any, long-term benefit does such involvement have? Is intervention prolonging the agony of those involved and delaying the inevitable demise of the Bosnian state? Or is it an indispensable component of a long-term democratisation process whose benefits need more time to become irreversible? What lessons can post-settlement international intervention in Bosnia teach to other cases of intervention in weak and failing states worldwide?

The arguments of this book

This book makes two main arguments, both of which address directly the debates briefly outlined above. The first major argument of this book involves the role of international agencies in sustaining and deepening the peace process. Post-Dayton international intervention has not been as successful as hoped for – at least in light of the high level of international political, economic and financial involvement. The criticism of international intervention put forward by historical determinists, strong interventionists and autonomists has at least some degree of justification. The compelling question is why intervention has been somewhat disappointing and how it could be restructured to meet the expectations and needs of other similar cases of multilateral intervention in weak and failing states.

Three main lessons can be drawn from more than a decade of experience in Bosnia. First, third parties' multiple objectives complicated the overall effectiveness of international intervention. International agencies have been oscillating between accepting the social disorder which emerged from the war and promoting diversity, pluralism and coexistence. In practice, this range of objectives delayed and complicated the local adoption of democratic reforms. Second, despite the robust and assertive international presence, intervention had a bias towards maintaining the status quo. The focus of international actors has been to preserve stability as much as possible while neglecting the more important need for change. This focus led international actors to support the dysfunctional political structures that emerged from the war, while failing to buttress the development of alternative political and social projects in civil society. Third, the focus on stability went hand-in-hand with a preoccupation with achieving visible and concrete short-term results. International agencies often focused on top-down discrete projects leading to clear and measurable outputs which could be touted as a 'success' (such as organising elections), instead of long-term structural initiatives (such as reforming the political system to make elections more than an ethnic count). In the process, they dictated priorities and forms of implementation – imposing short-term deadlines, preventing the development of meaningful partnerships between international and local actors, and blaming Bosnians for delays and setbacks.

The limits of international intervention in Bosnia point to the second main argument of this book. It is the vision and strategic commitment of international interveners that improve the chances that intervention will have a deeper and more lasting impact – not the mere amount of economic and financial resources involved. Such a vision and strategic commitment must include the careful consideration of at least two aspects. First, international agencies need to give far greater attention to the impact and sustainability of their actions – particularly on local institutional development. In the name of ensuring short-term efficiency, international agencies have often intervened to remove obstacles to peace implementation, thus creating a domestic culture of dependency and delaying the development of local political and institutional responsibilities. Although there is no easy solution to the dilemma between efficiency and domestic capacity building, between international assertiveness and the need for local autonomy and democracy, some version of 'shared sovereignty' (Krasner 2004) between international and domestic actors is the best option available. When domestic institutions cannot autonomously guarantee efficient policy-making, they can benefit from the presence of international staff guaranteeing professional standards and technical support. Shared sovereignty institutions are the alternative to both neo-colonial interventions relying on extensive international executive and legislative powers, and to naive calls for domestic autonomy.

Second, in addition to developing viable domestic institutions with international support, international intervention should encourage grassroots or bottom-up peace building initiatives aimed at re-establishing economic and social ties across different communities. As the experience of Bosnia confirms, physical separation in a context of massive human displacement caused by the war is only a temporary solution. Shifts in international policy following the signing of the DPA confirm that the separation of individuals into ethnic enclaves complicates the furtherance of peace. The first two years of post-DPA transition, when Bosnians displaced by the war could not repossess their properties and return to their homes, were particularly difficult and unstable. The precariousness of the situation led international agencies to increase their commitment to reserving at least in part wartime ethnic cleansing, and to re-creating a degree of ethnic inter-mixing. The very fact that, over time, international agencies were drawn deeper into local politics in order to remove obstacles to the implementation of the DPA indicates the non-sustainability of division as a solution to ethnic conflict and the need to move towards a more integrative model of intervention. Rather than providing the solution to conflict, ethnic segregation and partition risk perpetuating the problem.

In practice, the experience of Bosnia demonstrates that the preservation and strengthening of multi-ethnic and multi-national states requires a careful balance between group and individual rights. It is often noted that consociationalism guarantees group rights and a considerable number of self-governing prerogatives, but at the cost of immobility and inflexibility (see for example Reilly 2001). Less appreciated is the extent to which group rights and self-government over ethnically defined territories have other, negative far-reaching consequences. They entrench the power of those nationalist elites responsible for war and complicate the emergence of moderate political alternatives; they undercut the exercise of individual rights, particularly the right of ethnic minorities to return home after war; and they create considerable hurdles in undermining zero-sum notions of identity and establishing civic notions of citizenship (Bell 2000; Wippman 1998). Individual human rights, on the contrary, are an important means for challenging the ethno-national divisions that emerged from the war – in so far as they can provide an avenue for reforming the social disorder created by years of conflict. As Chapter 6 will show, the return of refugees and displaced persons to areas under the control of another ethnic group has often contributed to the marginalisation of extreme ethno-nationalists and the softening of tensions between different communities.

The analysis of international intervention in Bosnia generates broader hypotheses as to how international intervention in weak and failing states could be made more effective, as well as what lessons Bosnia can offer for other similar operations worldwide. While there is no single set of answers applicable to all cases, a few general principles can be identified. First, no long-term political solution to conflict can emerge from local ethno-nationalists (Kaldor 1999). As the case of Bosnia demonstrates, their proposed 'solutions' perpetuate the problem, and delay the implementation of local conflict-regulating practices. To the extent that international agencies accept domestic nationalist claims at face value, they ratify the status quo and prevent the development of those political alternatives international interveners attempt to strengthen. An alternative approach should attempt to transform the conflict by challenging ethno-nationalism and by promoting participatory democracy and individual human rights. Second, successful intervention needs more than the implementation of a set of discrete projects, which are typically implemented independently of each other. The ability to move from a short-term perspective to a long-term structural approach can make the difference between success and failure. Third, the long-term transformation of conflict requires the strengthening of local institutions, together with the active involvement and empowerment of domestic civil society groups. Instead of considering domestic society as a desolate blank slate, international agencies need to build on local resources and assets, which are available even in the aftermath of a devastating war. The involvement of civil society is not only a prerequisite for conflict transformation but also a strategy for avoiding the transformation of international intervention into an instance of Western neo-colonial control strategy of troubled frontier zones (Duffield 2001).

The problems posed by weak and failing states since the end of the Cold War have become the single most compelling issue on the international agenda. These states often abuse their own citizens, cause humanitarian disasters with cross-border repercussions (ranging from massive refugee flights to destabilising criminal activities) and even pursue aggressive foreign policies. The events of 11 September 2001 highlighted how weak and failing states can also be hijacked by terrorist networks and used to launch devastating attacks well beyond their immediate neighbourhoods. In sum, learning how to promote effective and legitimate governance in weak and failing states, improve their democratic legitimacy and strengthen their institutions has become one of the main projects of contemporary international politics. With increasing demands for democratic governance and peaceful coexistence in countries such as Afghanistan and Iraq, the questions and issues addressed in Bosnia take on greater urgency (Nazi and Rutzen 2003). The presence of international missions in war-torn areas across the globe confirms that multilateral involvement has become a strategic imperative to secure international peace and security, and is possibly an effective tool available in the fight against terrorism. Significantly, in late 2005 the United Nations (UN) approved the creation of a new Peacebuilding Commission with the task of facing these new global challenges. More than a decade of experience in Bosnia can provide important lessons to both policy-makers and scholars struggling to understand and improve upon the dynamics of international intervention.

Actors, identities and the assessment of international intervention

Throughout this work, when referring to the collective character of intervention, I use the phrase 'third parties', 'international agencies' and 'international intervention' interchangeably, as these expressions suggest the plurality of actors involved. I avoid the word 'community' which has positive connotations that are not always warranted. I focus particular attention on three international agencies, the Office of the High Representative (OHR), the Organisation for Security and Cooperation in Europe (OSCE), and the United Nations High Commissioner for Refugees (UNHCR), because of their leading roles in Bosnia.

While the choice of terminology for international agents is relatively unproblematic, this is not the case for domestic ones. One of the most complex problems raised by research in deeply divided societies is the possibility that external actors (policy-makers, international organisations, humanitarian workers, scholars, journalists, and so on) implicitly legitimise local violence by uncritically accepting and involuntarily reproducing the same categories of ethnic exclusivism that underpin the ethno-nationalist project. An example will illustrate the hazards involved in this possibility. In my first trip to Bosnia in 1996, I met a middle-aged man living in the north-eastern town of Bihać. He had been employed as a social worker at the local prison for twenty years and when the war broke out, he lost his job. I could not understand why he had been fired and was unsure whether this was one of the many cases of ethnic discrimination. His name suggested he was a Bosniak, and Bihać was (and still is) a predominantly Bosniak town. When I asked him about his ethnicity, he repeated he was 'Bosnian'. 'Yes,' I replied, 'but are you a Bosniak, a Croat, or a Serb?'

My question was naive. However, more than a decade after the end of the war such questioning which identifies individuals in a superficial and limited fashion is still common among most foreign researchers, journalists, international diplomats and civil servants. Although external actors believe they hold a perspective on ethnicity and identity diametrically opposed to that of Bosnian ethno-nationalists, they actually share many principles with the perpetrators of ethnic cleansing. Among these are the definitions of individual and group identity as inescapable and mutually exclusive, and the notion that the alignment between territory and identity is a 'natural' spatial organisation of political life (Campbell 1998). Thus, foreign observers often reify the same ethnic and discursive structures they try to understand – much in the same way I imposed my own categories on my interlocutor in Bihać.

The perspective adopted here is grounded in the belief that the researcher's reflexivity about his/her role can bring clarity of purpose and help him to avoid over-simplifying the problems that exist in a small but complex country (Smyth and Robinson 2001).[2] This perspective endorses the view that the nation, national belonging and identity are contingent and fluid, and thus changeable over time (Anderson 1991). I am under no delusion that the individuals' sense of belonging and identity will or even should change in the short term, but I do think that Southeast European peoples, like their Western European counterparts, can have multiple and non-exclusive identities. Somebody could be a Sarajevan, a Serb, a Bosnian and a European, just as I am a Bolognese, an Italian, and a European currently living in Northern Ireland. To have an identity limited to being a Serb or a Croat or a Bosniak (or an Italian), would be greatly impoverishing. The idea of transforming ethnic identities in less conflictual directions rests on the notion that individuals have many identities, and that a rigid and exclusive ethnic identification is a loss for the individuals concerned.

This last point has important implications for evaluating the effectiveness of international intervention. Intervention that prevents or hinders human development and constrains the individual and collective choices of the domestic population might preserve peace (understood as the absence of war), but does little to move the local political dialogue beyond antagonistic and irreconcilable identities, and thus it is a doubtful long-term approach to preventing war. The long-term success of the peace process requires the development of less antagonistic and zero-sum notions of identity, which are necessary for managing differences peacefully. The local development of institutional and societal tools able to channel potentially violent behaviour into non-violent compromise is the only road to durable peace and further democratisation.

As the following chapters demonstrate, the impact of international intervention on domestic social and political processes is very hard to gauge with any precision and raises difficult methodological questions. Extreme situations, scores or outcomes (such as Bosnia's devastation by the end of the war) have a tendency to transform themselves to less extreme ones – a phenomenon that statisticians have identified as 'regression to the mean'. Terrible conditions at the beginning of a study are likely to improve with the passage of time, while wonderful conditions are likely to deteriorate, even if there has been no change at all in the factors causing them. This circumstance can cause the measurement of change, leading to a misunderstanding of the amount and type of change that has actually occurred and even to arguments to explain changes that have not occurred – or were not due to an independent variable such as international intervention. More importantly, this situation can lead analysts to attribute improvement (or deterioration) to their preferred conditions among the intervening events – as evident in the arguments of historical determinists, strong interventionists and autonomists. The way out of this methodological conundrum resides in identifying and isolating the local conditions existing prior to intervention, followed by a careful assessment of the impact of international involvement. In order to allow for a longitudinal comparison, each chapter of this study is roughly structured in the same way: the analysis of international intervention is preceded by a brief assessment of the local constraints and possibilities. This approach will minimise the possibility of mis-measurement and lead to a more reliable evaluation of the impact of intervention – particularly the reasons for its limited effectiveness.

Still, the diversity and fragmentation of international agencies makes improvements (and setbacks) the result of discrete, localised actions. The cumulative effect of these actions is very difficult to determine. In this context, progress is better understood as involving various and possibly contradictory dimensions – what has been termed 'pieces of peace' (Ross 2001: 35). Accordingly, this study endorses the idea of 'progress' instead of 'success' because the former suggests a process, while the latter implies a rarely attainable end-state. Unlike that of success, the notion of progress is inherently relative and has the obvious advantage of not requiring an unequivocal, and hardly attainable, successful end-state. At the very beginning of the peace process, for example, the withdrawal of armies to their barracks and the gradual demobilisation of the former enemies is clearly an achievement, but it is only a partial one.

Bosnia's long-term survival requires the development of effective and representative political institutions. Many recent examples of state collapse, from Somalia to Afghanistan, show how the alternative to states can be extremely oppressive, abusive and generally unattractive. Representative and democratic states are more likely to protect human rights than are decentralised regions run like fiefdoms. A functioning state creates stable rules and expectations that can serve the interests of all of its citizens, and is an indispensable interlocutor for civil society groups. The rule of law and the protection of human rights require an effective state authority, the very condition that the DPA failed to create.

Overview

Chapter 2 reviews Bosnia's stateness problem, that is, how domestic differences limit the state's ability to provide security, goods and services to its citizens. The DPA ended the war, but did not address the question of what the state is for, and whom it represents. Instead, extensive local self-governing prerogatives have been granted to the main communities, leaving the central state institutions either non-existent or with very limited powers. The inefficient performance of Bosnian institutions was balanced by an assertive international presence, and triggered a lively debate about different options for solving Bosnia's stateness problem. Strong interventionists, historical determinists and autonomists have put forward competing perspectives, but have failed to identify workable alternatives to improve international intervention.

Chapter 3 focuses on the structure of the post-war Bosnian state – a core aspect of the stateness problem. The consociational institutions established at Dayton created profound elements of ethnic discrimination. Several proposals have been put forward to change or reform the DPA. The analysis focuses on the July 2000 Constitutional Court decision that set in motion a far-reaching process of revision of the institutional structure. While the changes resulting from this decision have greatly improved the multi-ethnic character of central institutions, they have not solved Bosnia's stateness issue. Rather, they have entrenched the ethnic character of Bosnian institutions and have further complicated policy-making. As a result, the efficiency of domestic institutions remains limited.

Chapter 4 analyses the attempt to foster moderation and compromise through electoral engineering. Elections are universally recognised as an important conflict management tool. Not only do elections permit the creation of legitimate and representative institutions, but also electoral laws can be instrumental in facilitating multi-ethnic coalitions and political compromise. Accordingly, this chapter focuses on the impact of the electoral process on building cooperation and compromise, with particular reference to the process of adopting a permanent election law. Unfortunately, international agencies have designed an electoral system which reinforces ethno-nationalist domination, while marginalising multi-ethnic, non-nationalist parties.

The stateness problem of weak and failing states such as Bosnia cannot be addressed only at the institutional level but must be tackled at the social level as well. Chapter 5 considers the potential and actual contribution of civil society to further democratisation and peace by re-establishing ties across ethnic communities. This contribution can take two forms. First, the self-interest of individuals and groups can lead to ethnic cooperation and re-integration through economic incentives. Second, civil society can also be the realm of altruism, where individuals and groups promote the well-being of society at large. Particular attention is paid to the role of non-governmental organisations (NGOs) that are often recognised as the most visible and important indicators of a healthy and effective civil society. The revitalisation of civil society, while sound in principle, was implemented under the mistaken assumption of an environment resembling a *tabula rasa* with little or no human and political resources to contribute to the post-Dayton transition. As a result, international intervention has stifled the capacity of local groups to posit an alternative world-view to that of nationalist fragmentation and division. A broad conclusion is that a diverse and healthy civil society is the sign of a well functioning state, not its cause.

Chapter 6 focuses on the problem of the presence of a high number of refugees and displaced persons (DPs). The fate of those displaced by the war is the single most pressing problem of post-settlement societies. It is particularly crucial, in a case like Bosnia, where war was waged against the civilian population to change the ethnic character of the state. Because more than half of Bosnian citizens were displaced by the conflict, no lasting peace will be achieved until the DPs find a durable solution. International agencies in the first post-war period considered ethnic separation into homogeneous enclaves indispensable to the preservation of peace. Confronted with the non-sustainability of such a choice, international agencies began promoting the return of displaced Bosnians to their pre-war homes in areas under the control of another ethnic group (so-called 'minority return'). The return process is assessed in terms of its contribution to the calming of inter-ethnic tensions. This chapter suggests that it is unlikely that the pre-war ethnic mix can ever be recreated, but that limited returns are essential to ensuring peace, stability and democratic governance. Moreover, it argues that the sustainability of minority return (requiring intrusive social and economic engineering) is at odds with the broader intervention template (based on political and economic liberalisation).

Chapter 7 considers future prospects. First, the potential for Bosnia's gradual integration into European institutions is assessed. 'Europeanisation' can provide a long-term answer to Bosnia's stateness problem by replacing the post-Dayton short-term, ad hoc international approach with a clear vision grounded on the country's future inclusion into European political, economic, and security institutions. By making political boundaries less important, inclusion in European institutions can help 'soften' local identities and mitigate domestic competition over control of the state. Moreover, as the experience of other Central and Eastern European states suggests, the process of accession to the EU can have a profoundly positive impact on both political and economic development. For Bosnia, however, the benefits of Europeanisation might require a long time to materialise – thus complicating the short-term domestic endorsement of reforms. Second, this chapter considers which reforms are needed to put Bosnia on a steady course towards further democratisation. Central to the country's democratic consolidation is the reform of the Dayton constitution and the creation of viable domestic political institutions.

Chapter 8 assesses more than a decade of international intervention. It identifies three main reasons why intervention has been less effective than hoped for: it has pursued contradictory objectives, it has focused too much on stability rather than change, and it has narrowly concentrated on short-term policies at the expense of long-term structural intervention. This assessment concludes with the identification of broader lessons to be applied to other cases of international intervention in weak and failing states. In particular, it argues that successful intervention requires a coherent approach to strengthening political institutions, the rule of law, and, more broadly, the legitimacy of domestic decision-making bodies. In this regard, shared-sovereignty institutions have an important role to play. At the same time, the Bosnian experience shows that even under the most unfavourable circumstances there exist important local resources that can be mobilised for more effective peace building.

2 Bosnia's and international intervention

International intervention in weak and failing states has been at the top of the international agenda since the end of the Cold War. International operations have been deployed in almost all corners of the globe, from Afghanistan to Bosnia, Cambodia, Kosovo, East Timor, Iraq and Somalia – just to cite a few of the most prominent cases. These operations have taken place in different circumstances. Some of them have been justified in the name of the war on terror, while others were conducted in view of implementing a recently achieved peace agreement. All of these operations face similar constraints and dilemmas. The context where international intervention takes place is one of extreme political, economic and social instability. Years of war destroy the physical and economic infrastructure, provoke mass human displacement, and leave the population traumatised. Moreover, rarely does war end with a clear victory of one of the parties involved. Instead, conflicts frequently terminate with the signing of a peace agreement reflecting a difficult and unstable compromise.

After a negotiated settlement is reached, the 'stateness problem' remains to complicate the implementation phase. In weak states, national/ethnic differences prevent the universal acceptance of the state by its population. The lack of social cohesion further undermines the state's ability to formulate and implement policy. Weak states are unable to provide internal and external security for their citizens or meet their economic and social needs, and they often remain subjected to parochial and sectarian interests, preventing the development and consolidation of a bureaucratic structure. Social order is not guaranteed through formalised procedures and the rule of law, but through informal, clientelistic channels. The absence of an organisation with the characteristics of the modern state prevents democratic governance, although it does not preclude the presence of areas of segmented political authority (Linz and Stepan 1996: 16–37). The former warring parties maintain the capacity to resort to violence whenever they wish – and they often do so. Thus, negotiated settlements to identity civil wars, such as the DPA, have a higher risk of breaking down than settlements imposed by military victories (Licklider 1995).

This chapter begins with a brief overview of Bosnia's stateness problem. Bosnia at the time of the signing of the DPA was a typical weak state, existing in large measure only on paper, internally divided and contested by most of its population. Although the DPA terminated open hostilities between the main warring parties, it did not prevent continuing differences from hampering the implementation of the agreement. In this context, international intervention attempted to support the transition from war to peace and self-sustaining democratic institutions. The international mission deployed in late 1995 was massive in size, but ill conceived for the purpose of carrying out a complex mandate in a difficult environment. A clear separation between the military and the civilian component prevented coordinated action; exogenous priorities were often superimposed on domestic needs; and much time was lost in attempting to devise a workable intervention strategy.

Second, this chapter considers the liberal-interventionist template adopted by international interveners. Since the end of the Cold War, all international missions have pursued a neo-Wilsonian approach aimed at the simultaneous liberalisation of the political and economic sphere. Political democracy and a market economy have been put forward as the solution to the problems faced by weak and failing states. This approach has had limited success, in some cases even exacerbating the problems it sought to address (Paris 2004). In Bosnia, liberalisation has entrenched the power of those ethno-national elites most likely to complicate the post-settlement transition, and failed to reform the economy in a way that meets Bosnians' needs. Critics have drawn different lessons from this experience. But while strong interventionists, historical determinists, and autonomists have all provided important insights in the working and impact of international intervention, they have failed to put forward a clear and workable alternative strategy. The chapter ends with a critique of these three approaches, arguing that their solutions for overcoming the weakness of the Bosnian state are not practicable options.

The Dayton deal: between partition and reintegration

The Bosnian war made headline news worldwide almost every day between the spring of 1992 and the autumn of 1995. The siege of Sarajevo and the use of ethnic cleansing as the main policy of at least one of the parties to the conflict compelled international attention at a high level. Furthermore, because the war involved individuals and groups who were culturally and ethnically European, it was not uncommon for the Western public, journalists and aid workers to feel emotionally connected to the Bosnians' plight. Despite the enormous interest and pressure to intervene, the great powers could not summon the necessary political will until the summer of 1995, when the United States took the lead by intervening militarily to create the conditions for a negotiated settlement to the crisis and opened the way to the most important international peace operation of the second half of the 1990s (Chollet 2005).

American-led NATO bombing, combined with the shifting military balance among the parties, contributed to the creation of the conditions for successful peace negotiations. In early September 1995 at Geneva, the parties under international pressure agreed to three basic principles for a settlement

(Owen 1995: 359). First, there would be two Entities within Bosnia, Republika Srpska (RS) and the Croat/Bosniak Federation, each with its own constitution and extensive self-governing powers, and separated by an Inter Entity Boundary Line (IEBL). Each Entity would be allowed to establish special relations with neighbouring Croatia and Serbia (see Map 2.1). Second, the territorial split between the Entities would be based on the 51–49 per cent proposal already put forward by international negotiators two years earlier. While the Serbs would be granted 49 per cent of the territory, the Bosniaks obtained 33.3 per cent, and the Croats 17.7 per cent. Third, Bosnia's internationally recognised borders would be preserved. Agreement on these principles opened the way for a peace conference. The Americans assembled the parties at the Wright-Patterson air force base at Dayton, Ohio. The talks in Dayton, which lasted from 1 to 21 November 1995, led to a settlement whereby Federation leaders reluctantly accepted the right of the RS to existence, and the Serbs conceded that there should

Map 1 Bosnia and Herzogovina (source UN Cartographic Section)

be a 'thin roof' of central institutions to carry out those state activities not assigned to the Entities. Despite lip service paid to an integral Bosnia, the post-war settlement was for the most part founded on the division of territory on an ethnic basis. Bosnia's new constitution, contained in Annex 4 of the Dayton Peace Agreement (DPA), sanctioned Bosnia's political divisions.

Some divided states, such as Belgium, can be internally divided but quite stable and can even provide a model of how to facilitate compromise in divided polities (Stroschein 2003). However, Bosnia's recent history of violence complicates co-existence among the main groups. Moreover, inconsistencies embodied in the peace agreement set further hurdles in the way of the post-war peacebuilding process. The DPA proved to be a contradictory document where both partition and ethnic reintegration were present. The rights of the ethnic groups and their physical separation were made predominant in the document. At the same time, the parties agreed to 'ensure the highest level of internationally recognised human rights and fundamental freedoms' (Annex 4, art. II, 1), most of which are cast in terms of protecting individual human rights, and imply the preference for the reintegration of the country along multi-ethnic lines. Provisions for human rights included the direct application of over twenty international human rights instruments in the domestic legal framework, the establishment of human rights courts, ombudspersons, and international human rights monitoring missions. The right of all Bosnians to return home to areas under the control of another ethnic group was solemnly affirmed. While at the time of the DPA's signing few thought about the long-term impact of these provisions, they proved important in justifying further international intervention in Bosnian politics and in creating at least some avenues to affirm the rights of all Bosnians regardless of their ethnic belonging.

Bosnia's uncertain stateness

Bosnia's post-war democratic development is intertwined with the question of how to build and consolidate a functioning state. According to Juan Linz and Alfred Stepan, 'modern democratic governance is inevitably linked to stateness. Without a state, there can be no citizenship; without citizenship, there can be no democracy' (1996: 19). Unless a state exists, elections cannot be held, governments cannot exercise the monopoly of legitimate force and citizens cannot have their rights protected by the rule of law. The more the residents of a territory identify with one national group, the more a state is likely to come into existence and to consolidate itself. In other words, the congruence between the *demos* (the 'people') and the *polis* (the political community where the people resides) contributes to the creation of a nation-state and constitutes a supportive condition for democratic consolidation (Linz and Stepan 1996: 25). Conversely, a stateness problem exists when there remain profound discrepancies between the boundaries of the political community and the rights of citizenship within that community.

As Linz and Stepan point out, democracy can still be consolidated in multi-ethnic states, but it requires considerable political crafting in terms of democratic norms and institutions.

Similarly to other weak and failing states, Bosnia's performance as a state can be assessed in terms of its capacity to deliver crucial political goods, especially human security (Rotberg 2004). The DPA succeeded in transferring the conflict between Serbs, Croats and Bosniaks from the military to the political realm, but did not resolve the underlying stateness issue, with significant consequences for state capacity. Both Croats and Serbs prefer high degrees of autonomy within the state and close ties with Croatia and Serbia respectively. Bosniaks believe that the preservation and consolidation of the state is the best avenue for their political and national survival. Since the signing of the DPA, little common ground has been found between these competing positions. As a result, political institutions remain divided and often deadlocked; elections regularly provide access to office for the very same political parties responsible for the war, and most likely to boycott the implementation of the DPA. The economy is not only unable to provide jobs and growth, but is largely prey to parochial and often illegal interests. Civil society is weak and fragmented, with most local non-governmental organisations (NGOs) dependent on foreign resources and unable to project a political and social vision alternative to nationalist fragmentation. Finally, most Bosnians continue to live in ethnically homogeneous enclaves. When they venture into areas controlled by an ethnic group other than their own, they face discrimination and occasionally even physical harassment.

Bosnia's stateness problem did not arise as a result of the 1992–95 war. Rather, the war itself could be interpreted as a consequence of the existence of different national identities. While sharing the same physical territory, Bosnia's three main national communities developed largely in isolation from one another. Islam, Roman Catholicism and Orthodox Christianity shaped the life of a population with a similar ethnic background and a common language. The Muslim-Bosniak cultural identity was shaped by Turkish-Islamic influences (Bougarel 2003); the Serb Orthodox tradition owes much to the Byzantine religious tradition; and the Croat Catholics are linked to the Western Christian influence. A complex religious and cultural picture crystallised in Bosnia well before the outbreak of the 1992–95 war, turning Bosnia into 'an exceptionally complicated and ambivalent society, characterised on the one hand by cultural and spiritual isolationism, on the other by tolerance for difference as a normal aspect of life' (Lovrenović 2001: 108; see also Bougarel 1996; Donia and Fine 1994; Malcolm 1996).

The post-World War II Yugoslav state attempted to strike a balance among Yugoslavia's many national groups. Yugoslavia was a Federation of six republics: Slovenia, Macedonia, and Montenegro were the smaller federal units, each located at a different edge of the state, while Serbia, Croatia, and Bosnia-Herzegovina were in the centre. In each of the republics, ethnic and religious differences overlapped. Serbia was mostly Christian Orthodox,

Croatia was mostly Catholic, and Bosnia had a relative majority of Muslims. Tito's socialist doctrine helped to preserve peace and harmony for much of post-World War II history, both between and within the republics. 'Brotherhood and Unity' was Yugoslavia's official ideology. Tito opposed ethnic conflict in the name of a proletarian revolution extending, by definition, across national lines.[1] At the same time, national identities were never suppressed but constituted the building blocks of the federal state; each nation possessed a hegemonic status within its own republic, with the exception of Bosnia with its mixed population. The federal system was based on a balance between national groups and on the role of Tito as the final guarantor of stability.

In Bosnia, the balance was enforced more rigidly than anywhere else in Yugoslavia. All functions and institutions were filled according to the principle of rotation of nationality – the *ključ* (Silber and Little 1996: 207). The ethnic key was a forerunner of consociational democracy (see Chapter 3), but with an important difference. Although political leaders were chosen on the basis of nationality, they acted as leaders of the whole Bosnian political nation, instead of acting as ethnic representatives (Andjelić 2003: 19). Over time, however, demographic changes strained the social and political stability ensured by the ethnic key policy. Between 1971 and 1991, the proportion of Bosniaks in the population increased from 39.57 per cent to 43.67 per cent, while the Serb population declined from 37.19 per cent to 31.37 per cent. These changes led to a transfer of jobs, allocated on the basis of the percentage of each ethnic group, from the Serbs to the Bosniaks, increased competition for resources and escalated inter-ethnic tensions (Slack and Doyon 2001: 146, 150).

Artificial or natural?

The fact that Yugoslavia dissolved violently should not suggest that it was an artificial country (Denitch 1996; Rusinow 1995), a view often expressed by nationalists who wanted to dismantle it and supported by historical determinists who consider the creation of ethnically homogeneous nation-states as 'inevitable'. Instead, Yugoslavia was created first in 1918 and then re-established in 1945 because patriotic South Slavs reasoned that some form of even imperfect union would be preferable to small, weak and divided nation-states, which were easy prey to great powers' influence. The creation of Yugoslavia was also a way to address the Serb political question by including all Serbs in one state. To be sure, there were always nationalists who were opposed to the Yugoslav idea, but this opposition did not make the state any less legitimate than any other European state. Nor did it make the state constantly subject to nationalist outbursts. The different national communities coexisted in relative peace for long periods.

But even if one accepts the idea of Yugoslavia's 'artificiality', there remains the problem of explaining the relationship between the end of a supposedly artificial federation and the war in Bosnia. The notion that Bosnia was Yugoslavia 'writ small' with its mix of different ethnic groups, and that 'there would have been no war in Bosnia and Herzegovina if Yugoslavia had not first collapsed' (Woodward 1999: 75) implies an excessive degree of inevitability. As Noel Malcolm argues, Bosnia had a strong historical identity that pre-dated the creation of Yugoslavia and, for that matter, all European states (Malcolm 1996). All of its borders have a considerable historical continuity, either as internal administrative borders or international ones. Bosnia was an independent kingdom in the Middle Ages and, after 1580, it was a distinct administrative unit within the Ottoman empire. Only during World War II was Bosnia briefly partitioned. In view of the fact that political and administrative units in the Middle Ages are hardly comparable to modern European states, Malcolm engages in a case of 'conceptual stretching' – transporting modern concepts like the state back to a time when such an institution did not exist. However, his broader insight is an important one: if Yugoslavia was 'artificial', Bosnia was 'natural', a location shared by different individuals and groups for generations.

International aspects of the Dayton Agreement

The 1992–95 war could only heighten Bosnia's complexity and exacerbate its stateness problem. A large international mission, composed of both a military and a civilian component, was deployed to help implement the DPA, stabilise Bosnia and sustain a process of democratic consolidation. Even a cursory overview of the structure, composition and mandate of international organisations reveals the limits of an ill planned operation.

International deployment and mandate

International deployment had more to do with the interveners' own interests than the reality on the ground. Even before the peace talks began, the US administration announced that it would allow its troops to remain in Bosnia for no longer than twelve months (Chollet 2005: 77). According to American chief negotiator Richard Holbrooke, this decision was less an 'exit strategy' than an 'exit deadline', which complicated the negotiations and, even more so, the implementation of the agreement (1998: 211). This short timespan was due to American reluctance to deploy its troops in potentially dangerous combat situations. The US government was consumed by the 'Vietmalia syndrome' after the trauma created by the foreign policy debacles in Vietnam and in 1993 in Somalia (Holbrooke 1998: 219), and feared that the American public would not be supportive of a deployment in a region devoid of strategic interest. As a result, as one commentator aptly put it, 'the Bosnia deployment resembles nothing more than the moon landings, with the principal objective being to send men far away and bring them back safely' (Rose 1998: 66).[2]

Accordingly, A NATO-led peacekeeping force of 60,000 troops, the Implementation Force (IFOR) was authorised under Chapter 7 of the UN Charter and expected to complete its mandate within twelve months from the signing of the agreement, that is, by December 1996. IFOR's mandate was limited in scope. Its core task was to separate armed forces, stabilise the ceasefire, and oversee the cantonment of troops and heavy weapons (Annex 1A). In substance, IFOR's 'primary role was that of a classic, if particularly well armed peacekeeping force' (Cousens and Cater 2001: 37). IFOR had the authority, but crucially not the obligation to undertake tasks beyond those expressly identified in the peace agreement, such as arresting indicted war criminals (Chollet 2005: 127–28). The NATO leadership interpreted its mandate restrictively, to the despair of both ordinary Bosnians, who hoped foreign troops would be effective security providers, and of the civilian component of the peace operation, who wanted IFOR to be more active.

Because of NATO's limited role, a strong international policing task force would have greatly facilitated the peace implementation process. Instead, a weak police force with only monitoring and training responsibilities was established. Holbrooke writes that the reason for this choice was not the local parties, who distrusted each other and thus favoured an external force able to ensure compliance, but European leaders, who feared that the possibility of a long-term policing commitment could embroil them in a dangerous quagmire.[3] As later developments would make clear, the limited tasks assigned to both the international military and the police forces created a serious enforcement vacuum with tragic human rights consequences – in particular for those Bosnian refugees and displaced persons (DPs) who attempted to return to their pre-war homes but often faced overt discrimination if not violent opposition.

Even the separation of the military and civilian components of the peace operation can be traced to the diversity of opinion between the US and European states. After the Americans obtained command over the military aspects of the peace operation, the Europeans were determined to obtain the civilian counterpart. Negotiations over the appointment of the head of the civilian mission resulted in a stalemate. In the end the decision to leave this important post to a non-American was made for financial reasons, as the Europeans had agreed to meet most of the costs (Chollet 2005: 142; Holbrooke 1998: 174). Once this had been agreed, the US attempted to thwart the allocation of substantive powers to the head of the civilian mission – the High Representative of the International Community (Neville-Jones 1996–97: 50). Eventually, the military and civilian elements were separated, with the US focusing on military matters and the Europeans concentrating on civilian aspects (Bildt 1998: 109). The limited cooperation between the military and civilian component of the operation undermined the implementation of important clauses of the agreement. For example, civilian agencies would work with DPs to help them return home, but could not rely on NATO to provide security for the returnees. Because of the lack of enforcement mechanisms, the first High Representative, Norwegian politician Carl Bildt, initially had to rely on the tacit support and cooperation of local politicians, rendering him practically powerless.

Not only was the High Representative and his Office (OHR) not granted authority over the military commander, but also his powers were limited to 'overseeing and coordinating' the activities of the civilian organisations. Given OHR's loose coordinating role, international civilian agencies maintained their chain of command and reporting requirements with their respective headquarters. Even the allocation of roles between international agencies was not decided by organisational competence and previous experience, but rather on the basis of institutional and national bargaining (Kostakos 1998). Predictably, the OHR's later attempts to increase its role in the name of 'strategic coordination' and greater effectiveness were regularly met with resistance and opposition from other international organisations, in particular the US-controlled Organisation for Security and Cooperation in Europe (OSCE).

In addition to having no authority over either the military or civilian components of the peace operation, OHR was also deprived of political support and direction. The Peace Implementation Council (PIC), composed of representatives of more than fifty governments, was supposed to provide coordination and strategic direction to the work of OHR. In practice, many important decisions had been taken outside the PIC framework, thus undermining the legitimacy and effectiveness of this body. Bilateral initiatives have constantly complicated the PIC's directive role. For example, American negotiators at Dayton secretly agreed with the Bosniak delegation on a military programme aimed at improving the Bosniaks' position in the event of a new war. The 'train-and-equip' programme was criticised by most European allies, who feared the increase in weapons in the region (never endorsed by the PIC) and questioned by the first High Representative, Carl Bildt, who wondered whether arming the most aggrieved party (which was thus relatively more likely to restart the war) was an appropriate peace building strategy.

In the first few post-Dayton years, the PIC meetings were attended by prime ministers and foreign ministers, later replaced by political directors of foreign ministries attending the meetings of the PIC Steering Board (PICSB) composed of the G8 states, Turkey, and the EU Presidency. OHR is formally accountable to the PICSB, but the real influence of the latter over the former cannot be conclusively determined, since the PICSB meetings are not public and the minutes are not published. In general, however, the PIC's loss of prestige led to an expansion of the discretionary powers of OHR. The PICSB has increasingly come to endorse strategy documents devised by international officials in Bosnia, instead of giving its own strategic direction to OHR. Left with a wide and flexible mandate, OHR proceeded without a comprehensive strategic approach until the High Representative devised a Mission Implementation Plan in January 2003 (revised and updated in 2004 and 2005) identifying the core objectives for successfully completing the peace building mission. In sum, the architecture of international intervention adopted at Dayton kept a sharp separation between the military and civilian aspects of intervention, maintained a very loose coordination among civilian agencies, and failed to provide the High Representative with strong political support. This model would prove sufficient to preserve the absence of fighting but inadequate in addressing Bosnia's stateness problem.

The rise and fall of international intervention

Post-Dayton international intervention can be divided roughly into three phases. During the first phase (1996–98), third parties' passive, short-term and less than daring approach did little to help a population traumatised by years of war. Despite the presence of thousands of international interveners and a vast financial commitment to rebuild the destroyed infrastructure, Bosnian nationalists were able to continue the process of ethnic cleansing and separation. Many Bosnians who stayed put during the war were convinced that they should leave shortly after the signing of the DPA as a result of residing on the 'wrong' side. The lack of third parties' interest in individual human rights allowed the final separation of Bosnian groups in ethnically homogeneous enclaves and created Sisyphean obstacles for later international intervention.

The first High Representative of the International Community, Carl Bildt, concluded that the post-war return of the displaced population could destabilise the peace. Accordingly, he overlooked the human rights components of the DPA, preferring instead to recognise the de facto partition of the country. The deployment of international military and civilian personnel confirmed the priorities of international agencies. NATO focussed on patrolling the IEBL, thus cementing the separation of the parties. The OSCE, which was given considerable responsibilities in the organisation of the elections, monitoring of human rights, and supervision of the arms control clauses of the DPA, was organised in a field structure that closely followed the separation lines among ethnic groups.[4] The weak international presence neither prevented the completion of ethnic cleansing, nor did it improve communication and develop trust between former combatants. The separation into ethnic enclaves perpetuated ethnic insecurity and mistrust, and put the peace process at risk of collapse.

In the second phase (1998–2000), international agencies became more assertive in order to overcome the very same local obstacles that previous intervention had helped create. In May 1997 the PIC met at Sintra, Portugal, where it emphasised it would not 'tolerate any attempts at partition, *de facto* or *de iure*, by anyone' (PIC 1997b). The meeting set the stage for a more assertive foreign military presence. The Stabilisation Force (SFOR, which replaced IFOR in late 1996) became increasingly active in the implementation of the civilian aspects of the peace operation. The first military action against an indicted war criminal came on 10 June 1997, when British troops in Prijedor captured one Serb and killed another one who had been named by the International Criminal Tribunal for the former Yugoslavia (ICTY) in a sealed indictment (on the importance of this episode in opening the way for refugee return, see Chapter 6).

The PIC met again in Bonn in December 1997, where the peace operation was transformed in practice from one of providing assistance to local parties to an undeclared protectorate. The second High Representative, Spanish diplomat Carlos Westendorp, was given the authority to impose laws 'until the Presidency or Council of Ministers has adopted a decision consistent with the Peace Agreement on the issue concerned' and to sack politicians who obstruct the implementation of the DPA – or, as the PIC (1997a: ch. 11, para. 11) put it, to take actions against persons 'in violation of the legal commitments made under the Peace Agreement or the terms of its implementation'. The Bonn decision put Bosnia under strict international direction and elevated state building to the top of the agenda. The goal of third-party intervention had become that of reinforcing the state's capacity to stand on its own. Westendorp assertively used his new powers by imposing laws and sacking elected politicians. The third High Representative, Wolfgang Petritsch, appointed in August 1999, continued to impose decisions from above when confronted with local obstruction. Petritsch adopted a dual strategy of using his Bonn powers more assertively, frequently and strategically than his predecessor, while at the same time pursuing 'functional integration' through the creation of state institutions (Petritsch 2002a: 151–58).

The third phase (2000 to the present) has been marked by both state building and the gradual downsizing of the international presence with a view to withdrawal. Meeting in Brussels in May 2000, the PIC recognised that Bosnia's survival depended on the presence of effective state institutions (PIC 2000) – marking a 'dramatic shift in international priorities' (ESI 2000: 1). In June 2001, the Steering Board of the PIC began debating a radical plan (the so-called 'streamlining process') to merge international agencies in order to improve their efficiency and make better use of resources at a time of declining international interest. Under the plan, international agencies (in particular the OHR, the OSCE, and the UN mission) were expected gradually to merge into a single organisation with a single budget and unified structure (OHR 2001a). To improve the efficiency of the international presence, and compensate for the reduction of international resources, the High Representative was tasked with directing a cabinet coordinating the work of various international agencies. The plan's existence revealed that the countdown to international withdrawal had begun, although several organisations bent on preserving their own influence and visibility resisted it – complicating and delaying international restructuring.

After Wolfgang Petritsch left his post as Bosnia's third High Representative in June 2002, the fourth High Representative, British politician Paddy Ashdown explicitly adopted as his goal the effort to 'wind down the interventionist peacebuilding process' (2002a). Ashdown's concrete agenda to complete the peace building task was to focus on the rule of law, economic liberalisation, and government restructuring. Legal and judicial reforms were particularly sensitive, as they were meant to undermine the power structure of the nationalist parties thought to be based on corruption and organised crime. Ashdown's overall strategy concentrated on downsizing his office while putting Bosnia on the road to statehood and eventual European integration. In the summer of 2005 the PIC endorsed this agenda, announcing a number of important changes, including the transfer of responsibilities to Bosnian authorities, the intention to limit the use of the Bonn powers, and the transition from the OHR to the office of the EU Special Representative (EUSR) responsible for monitoring and assisting Bosnia in her progress towards EU integration (OHR 2005b). Christian Schwarz-Schilling, a veteran German politician with extensive experience of local level mediation in Bosnia, became the fifth High Representative in February 2006. His stated priority was to 'phase out the post-war protectorate' (Schwarz-Schilling 2006). While Schwarz-Schilling maintained the same prerogatives granted to his predecessor, he did not impose legislation on the Bosnian Parliament.[5] At the time of his appointment, it was expected that Schwarz-Schilling would be Bosnia's last High Representative, and that OHR would be closed down sometime in 2007, to be replaced by a much less intrusive EU mission. However, throughout Schwarz-Schilling's tenure little progress towards state building and European integration was achieved. The German official was widely criticised for his alleged lack of energy and attentiveness. In January 2007 Schwarz-Schilling abruptly announced his resignation and intention to leave Bosnia at the end of June 2007 (Traynor 2007). A sense of destabilising crisis involving both Bosnia and neighbouring Serbia led the PIC to postpone OHR closure until June 2008 (PIC 2007). In May 2007, Miroslav Lajčák, a polyglot Slovak career diplomat known for his role as personal representative of the EU Representative for the Common Foreign and Security Policy, Javier Solana, in Montenegro (where he oversaw the 2006 referendum on independence) was appointed to replace Schwarz-Schilling.

The intervention template

Since the end of the Cold War, all peace operations have pursued the same general template to establish stability and peace in weak and failing states – and Bosnia is no exception to this broader trend. With the victory of Western-style democracy over its main twentieth-century ideological alternative, liberal democracy became the blueprint for international intervention.

Wilsonianism and its limits

Roland Paris (2004: 40–42) has defined this blueprint as 'Wilsonianism' – after Woodrow Wilson, the twenty-eighth president of the United States, who argued that liberalism and democratic forms of government were the key to peace and security in both international and domestic politics. Wilsonianism informed the peace building efforts following World War I and World War II, and was re-affirmed at the end of the Cold War. Political liberalisation involves the promotion of periodic elections, constitutional checks and balances, and respect for civil liberties. In the economic sphere, liberalisation involves marketisation, that is, the development of a viable market economy where private investors, producers and consumers freely pursue their economic self-interest unhindered by government intrusion (Paris 2004).

The problem with Wilsonianism is that it does not take into account the specific nature of identity conflicts and the stateness problem they give rise to. When political and economic liberalisation are advanced as key intervention strategies in a context dominated by ethno-national mobilisation on the basis of identity, they are unlikely to work. The presence of political and economic corruption and a political leadership bent on plundering the assets of the state and those of ordinary people makes quick elections and economic liberalisation counter-productive. Moreover, because markets increase competition and inequality, in the short term they can exacerbate conflict instead of alleviating it. Similarly, political liberalisation and elections in conditions of ethnic insecurity typical of weak and failing states can result in an ethnic census instead of an expression of democratic principles. In a society deeply divided along ethnic lines, Wilsonianism has little chance of success. Unsurprisingly, in his thorough examination of post-Cold War peace building efforts, Paris (2004) finds that the practical impact of international intervention reveals a disconcerting chasm between expectations and actual outcomes.

At its core, the limits of Wilsonianism are due to the fact that international operations are deployed to areas where the very stateness of the country recovering from war is in question (Belloni 2007). By pushing for political and economic liberalisation without taking into account the particular context of intervention, contemporary Wilsonianism assumes that the stateness problem has been addressed or will solve itself during the transition process – a dangerous and untested assumption. By contrast, Wilson himself was keenly aware of the weakness of states composed of national and ethnic groups competing for the control of central institutions. Wilson's remedy in the aftermath of World War I was the attempt to match as much as possible the *demos* with the *polis* by creating ethnically homogeneous nation-states. The peace conference at Versailles, which ended World War I, attempted to reach this goal by adopting the principle of national self-determination fervently championed by Wilson. No other attempt was ever made to this degree, before or since, to make the ethnically homogeneous nation-state not simply an ideal but as close as possible to empirical reality. Each state in Central and Eastern Europe was effectively assigned to a dominant ethnic group. Many minorities were expected to move to a state where they would be part of an ethnic majority. Those who remained hoped that their state would respect the minority rights system established at Versailles. As Michael Mann explains,

> cleansing by resettlement – partly voluntary but mostly coerced deportations – was officially ratified by the 1918 peace treaties implementing Woodrow Wilson's doctrine of *national self-determination* ... Citizenship was now substantially identified with ethnicity, with minorities in danger of becoming second-class citizens. It was believed that this was better than keeping the ethnicities mixed.
>
> (Mann 2004: 66–67)

The Wilsonian agenda of democracy promotion actively endorsed a state-centered approach, which sat uneasily with the defence of group and individual rights. As we shall see shortly, this solution to the stateness problem is still advocated by 'historical determinists' who believe that only by matching national with political boundaries in weak states such as Bosnia will stability and democratic development be ensured. However, the very creation of multinational Yugoslavia in 1918 and its re-establishment in 1945 testifies to the logistical difficulties of creating ethnically homogeneous nation-states. Wilson failed to realise how indeterminate the criterion of national identity was in demarcating states' frontiers. In fact, not all claims to self-determination could be recognised at the end of World War I, thus creating the conditions for ethnically-based dissatisfaction with the territorial status quo (Jackson Preece 2005: 166). Moreover, in addition to proving logistically impractical, since the end of World War I the creation of homogeneous nation-states has been normatively discredited. Policies of national homogenisation and population transfers, which produce large scale of human suffering and personal and societal upheaval, no longer fit the legitimate menu of choices available to policy-makers for addressing issues related to stateness. Rather than being perceived as a threat, diversity has become a value to preserve, even when it implies limiting state sovereignty (Jackson Preece 2005: 160–63). While classic Wilsonianism viewed security as pertaining to the relations between sovereign states, leaving the internal configuration of states entirely under the control of national governments (Richmond 2002: 22–23), an alternative perspective, centred on the security of individuals and groups, has begun to take root. At least at the level of rhetoric, human security and individual and group rights contend with state security in the constitution of order.

The distinctiveness of contemporary interventions

In addition to their rhetorical commitment to individual and group rights, contemporary post-war interventions differ from previous ones because of the context in which they take place. Although the reconstruction of Germany and Japan are often hailed as possible blueprints for international intervention in countries such Bosnia (Šabić 2005) there are important differences between international intervention after World War II and contemporary missions. To begin with, Germany and Japan at the end of World War II were conquered states, not weak or failing ones. Neither Germany nor Japan had any significant stateness problems. For many years prior to foreign occupation, a strong state apparatus and bureaucracy were able effectively to provide public goods to citizens. Moreover, both countries had a long history as nations, where citizens had recognised loyalty to the state as opposed to a clan or a sub-national group.

By contrast, contemporary international intervention takes place in weak and failing states, not conquered ones. Weak and failing states are internally divided along national, religious or ideological lines. A peace agreement might be in place, but local parties are likely to remain divided and continue to fight their war through political means. Citizens do not recognise each other as belonging to the same political entity; instead, the very existence and nature of the state remains in question – as vividly illustrated by the difficulties in the implementation of the DPA. Divided institutions, the absence of a functioning state, the weakness of civil society and the mass displacement of the population (especially groups directly targeted during the war), place specific constraints on international actors and shape the nature of the choices they face in the post-settlement process.

The intervention debate

There are three main scholarly and policy approaches to solving the stateness problem of weak and failing states – 'strong interventionism', 'historical determinism' and 'autonomism'.[6] Each approach has been widely debated in the context of intervention in Bosnia, but is more relevant for other interventions as well. Strong interventionists argue that the goal of preserving and consolidating a multi-ethnic state such as Bosnia is a sound one. The problem with the limited impact of international intervention does not lie in the goals it tries to achieve, but in the weak enforcement powers available to interveners. Historical determinists claim that the preservation and consolidation of multi-ethnic states is contrary to the historical experience of Western democracies and thus is inevitably bound to fail. Rather than preserving an internally weak state unwanted by large sections of its own citizens, international intervention should acknowledge the inevitable, that is, the eventual partition of Bosnia into mono-ethnic states. Autonomists contend that, whatever the limited merits of international intervention,

Bosnians are ultimately responsible for sorting out their own fate, freed from external constraints. The imposition of external priorities makes a sham of democratic self-government and is not justified by domestic needs – particularly since the war has been over for more than a decade and there is no short-term concern over a relapse into fighting. As a brief analysis of these views will show, none of these approaches is entirely satisfactory.

The strong interventionist approach

According to the strong enforcement view, long-term democratic self-government, economic recovery and greater protection of individual and group rights require extensive international involvement and authority. The absence of functioning and efficient domestic institutions – in conjunction with the broader consequences of war on the fabric of society – legitimises an assertive international presence in weak and failing states worldwide. According to Michael Ignatieff (2003) intervention in war-torn countries such as Bosnia constitutes an imperial enterprise because its ultimate purpose – that of creating order in border zones important for the security of great powers – requires the deployment of military might and occasionally the use of international autocratic powers. For liberal interventionists such as Ignatieff, imperial rule is legitimised by the public goods it provides to weak or failing states, primarily 'good governance' and greater respect for human rights. International organisations, it is argued, contribute decisively to the success of intervention. These organisations embody liberal values such as human rights, democracy and the rule of law and transmit them to weak states struggling to develop and consolidate viable institutions. International agencies

> often act as conveyor belts for the transmission of norms and models of good political behavior. There is nothing accidental or unintended about this role. Officials ... often insist that part of their mission is to spread, inculcate, and enforce global values and norms. They are the missionaries of our time.
>
> (Barnett and Finnemore 2004: 33)

Interventionists believe that the weakness of local institutions justifies this imperial mission and a generally top-down approach to intervention. According to Roland Paris (2004), because war-shattered states possess neither the institutional capacity nor a tradition of peaceful conflict resolution, international agencies should assume the lion's share of responsibility and promote a strategy of Institutionalisation Before Liberalisation (IBL). Instead of rushing into elections, peacebuilders should get more involved in the domestic affairs of war-shattered states, limiting political and economic freedom in the short term while creating better foundations for peace and democracy in the long term. Although Paris does not mention the need for a protectorate, his strategy for international involvement nonetheless calls for extensive international powers. Fearon and Laitin (2004) add that a lead state or regional organisation should be granted a management role in carrying out the international mission, setting the terms of coordination among international agencies, and preventing local parties from playing international interveners one against the other.

Bosnia is a case where a more assertive international stance from an early stage could have built better foundations for a self-sustaining state. The post-Dayton international peace operation should have been more forceful and wide-ranging in order to overcome local obstacles and put Bosnia on a course to self-sustaining peace and democracy. Strong interventionists argue that the international administration should have been granted 'full executive authority' to overcome the opposition of local actors (Caplan 2005: 179–80; ICG 2003b). Instead of empowering weak and divided institutions, international agencies should have created an international protectorate with full executive and legislative powers to promote liberal values, such as tolerance, equality and human rights. This view has widespread appeal among Bosnians of all ethnic groups, who have often expressed more confidence in international authorities than domestic ones and trust the ability of international rule to identify and address Bosnia's needs (Alić 2003c). Džemal Sokolović (2001) has proposed the creation of an 'educational protectorate', which would suspend institutional political life for a considerable period of time and 'teach goodness' to the Bosnian people(s). Along similar lines, the editors of the influential Sarajevo magazine *Dani* (2000; see also Pecanin 2002) echoed this appeal by presenting international authorities with ten action points for Bosnia. In order to save the state from continuous mismanagement, corruption and economic collapse, the editors called on international agencies to disband local institutions and establish a one-year protectorate.[7]

Despite these agencies' lack of accountability to Bosnian citizens, the broad support among Bosnians for assertive international involvement in domestic politics suggests the prima facie attractiveness of this option. Whatever the appeal of this solution, however, there are both normative and practical reasons for rejecting it. Normatively, the formal suspension of democratic procedures (even for the noble goals of creating better foundations for democracy itself) is reminiscent of dubious 'civilisational politics' whereby enlightened Western officials transmit superior knowledge to backward local groups. Similar to the eighteenth- and nineteenth-century European powers' justification for their colonial possessions (Jackson Preece 2005: 79–84), the call for a 'new Western imperialism' is justified in paternalistic terms in order to 'convert' backward groups in order to 'save' them from war, annihilation, corruption and mismanagement. The very fact that this proposal often comes from Bosnian intellectuals is a clear sign of how ingrained this argument is locally, a signal of the internalisation of a dependent mindset that, as Frantz Fanon (1991) famously pointed out in his analysis of populations living under European colonial rule, characterises those who have been effectively colonised. Moreover, liberal interventionists never acknowledge the extent to which the present circumstances requiring an imperial rule are themselves the consequences of older imperial experiments or counter-productive international policies (Rao 2004). Yugoslavia itself was weakened in the 1980s by the package of austerity measures imposed by international financial institutions – undermining the ability of the federal government to deliver public goods (Woodward 1995). More generally, although there might be some localised domestic support for international administration, most weak states view with suspicion international intervention because of the issues of sovereignty it raises, and the possibility that intervention can be used (and abused) as a political tool of Western states (Ayoob 2004).

In addition, Bosnia shows how the limits of a protectorate are also very practical. Bosnia has, in practice, had a protectorate for years, even though international officials have always resisted using this label (Everly 2006). The High Representative's controversial use of the Bonn powers illustrates the dangers involved in granting unchecked international authority. For example, on 30 June 2004, the then High Representative Paddy Ashdown dismissed sixty democratically elected politicians for their obstruction of the peace process. Fifty-nine of them were Serbs allegedly involved in the criminal network of silence and complicity keeping wartime leader Radovan Karadžić safe from arrest and transfer to the ICTY in The Hague. By human rights standards, the dismissals were problematic. The politicians were democratically chosen though 'free and fair' elections, while those who fired them were appointed bureaucrats free of the constraints of direct accountability to the Bosnian population. Even more troubling, the possibility of appealing the decision was not even considered, nor was any criminal prosecution anticipated for those politicians allegedly involved in the mismanagement and embezzlement of public funds.[8] Criminal prosecution sometimes does occur when domestic courts follow up allegations by international officials, but this remains the exception instead of the rule.

Several observers have criticised this and other similar decisions which seem to neglect democratic principles and procedures. Doris Pack, member of the EU Parliament and Chairperson of the Delegation for Relations with the countries of Southeastern Europe, has vociferously attacked the arbitrary powers of the High Representative, but she is not the only one. Just a week prior to the mass dismissal, the Council of Europe (CoE) issued a report that described the powers of the High Representative in these terms:

> such powers run counter to the basic principles of democracy and are reminiscent of a totalitarian regime. Their use, no matter how seemingly justifiable on public-interest grounds, has an extremely harmful effect on the democratisation process in Bosnia and Herzegovina, since it causes feelings of injustice and undermines the credibility of democratic institutions and mechanisms.
>
> (CoE 2004)

In early 2007 the Bosnian Constitutional Court published its ruling declaring that the lack of any right of appeal for those individuals sacked by the High Representative constituted a violation of the European Convention on Human Rights. This ruling represents a healthy development, since it is a significant attempt by a Bosnian institution to assume ownership of a controversial subject from OHR. Nevertheless, the ruling could have far reaching consequences, since it directly challenges the Bonn powers and could put domestic and international institutions on to a collision course (ESI 2007).

Also, Bosnian citizens themselves do not always agree with the way the Bonn powers are used. In Han Pijesak, a hard-line municipality in the eastern part of the RS, 600 citizens signed a petition to reinstate the Serb mayor fired by Ashdown. The citizens' initiative is particularly interesting for two reasons. First, Han Pijesak has a complicated labyrinth of underground tunnels and caves where Karadžić is said to occasionally hide. For this reason, this municipality is politically and militarily extremely important. Second, the petition was also signed by many Bosniak returnees who perceived the Serb mayor as a respectable and trustworthy person – at least compared to the alternatives (Belloni 2004). These problematic aspects of international administration would only have been accentuated if international agencies had established a fully fledged protectorate.

In general, as the analysis in this book will show, a top-down approach makes it difficult to place the local population at the heart of the post-settlement democratisation process, but can lead international interveners to overlook local knowledge, talents and aspirations in the name of short-term efficiency. At the same time, the external imposition of policy creates the impression that the system is 'working' – alleviating pressure for reform. International agencies devote considerable attention to selling their achievements, rather than addressing deep-rooted problems and undertaking long-term structural projects that might have a more profound impact. This tendency to 'show results' combines with the inclination to blame local actors for delays, obstacles and drawbacks in the process. Slow progress is frequently blamed on narrow-minded and uncooperative local elites or on the 'Balkan mentality', the supposed combined effects of socialism and war. Moreover, many of the results that a protectorate could have achieved in Bosnia could have been reached with a more aggressive interpretation of the existing international prerogatives. The policy towards indicted war criminals, leaving international forces with the choice but not the obligation to arrest them, is probably the best example. Finally, although imperial power is sometimes regarded as the only form of foreign support to failing or weak states, there are promising alternatives. When local institutions cannot guarantee effective domestic governance, 'shared sovereignty' arrangements involving the appointment of international experts to local institutions can provide more efficient and transparent policy-making (Krasner 2004). In the long term, as Chapter 7 will argue, association agreements with the EU and eventual EU membership are preferable to the Western neo-colonial rule of troubled borderlands. But alternatives exist also for the post-colonial world further from Europe. Technology transfer, debt forgiveness and increased aid are often debated in international fora but regularly passed over or neglected.

The historical determinist approach

Some commentators argue that the creation of ethnically homogeneous nation-states is a necessary and inevitable historical development. Rather than forcing ethnic groups to share an unwanted state, international agencies should favour the groups' separation along clear lines and the creation of defensible borders. While the immediate human costs of this policy might be high, the long-term effects are more conducive to peace and stability.

According to Chaim Kaufmann (1999), structural circumstances complicate the co-existence of different ethnic and national groups in a single state. Whether groups want to cooperate or not might depend less on their goodwill and more on the structural conditions for collaboration. The dynamics of the security dilemma greatly affect groups' choices. Plausibly, in an environment dominated by an ineffectual central government, ethnic groups can rely only on themselves to guarantee their physical safety. As one group organises itself for self-protection, rival groups feel threatened and, in response to this real or perceived threat, decide to arm themselves. Even though arming may, theoretically, be only for defensive purposes, it can set in motion a dangerous spiral, particularly in a context such as Southeastern Europe where memories of the atrocities of World War II still haunt individuals and groups. In the aftermath of a bloody war, the parties suffer from a 'security dilemma in reverse', making matters even worse. Even when the former enemies want to implement a peace agreement in good faith, they need assurances that their willingness to cooperate will not provide an excuse for one of the parties to seize an opportunity to resume the war. As Barbara Walter explains,

> as groups begin to disarm, they create an increasingly tense situation. The fewer arms they have, the more vulnerable they feel. The more vulnerable they feel, the more sensitive they become to possible violations. And the more sensitive the less likely they are to fulfill their own side of the bargain.
> (Walter 1999: 43–44)

According to historical determinists, the dynamics of the security dilemma are so compelling as to make inter-ethnic coexistence impossible and the creation of mono-ethnic nation-states both inevitable and desirable. Only partition, the transfer of people and the homogenisation of states will succeed in addressing the security dilemmas affecting weak and failing states and and solve their stateness problems.

Historical determinists argue that the historical development of the nation-state in Europe confirms that ethnic and national homogeneity is inevitable – and that Bosnia will follow the path of other European countries. The wars that engulfed the former Yugoslavia for most of the 1990s represent the 'final working out of a long European tradition of violent ethnic homogenization' (Stokes 2003: 204) driven by the formation of nation-states on European territory. State-making wars are impossible to stop until they have completed their 'natural' course, that is, until they result in the creation of ethnically homogeneous nation-states. The idea of preserving ethnic diversity is therefore perceived to be whimsical and illusory. As Robert Hayden boldly states, the possibility that Bosnia will survive as a joint state of equal nations and citizens is 'virtually nonexistent' (1999: 18). For Gale Stokes, 'stability will come only when state borders ... are redrawn on ethnic lines, as they have been in the rest of Europe' (2003: 204). On similar grounds, Timothy Waters (2004) and Alexander Downes (2007) argue that Bosnia will achieve peace and stability only after its formal dismemberment. In sum, as long as international intervention stubbornly persists in preserving multi-ethnicity, Bosnia and the wider region will continue to be politically, socially and economically unstable.

The view that ethnic diversity is a recipe for instability and that partition is a solution to the stateness problem is open to a number of objections (Licklider and Bloom 2007; Stroschein 2005). The experience of Bosnia during the 1992–95 war suggests caution. When international diplomacy proposed partition to stop the war, it provoked further fighting. For example, the 1993 Vance–Owen Peace Plan (VOPP), named after its two main drafters (Cyrus Vance representing the UN and David Owen representing the EC), proposed the division of Bosnia into ten ethnically based provinces, the boundaries of which would be drawn on the basis of national and historic criteria, and maintained by a relatively centralised federal government (Owen 1995: 65). The perception that partition along ethnic lines was going to happen increased the incentives for local extremists to raise the level of violence and create a fait accompli as the basis for negotiating the separation. Despite Owen's disingenuous claim that the plan did not explicitly assign territories to any of the parties nor label the provinces with an ethnic character, it was very clear how the territories would be assigned. In particular, because the plan gave the Croats territories they neither controlled nor could claim on the basis of their numerical strength, it broke down the Muslim/Croat alliance which had been the only effective barrier to the advances of the Serbs, and it provided an incentive for the Croats (encouraged and supported by their kin in Croatia proper) to launch their own land campaign (Malcolm 1996: 248–49). As a result, 'proposals for the ethnicisation of Bosnia and its partition constitute a dangerous idealism, rather than the sober realism they style themselves as' (Campbell 1998: 163). Peace proposals that recognised ethnic groups as entitled to exclusive control over territory endorsed the logic of establishing ethnically homogeneous nation-states and gave free rein for violence against those individuals who inadvertently stood in the way.

If partition was back on the political agenda, it would probably lead to a renewal of fighting both in Bosnia and perhaps in other post-Yugoslav states. Moreover, partition is diametrically opposed to the post-World War II principle that law and security are incompatible with changing borders by force. After 1945, the right to self-determination was recognised only as a right to independence from a colonial power and freedom from foreign intervention and control, not border re-arrangement (Orentilicher 1998).[9] Granting the right to revise frontiers could set a precedent for dissatisfied minorities hoping to gain their own independence, effectively overturning the existing norm of self-determination with potentially far-reaching and dangerous consequences. Finally, any future partition of Bosnia would fail the significant number of Bosnian citizens who returned home after the war in an area under the control of an ethnic group other than their own, once again opening the possibility for their systematic harassment and possible expulsion.

In addition to these oft-cited reasons, advocates of partition ignore the fact that most states worldwide are both ethnically diverse and peaceful, underestimate the role of domestic elites in creating and sustaining the security dilemma, take no notice of the positive role international intervention can have in addressing such dilemma, and rely on questionable assumptions concerning the necessary historical development of states in Southeastern Europe.

First, historical determinists assume that diversity is a problem that will be resolved by the inevitable historical development of the ethnically homogeneous nation-state. However, examples from other Former Yugoslav Republics demonstrate how ethnic diversity is not a problem per se. When Yugoslavia dissolved, many predicted that Macedonia, with its sizeable Albanian population in a predominantly Slavic state, would soon fall into anarchy and civil war. According to Misha Glenny, 'Macedonia was the most fragile of the new states to emerge from the former Yugoslavia, less secure even than Bosnia-Herzegovina' (1999: 655). The fact that war broke out in the 1990s in Bosnia and not in Macedonia raises the question of whether the problem of multi-ethnic states is caused by their diversity or the choices made by political elites. Supporters of ethnic partition fail to consider this issue, or apply different standards to Bosnia and its neighbours. Thomas Friedman (2001), for example, has praised democratisation in Croatia and Serbia following the disappearance from the political scene of nationalist leaders Franjo Tuđman and Slobodan Milošević in 2000. When analysing Bosnia, however, he surprisingly argues that multi-ethnicity, and not Bosnian elites, is responsible for the slow progress towards democratic consolidation. Changes among elites in Croatia and Serbia helped the democratisation process, but similar changes are not considered useful in Bosnia where, Friedman argues, ethnic diversity makes progress very difficult, if not impossible. Although Friedman is correct to point out that elites should not be blamed for each and every crime committed since Yugoslavia's dissolution, it is unclear why what applies to Serbia and Croatia is not equally applicable to Bosnia.

Second, historical determinists underestimate the role of international intervention in addressing the security dilemma. The willingness of international actors to pursue coercive strategies can make the difference between maintaining peace (understood as a truce between two wars) and building the conditions for long-term democratisation and development (Stedman 2002: 667). The presence of spoilers, individuals whose inclination to cooperation and compromise cannot be improved through mediation and diplomacy, makes the use of coercive mechanisms indispensable. An assertive foreign military presence targeting local spoilers might be the precondition for implementing various clauses of a peace agreement. Even in the absence of local spoilers, the presence of international organisations can still be indispensable for guaranteeing the verification and enforcement of the peace treaty during the possibly treacherous period of post-war demobilisation. Finally, as Chapter 6 will show, post-war ethnic separation does not solve the security dilemma, but rather it can exacerbate inter-group tensions. Contrary to Kaufmann's main argument, it is the return of refugees and displaced persons to their pre-war homes that ensures the successful transition from war to peace and democracy.

In sum, one is led to believe that the historical determinists' underlying perspective is not grounded in the teleological idea that the ethnically homogeneous nation-state is historically inevitable, but instead on the principle that history in Southeastern Europe progresses in a circular rather than a linear fashion. The belief that Bosnian peoples will keep fighting until they attain their ethnically pure nation-states can only be justified from a perspective which can be described as 'historical recidivism'. Like inmates who, once freed from jail, are statistically more likely to commit crimes than the general population, Bosnians are supposedly doomed to perpetual conflict. A view popularised by the media sees Southeastern Europe as an area with unique traits of violence which set the region apart from other states and peoples. Often those analysts who use the term 'Balkans' rather than other possible labels, such as the more politically neutral 'Southeastern Europe', implicitly and indiscriminately adopt this view.[10] The 'violent and primordial' character of Southeastern European peoples is supposedly accentuated by the fact that they have rarely experienced democracy, self-government, and the recognition and protection of individual and group rights. When taken to its logical extreme, this kind of historical determinism dooms the project of building peace and democracy from the start. By denying the prospect that ethnic and national groups can manage their differences peacefully, historical determinists maintain a complacent, implicitly racist attitude of low expectations. However, recidivism is not destiny. Like former prison inmates who need a social and economic network of support to escape the traps of recidivism, deeply divided societies such as Bosnia need a similar support system in order to sustain peaceful coexistence.

The autonomist approach

Autonomists share with historical determinists the view that states cannot be made to work from the outside. Rather, success in state-building requires enlightened local leadership and domestic institutional responsibility – both very difficult to create exogenously (Chesterman *et al.* 2005). Some critics go as far as arguing that domestic institutional and local capacity is actually being destroyed by international intervention in weak and failing states. According to Francis Fukuyama, despite the rhetoric of 'capacity-building' the reality of international intervention shows a kind of 'capacity sucking out' (2004: 139). Instead of favouring the development of effective local institutions, rich and comparatively efficient international agencies crowd out weak state capacities.

However, while historical determinists argue that ethnic separation and the creation of mono-ethnic nation-states are ultimately unavoidable, autonomists focus on the means rather than the ends. Instead of pre-judging Bosnia's long-term political outlook, they stress the importance of procedural issues. They argue that only less international intervention will give the different local parties the indispensable breathing space to achieve locally rooted solutions to the post-Yugoslav political crisis. Local autonomy is needed to achieve stable political units able to develop and consolidate themselves in full-fledged democracies. There are two main versions of this argument, one highlighting the dangers of stopping a war before it is clearly won by one faction or group, and the other stressing the limits of international post-settlement intervention and the need to terminate foreign intrusion in Bosnian politics.

Autonomists argue that wars should run their course. The surest way to achieve lasting peace is not to impose a negotiated settlement from the outside, but to let the fighting achieve its 'natural' conclusion by allowing the stronger party to achieve a clear victory and enforce its own vision of reconciliation (Luttwak 1999). If a war does not exhaust its 'natural course' and a peace settlement is imposed by international interveners, then such a settlement is not really agreed upon by the local parties, and the possibility is real that war will start again soon after international interveners leave. In the absence of a clear victor, peace is better understood as an armistice and war is destined to start again sooner or later. Indeed, cross-country evidence suggests that negotiated settlements of identity civil wars are less likely to be stable than settlements resulting from military victories. Negotiated settlements create internal balance-of-power situations where groups maintain a power of veto which makes it unlikely that any major problems will be addressed and resolved. Crucially, each group will retain the military capacity for resorting to war, and will do so if it judges that its interests are better served by military action (Licklider 1995). According to the autonomists, the DPA embodies these contradictions – an example of 'how not to end a civil war' (Woodward 1999). It forces ethnic groups to recognise each other's right to existence and share power, and creates a domestic balance of power, but it leaves unresolved the underlying political problems that led to the war. Consequently, in the present circumstances the long-term chances of succeeding in building a democratic and multi-ethnic society are slim.

This view is problematic not only in moral terms, as it suggests that outsiders should not be concerned about mass killing and attempt to stop it, but, more importantly, it suggests an illusory recipe for building lasting peace. In the era of terrorism and weapons of mass destruction, permitting groups to fight a war to its 'natural conclusion' is a highly dangerous proposition. Moreover, leaving the parties to find a military solution until one ethnic group achieves a victory might take a very long time. And even when a faction is able to impose its own institutions and political identity, its victory can create a dynamic of competing national claims and counter-claims that are a continuing source of instability.[11] If the lessons of history in Southeastern Europe are worth learning, they teach that military victory does not lead to stability and order. Military success has provided the opportunity for the defeated party to reorganise to take revenge, and in turn to impose its own version of peace. Despite its numerous limitations and flaws, the DPA breaks this vicious circle. It provides an opportunity for the parties to negotiate their differences, thus potentially enabling them to acquire a stake in the maintenance of peace.

A second, subtler version of the autonomist perspective criticises the post-Dayton continuing external regulation of Bosnian political, social and economic affairs. International agencies justify this regulation on the grounds that they are engaged in the creation and promotion of local democratic institutions – an argument that fails to satisfy autonomists. David Chandler argues that the international consensus on democratisation and peace building 'has little to do with either democracy or Bosnia itself' (1999: 188). Rather, intervention in Bosnia is the instrument through which international agencies in danger of being rendered obsolete by the end of the Cold War were able to transform themselves and acquire a new strategic role. It is through the operation of these international agencies that great powers achieved a new partnership and grounds for cooperation, but at the expense of genuine democracy in Bosnia. Consequently, Chandler calls for less intervention and for 'letting the Bosnian people begin to work out their own way forward' without external and supposedly undue influence (1999: 198).

The contradictions inherent in the international imposition of decisions on the local parties, as mentioned, provide initial support for the autonomist views. The fact that the High Representative is unaccountable to, and that his powers are largely unchecked by, the local population, is worryingly reminiscent of the European colonial experience (Knaus and Martin 2003). The High Representative exercises his prerogatives on behalf and for the benefit of the Bosnian people. His interpretation of the 'will of the people' can be, and often is, in contrast to that of elected officials. The international imposition of decisions can frustrate the will of Bosnian citizens, who have chosen their leaders through (reasonably) free elections. The fact that these leaders do not always cooperate with the goals and aspirations of international agencies does not make them less legitimate than elected officials in, say, Italy or the United States. Accordingly, autonomists suggest that after more than a decade of international intervention, the assertive international presence should simply be terminated (in addition to Chandler 1999, see Knaus and Martin 2003; Bose 2002; Ivanić 2005). Since most observers believe that the end of international intervention will provide Serb and Croat nationalists with an opportunity to make the groups' separation permanent, the autonomist position is a de facto association with that of the historical determinists.

Despite the superficial appeal of notions of greater 'local democracy', less international intervention is not a solution to the Bosnian conundrum. There are two important problems with the currently fashionable view that Bosnia needs more self-government. First, it fails to take into account the reality of political life. Autonomists give little consideration to the environment where intervention takes place, or how local constraints affect the opportunities for international engagement. As Tihomir Loza points out, 'Bosnians don't take ownership of their country's future, not because the foreigners won't let them, but because they don't agree among themselves what the future should be like' (2004: 209–10). Autonomists mistakenly believe that domestic political disagreements would naturally be mediated and solve themselves. This view is not shared by local actors, who have been conspicuously absent from the debate about the possible end of international powers, despite the fact that they would benefit from the end of foreign prerogatives and the establishment of domestic institutions free from international supervision (Belloni 2003). Thus, an interventionist international presence is not the reason why Bosnians have failed to take responsible ownership over their own affairs, as demonstrated by the setbacks following changes in international strategy. While Paddy Ashdown assertively imposed his authority over Bosnian institutions, Schwartz-Schilling adopted a radically different approach, leaving Bosnian politicians to sort out their own problems. As a result, by the end of 2006 state building was stalled: constitutional reform faltered, the adoption of a unified police force was called into question, and lack of cooperation with the ICTY continued to delay integration within European institutions (ICG 2007).

Second, the procedural suggestion that international intervention has simply run its course is not a blueprint for what should replace it. Autonomists shy away from providing a workable alternative to the current political stalemate. This is unsurprising, since they believe that outsiders should simply be excluded from the domain of local politics. But as experience in Bosnia confirms, outsiders can play an important role. The question is not so much whether outside regulation should be terminated, but how to refine it to sustain the conditions for both the consolidation of democratic and inclusive political processes and increased domestic responsibility for policy-making. In short, the task is not to grant 'autonomy' (which no state in the world, with the possible exception of the United States, enjoys), but to shift international engagement from imposition to partnership and coopera-tion, progressively transferring the burden of policy-making to domestic authorities.

Towards better intervention

Much of the debate over international intervention in Bosnia has been framed in terms of more or less intervention. Strong interventionists con-sider continuing failures in local governance to be the result not of too much interventionism, but of too little. By contrast, historical determinists and autonomists lament excessive international involvement and urge the establishment of more locally ingrained political and social institutions. This debate over the proper dose of international involvement overlaps with the one about how to solve Bosnia's stateness problem. Strong interven-tionists trust the possibility that continuing international engagement and the removal of 'bad' domestic elites will keep secessionist tendencies in check and build strong foundations for Bosnia's democratic development; historical determinists foresee that only close symbiosis between the *demos* and the *polis* will guarantee stability and democratic development, and favour the creation of ethnically homogeneous nation-states; finally, autonomists do not take a stand on the question of ethnic and national diversity, arguing instead that Bosnians should simply govern themselves in the name of local self-determination.

Over time the debate has deteriorated into a rhetorical battle, with each side accusing the others of misinterpreting the reality of intervention. Lim-ited international impact is either understood as evidence of the uselessness of intervention, or of the need for a more assertive international presence. Sometimes academic and policy debate has even degenerated into personal attacks. Sumantra Bose, for example, describes Kaufmann's historical determinist argument in favour of partition as 'breezy and incorrect', 'crude, shallow', 'limited and static', 'inherently ahistorical, teleological' and 'lit-tered with factual mistakes'. He scolds the 'security dilemma fetishist', finally declaring that ethnic partition is 'ludicrous' and that 'Kaufmann's ignorance does not stop at matters of detail' (2002: 174–89). Examples such as this illustrate how the debate has stalemated between irreconcilable positions. More importantly, it has failed to identify the conditions under which international intervention can have a positive and lasting impact. In particular, the question of determining the proper balance between inter-national assertiveness and local ownership of the peace process is left unanswered. International agencies have to navigate the Scylla of excessive and potentially counter-productive actions that might undermine the foundations of state autonomy, and the Charybdis of weak intervention unable to create a concrete and lasting impact. The real dilemma is not only that of determining the extent to which unaccountable international administrators should use coercive powers, but that of fostering and sustaining the emergence of a democratic and inclusive domestic political process. Reaching this goal is an art, not a science, requiring long-term vision and commitment and a creative partnership between international and domestic forces.

Of course, how social and political institutions develop, and how human action can influence such development, is not a new question. In *The Poverty of Historicism* (1961), Karl Popper focused much of his attention on attacking historicism, the deterministic view that history moves inevitably and inexorably towards a specific state of affairs – a view still reflected in the historical determinists' views. Popper also considered and rejected an alternative position, labelled 'utopian social engineering' (1961: 42–45). This view, like historicism, requires the acceptance of deterministic connections between one social state of affairs and another. Strong interventionists and autonomists share this perspective in their prescription for strengthening weak and failing states. Strong interventionists aim at remodelling the whole of society in accordance with a specific blueprint – liberal internationalism. Autonomists argue instead that intervention prevents the 'natural' unfolding of the domestic political process, in particular the consolidation of democratic conflict management practices. According to Popper, historicism and utopian social engineering are ultimately flawed because they adopt a strong version of causality and prediction that is untenable in the social sciences.

Popper's alternative to historicism and utopian social engineering is 'piecemeal social engineering'. This approach accepts that social phenomena cannot be predicted with the degree of certainty found in the physical sciences: social scientists cannot predict the signing of a peace agreement in the same way an astronomer can predict a solar eclipse. However, piecemeal engineering accepts a weak version of prediction. Not all political and social institutions can be designed, but the piecemeal engineer can estimate the effect of any measure on society, learn from previous mistakes and make adjustments to achieve desirable ends (Popper 1961: 64–70). Piecemeal engineering in the context of weak and failing states calls for the careful examination of the impact of international policies and the identification of alternative strategies. As argued in Chapter 8, a balanced assessment of international intervention in Bosnia demonstrates that important mistakes were made, particularly at the beginning of the peace process, but that much has been accomplished as well. The Bosnian experience shows that the impact of intervention is likely to be more lasting the more it is aimed at improving the efficiency of domestic institutions, even at the cost of short-term delays or wastefulness.

Conclusion

Since the early 1990s, and even more so since the events of 11 September 2001, international intervention in weak and failing states has been at the top of the international agenda. More than a decade of experience in Bosnia can teach important lessons for other similar cases. Bosnia suffers from an intense 'stateness problem', whereby the different groups and citizens composing the Bosnian state have radically dissimilar views about the boundaries of the political community and the question of who should have citizenship rights in it. The 1995 Dayton Peace Agreement did not create this stateness question, but nor did it solve it. After three and a half years of war, Bosnia was maintained as a formally single state, but internally divided into two self-governing entities. A massive civilian and military mission was deployed to help implement the peace agreement. This mission was considerable in size and scope, but ill conceived. Its civilian part was composed by myriad international organisations and agencies only very loosely coordinated by a High Representative and his Office. Moreover, a clear separation was established between this office and the military and police component of the international operation – limiting the overall ability of international organisations to have an impact on events on the ground. Predictably, as Holbrooke foresaw, 'implementation [of the DPA] would be at least as difficult as the negotiations themselves' (1998: 205).

The resulting weakness and limited impact of the international mission has led to a lively debate on how to establish solid foundations for democratic development. Strong interventionists, historical determinists and autonomists have all put forward conflicting views, but rarely have they succeeded in identifying the conditions for effective international intervention. Instead, their debate has highlighted gaps and inconsistencies, but eventually stalemated into irreconcilable positions. At the heart of these differences lies the question of how to design local institutions to allow different groups to co-exist peacefully within a democratic, multi-ethnic institutional framework – a question addressed in the next chapter.

3 Democracy from scratch

The question of whether Bosnia is doomed to partition or can survive as one state – and in what form – largely depends on its institutions and citizens' commitment to them. Because conflict inevitably hardens the identities of those involved, mistrust among local parties complicates the process of institution building. Having endured three and a half years of fierce fighting, it is to be expected that local groups fear each others' intentions, and are very wary that one group might exploit the peace process to impose its own vision of the future with the sponsorship of international agencies. This imposes strong restrictions on the range of acceptable institutions that the local parties, at least initially, are willing to accept. Most of the Bosniak leadership has considered the DPA as a 'floor', that is, a document to be built on in order to strengthen central institutions. Both Serb and Croat nationalist parties have a diametrically opposite view, considering the DPA as the 'ceiling' that should not be further developed, and preferring the development of local autonomies and stronger ties with neighbouring Croatia and Serbia. This preference makes the Bosniaks nervous because of the spectre of a Poland-like scenario in which Serbia and Croatia agree to partition the territory lying between the two. When different groups within the polity have radically different opinions over the acceptable boundaries of the political community, and different preferences about issues of allegiance and identity, the nature of the institutions becomes the heart of the political struggle.

In these circumstances, the survival of the state depends on a careful balance of different views held by local parties. An elaborate set of checks and balances, grounded in the theory of consociationalism, was created at Dayton to guarantee the political representation of each national group at the institutional level, to protect groups' rights to self-government and to promote inter-ethnic compromise. Ethnic quotas ensure group representation at all levels of government and in the statewide public administration. Each group is also granted the right to veto decisions that might violate its own 'vital interest', while a proportional electoral system guarantees that all major groups in society are politically represented. There are strong reasons to suggest that this consociational framework was the only feasible model for Bosnia at the time of the signing of the DPA in 1995, and some argue that it still remains the only realistic institutional option for the country (Allcock 2004; Bose 2006).

This chapter first considers Bosnia's post-settlement institutions and their contradictory and inefficient nature, and continues with a review of the various proposals for changing these institutions. The chapter focuses on the 2000 Constitutional Court decision, known as the constituent peoples case, to end legalised ethnic discrimination throughout the Bosnian territory and its impact on the institutional structures. While the implementation of this decision did improve the quality of the political representation of the various ethnic groups and the legitimacy of Bosnian institutions, it was never intended to create a viable and functional state. Overall, Bosnian consociational institutions ensure equal representation of the main groups in society, but at the cost of efficient decision-making and governability.

Institutional promises

The consociational approach to conflict management is a group-based institutional mechanism centred on cooperation between political elites. Consociationalists argue that ethnic differences have to be taken as a given, recognised, and made integral in the institutional design. They argue that consociationalism provides for a share in decision-making and as such provides each main group with a little of what they want – power. According to consociationalism's main proponent, Arend Lijphart, consociational systems need to contain the following institutional arrangements: (1) the participation of representatives of all significant groups in the government in order to enable cross-community executive power-sharing; (2) the proportionality principle to serve as the basic standard of political representation; (3) a high degree of community autonomy and self-government; and (4) a minority or mutual power of veto that guarantees no group will be outvoted by the majority when its vital interests are at stake (1977: 25). Consociational institutions have worked successfully in divided societies such as Switzerland and Belgium, and it is at least plausible that they could provide an institutional solution for deeply divided societies such as Bosnia.

Bosnia's consociationalism

The post-Dayton institutional framework corresponds to a 'classic example of consociational settlement' (Bose 2002: 216; Bieber 2006a: ch. 4), with extensive power-sharing provisions and self-governing prerogatives given to the three main ethnic groups. The DPA created a complex political structure, composed of one state, two entities, three peoples, four million citizens, and five layers of governance led by fourteen prime ministers and governments, making Bosnia the state with the highest number of presidents, prime ministers and ministers in the entire world (see Figure 3.1). The DPA set up what Carl Bildt described as 'the most decentralised state in the world' (1998). As Sarajevans sarcastically put it, if one loudly says 'Good morning, Mr President!' in the main pedestrian street of the Bosnian capital, everybody turns around. Even a cursory overview of the institutions created by the Bosnian constitution confirms the judgment that it is a

'Frankenstein constitution' (Lyon 2000: 112). Annex 4 of the DPA outlines the responsibilities of domestic institutions (the parliament, presidency, and the constitutional court) and their ethnic composition.

Statewide institutions

The central government is weak and has limited powers. It was intended by the DPA to be sluggish and this is indeed the case. The Council of Ministers comprises a member of each of the three main groups, with the chair rotating every eight months. In December 2002, the High Representative imposed a provision that ended the rotation principle, made the appointment

BiH's Legislative and Executive Bodies

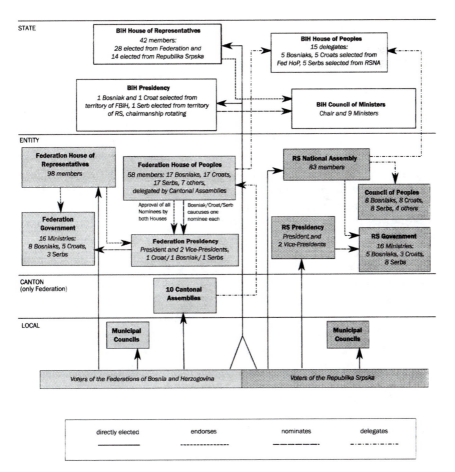

Figure 3.1 BiH's legislative and executive bodies. (Source: OHR)

four years long and thus provided more political stability. Only three ministries (Foreign Affairs, Foreign Trade, and Civil Affairs and Communications) were created at Dayton, prompting an observer to describe Bosnia as 'essentially a customs union with a foreign ministry attached' (Hayden 1999: 126). This situation prevailed until 2000 when three more ministries were instituted. These are the Ministry for European Integration, the Ministry for Human Rights and Refugees and the Ministry of the Treasury for the Institutions of BiH. In late 2002, two more ministries (Justice and Security) were added to the previous ones. The Ministry of Defence was established in 2004, raising the total number of ministries from the original three to nine. The weakness of the central institutions is perhaps best illustrated by the fact that not only are their budgets significantly smaller than that of the Entities, but they are also dependent upon transfers from them. Without an army, police force or judiciary, and with little economic and financial resources, the Bosnian state is very 'thin'.

Other divided states have equally weak unions. For example, in Belgium the central government has powers limited to budgeting, defence and foreign policy and the state structure is divided into three geographically defined regions – Flanders, Wallonia and the bilingual capital of Brussels – and three non-territorially defined cultural communities – the Flemish and French community and the small German-speaking community (Lijphart 1999: 195–97 and passim). In both Bosnia and Belgium, weak central powers and extensive decentralisation can serve a useful purpose, since domestic groups are often too divided to agree on a common policy (Stroschein 2003). Although group autonomy can serve to appease all groups, such autonomy in Bosnia clashes with individual human rights, in particular the post-war right to return home of those displaced by the 1992–95 conflict (see Chapter 6).

Moreover, the weak central powers and limited responsibilities of central institutions do not necessarily facilitate agreement and compromise among Bosnia's political leaders, who hold veto power in all institutions. Annex 4, art. V of the DPA provides for the direct election of a three-member collective state presidency composed of one Bosniak, one Croat, and one Serb. Crucially, the Bosniak and Croat members are elected in the Federation, while the Serb is elected in the RS. This method of election discourages officials from identifying themselves as representatives of the entire Bosnian body politic, and instead encourages ethnic over civic identity. The presidency functions on the basis of consensus, with any of the members having the right to block decisions by invoking the 'vital interest' of the respective group. As Robert Hayden points out, the Bosnian presidency 'seems to be an institution ... designed for deadlock' (1999: 131). When deadlock occurs, the RS National Assembly or the Federation Parliament can override a presidential veto with a two-thirds majority vote.

Bosnia's statewide legislature is bicameral. The House of Peoples, or Upper House, has fifteen members (five Croats and five Bosniaks from the

Federation and five members from the RS). Its members are appointed by the legislatures of the two entities. The House of Representatives, or Lower House, has forty-two members (equally divided between Bosniaks, Croats and Serbs) and is elected directly by proportional representation from the two Entities. The legislative process is cumbersome, slow, and produces frequent deadlocks. Any of the three communities can declare a proposed legislation 'destructive of a vital interest' if the majority of the delegates from that community so decide. In order to pass, a proposed parliamentary decision then requires a majority vote in the House of Peoples by each of the three communities. In practice, the legislative activity has been very modest.[1] In the first year of the parliament's existence, ten laws were passed. Between 1998 and 2000, an average of five laws a year was adopted. Since 2000, legislative activity has further increased. However, since the re-election of nationalist parties in late 2002, the work of the parliament has again been blocked (Bieber 2006a: 55). From mid-2004 domestic legislative activity has started again, prompted by the requirements of the process of European integration (see Chapter 7). Significantly, legislation was not imposed by the High Representative, although according to one estimate about 60 per cent of all laws are still drafted by international agencies, turning the Bosnian parliament into a rubber stamp for internationally drafted laws (Solioz 2005: 130).

The Entities

The Entities are granted all residual governmental powers and authority not expressly assigned to statewide institutions. Each is provided with self-governing institutions, including legislative, executive and judiciary organs. Significantly, defence responsibilities, an important indication of sovereign prerogatives, are vested in the Entities. Only in 2004 was a defence ministry established, competencies transferred from the Entity to the state parliament, and a unified chain of command for the three previously divided armies created.

The Federation has its own bicameral legislative institutions consisting of a House of Peoples and a House of Representatives. The House of Peoples has seventy-four members elected indirectly, thirty of whom must be Croats. The House of Representatives has 140 members elected directly by proportional representation. The two houses elect the president and vice president of the Federation, one of whom has to be a Bosniak and the other a Croat. Control of these two offices rotates between these groups on a yearly basis. Their powers are relatively modest. The Federation president nominates a government (headed by a prime minister) for endorsement by the legislature. Each minister must have a deputy who is not from their own ethnic group.

Power is even further decentralised and dispersed at the local level. Ten cantons exist, each with its own constitution, an assembly directly elected by the Federation voters, a prime minister, and ministries. Eight of the ten cantons have a clear ethnic majority. In the two mixed cantons, a special regime grants autonomy to those municipalities with an ethnic majority other than the majority at the cantonal level. An indication of cantons' strength is their budget, which for some cantons is ten times that of the Federation, and which derives from their power to tax (Fox and Wallich 1997). As of 1 January 2006 Bosnia introduced a value added tax (VAT) system to replace the Entity level sales tax. As a result, state-level revenues have increased, but at the cost of a considerable increase in inflation, which averaged 7.4 per cent in 2006. Consistent with the liberal economic template guiding international intervention, the VAT system came into effect with no preparation made to cushion the impact of higher prices on the poor.

Since its inception the Federation has been a paper tiger. Croats, supported by the president of neighbouring Croatia, Franjo Tuđman until his death in 1999, insist that the Bosniaks are trying to dominate them and thus are unreliable partners. In areas with a Croat majority a parallel statelet, 'Herceg-Bosna', effectively governs, despite repeated attempts by international agencies to dismantle it. Local authorities have repeatedly announced that Herceg-Bosna would cease to exist, but it is believed that it still effectively operates, perpetuating the weakness of the Federation's formal institutions. The international agencies' main response to the Croats' dissatisfaction with the institutional framework has been the attempt to abolish Herceg-Bosna and improve the functioning of the Federation. At Dayton, part of the negotiations revolved around making the Federation stronger and more united by dismantling these illegal structures.[2] In 1997, however, an OSCE internal study noted that Herceg-Bosna 'in every aspect from military and security matters to business ties is part of Croatia' (Burg and Shoup 1999: 377). When the main Croat nationalist party, the Croat Democratic Union (HDZ), declared Croat self-government in early 2001, the continuity between the newly established institutions and the wartime political structures was obvious (ICG 2001b). Not only do Croat parallel institutions still function outside the rule of law and the Dayton framework, but also the weak international effort to eliminate them can easily be exploited by Croat nationalists for their own interests. The HDZ leadership was able to use these feeble state building efforts to argue that they are attacks on the Croat people and their legitimate representatives. Fearing minority status within the Federation, the majority of ordinary Croats support their ethno-nationalist leaders.

The RS constitutional structure is more centralised and less convoluted than that of the Federation. The RS constitution is written in a rhetorical style reminiscent of state socialism, with a considerable 'credibility gap between rights proclaimed under the constitution and what is really practiced or observed' (Bose 2002: 70). The Serb predominance was at first guaranteed in Article 1 of the RS constitution, where it was stated that 'Republika Srpska shall be the state of the Serb people and of all its citizens', a provision that only changed after a 2000 Constitutional Court decision declared it unconstitutional (as further discussed later in this chapter). The RS maintains an eighty-three member unicameral National Assembly elected directly by proportional representation. Only after the 2000 Constitutional Court decision was an upper house created, composed of an equal number of Serbs, Croats and Bosniaks. The president is elected directly and exercises limited but politically significant powers. Among these powers is that of proposing to the RS Assembly a candidate for prime minister.[3] Unlike the Federation, the RS does not have cantons, making its structure centralised and simpler. However, municipal self-government both in the Federation and the RS adds an additional governance layer, with the special status of Brčko making the district almost like a third Entity in its own right.[4]

One key and potentially problematic aspect of the Entities' power is their right to regulate their own citizenship. While citizens of either Entity are automatically citizens of Bosnia, the reverse is not true. As Anna Morawiec Mansfield points out, in practice 'the citizenship provisions in the constitution effectively make citizenship, if not a function of, then certainly synonymous with, ethnicity ... these provisions are therefore quite likely to result in the discrimination that the state constitution prohibits' (2003: 2063). Instead of favouring reintegration, the citizenship regime facilitates segregation by encouraging citizens to move to the Entity controlled by their own ethnic group in order to gain greater influence and legal protection.

As a whole, Bosnia's institutions are expected to provide Bosnian groups with extensive self-governing prerogatives and with the possibility of sharing common institutions governing matters of joint concern. Supporters of consociational institutions claim that participation by former enemies in inclusive political structures can produce a more consensual political culture. As Lijphart argues, patience is the best counsel:

> In the Netherlands, it took about 50 years of power-sharing and autonomy to give the once hostile and antagonistic religious groups a sufficient feeling of security to moderate their attitudes toward each other and to create a less divided society. South Africa does not seem to have done badly under its power-sharing system in less than 10 years.
>
> (Lijphart 2003)

Although Lijphart trusts that consociational institutions will foster interethnic accommodation, there is only anecdotal evidence that this is the case (Roeder and Rotchild, 2005). Consociationalists never convincingly addressed the direction of causation between consociational institutions and cooperation: does consociationalism encourage cooperation, or is cooperation the result of a previous implicit agreement among the elites that they must reach a mutual accommodation? The example of South Africa actually highlights the limited and short-term usefulness of consociational institutions. South Africa's 1994 post-apartheid constitution contained extensive consociational measures, but these were scrapped in 1996 when South Africa became a majoritarian democracy. If a lesson can be learned from this example it is that consociationalism might have a role to play as a short-term institutional device to reassure numerically smaller groups that they will not be outvoted in the transitional period from one regime to another, but it is less useful in addressing the problem of stateness. Indeed, despite its internal divisions, the existence, autonomy and territorial integrity of the South African state were never called into question in the transition from apartheid to majoritarian democracy.

But even granted the short-term need for consociational arrangements, the reliance on elites' cooperation can be problematic. Bosnia's pre-war experience presents a clear warning of the precariousness of consociational democracy. The failed transition from communist rule to successful consociationalism in Bosnia in 1990 was due to lack of cooperation among the elites (Burg 1997: 135). In retrospect, the consequences for Bosnia were disastrous. The post-Dayton evidence confirms the difficulty of establishing a clear link between consociational institutions and elite cooperation. In more than a decade of post-settlement transition, consociationalism has had a limited impact on the commitment of Bosnian elites to cooperate in the implementation of the DPA. Perhaps this is due to the DPA's most striking paradox: 'in its attempt to integrate all people into a unified Bosnia and Herzegovina, the constitution bases such integration precisely on that which divides Bosnia and Herzegovina – ethnicity' (Mansfield 2003: 2058).

Institutional problems

What prevents consociational institutions from developing in a direction more amenable to inter-ethnic compromise? To begin with, the institutional/ electoral dynamics of the consociational system discourage cooperation among ethnic groups. Politicians and political parties have little or no incentive to appeal beyond their own narrow ethnic constituency in order to be voted into office. As Chapter 4 will illustrate, many rounds of post-settlement elections in Bosnia have confirmed they do not need to. Most offices are reserved for the representative of one ethnic group, and can be elected by residents of one Entity or the other, with little or no incentive for politicians to make cross-ethnic appeals. Without incentives for cooperation, it is easy for politicians to win popularity by defending their national group and by portraying the others as enemies. As a prominent Bosnian sociologist aptly observed, nationalist parties are very skilled in playing with nationalist and discriminatory sentiments: 'what they have to do is to say that the ethnicity they are supposedly representing does not have equal rights with other ethnicities' (Alić 2002).

When elites do compromise across ethnic lines, they are subjected to competition for group allegiance from counter-elites who can denounce compromise as 'selling out'. Politicians willing to seek or accept conciliation may find themselves open to the phenomenon of 'ethnic out-bidding', whereby extremist political fringes may accuse them of selling out the interests of the nation they are expected to represent. Instead of incentives for cooperation, consociationalism creates conditions for a centrifugal competition that severely limits inter-ethnic compromise, a point that consociationalists often fail to consider in proper depth (Reilly 2001). Without some degree of elite cohesion, consociationalism cannot improve the working of local institutions, but rather supports the election of those most likely to boycott them. Furthermore, ethnic elites often exploit their ethnic credentials for personal aggrandizement. Political analysts have long noted a symbiosis between nationalists and criminals, who are often one and the same, taking advantage of nationalism to hide their crimes. The March 2005 indictment of Dragan Čović, a sitting head of state, Mato Tadić, the president of the Constitutional Court and a number of prominent businessmen confirmed to Bosnian public opinion the limits of Bosnia's political class (Skrbić 2005). Perhaps this is why there has been remarkably little opposition among Bosnian citizens to the removal of obstructionist politicians, the arrest of indicted war criminals and the imposition of legislation following the 1997 international agencies' adoption of the Bonn powers.

Institutional inefficiency

The consociational institutional framework obscures responsibility and makes policy-making slow and likely to end in deadlock – problems Bosnia shares with most consociational democracies (see, for example, Roeder and Rotchild 2005). Because various ethnic elites maintain zero-sum views of each other, and institutions do not provide incentives for cooperation, effective governance is extremely difficult to achieve. Extensive autonomy and decentralisation increase the inefficiency of administration. For example, Bosnia has seventeen police services, but they refuse to cooperate, and crime is rising. Furthermore, ethnic guarantees, such as minority vetoes, have the perverse effect of increasing the possibility of mutual intransigence – entrenching the conditions for a perpetual stalemate whose long-term consequences are hard to gauge. The best-case scenario remains one in which intransigent elites are replaced over time by more accommodating political actors. This situation, however, is unlikely to occur in the near future, for the reasons inherent in the institutional dynamics just described.[5] In sum, ethnic quotas reinforce the salience of ethnic identity and cleavage, entrench many of the ethnic divisions that international intervention is supposed to reduce, and eventually come to perpetuate instability and inefficiency.

This inefficiency complicates the process of transition from international rule to local ownership. With institutions barely functioning, there arises the problem of knowing who will take over the responsibilities of international agencies as they downsize their presence with a view to exiting. In 1999, the

High Representative introduced the idea of 'ownership of the peace process' (Petritsch 2002a: 209–13). This was a conceptual sea change in the international approach to intervention, aimed at empowering local actors and introducing a breakthrough from dependency on international aid towards local sustainability (Sonn 2003: 49). The Stability Pact for South East Europe, launched on 10 June 1999, was presented to the world as expressing a similarly novel approach to the region. It attempted to replace a reactive crisis intervention policy with a comprehensive long-term approach consciously modelled on the post-1945 Marshall Plan which was so influential in rebuilding Europe after World War II. The Stability Pact aimed at developing a partnership between international and local actors, while creating the conditions for effective local ownership of the peace process. However, local ownership and the connected process of gradual international withdrawal are dependent upon the presence of functioning institutions, the very same condition that international intervention has only partly succeeded in creating.

Institutional discrimination

In addition to the problem of institutional inefficiency, there remains the question of the extent to which consociational institutions hinder the achievement of other objectives of the peace agreement. Because consociational institutions recognise and give priority to ethnic groups, they can undermine liberal human rights norms, which are typically cast in individual terms. While the DPA recognised and institutionalised group rights, at the same time it recognised extensive human rights provisions meant to protect individuals as such, not as members of a particular ethnic group. These two opposite rights-based approaches are in perpetual tension and, despite international agencies' efforts to assume this tension away, there is often a trade-off between group-based institutional components of a peace agreement and the defence of individual rights that are inevitably violated during war. Consociational arrangements violate at least three individual human rights norms: the regional autonomy conferred on groups can limit the capacity of individuals of one ethnic group to move (or return) to an area under the control of another ethnic group; institutions diminish the political power of individuals who are not members of the protected groups; finally, they openly discriminate among members of groups on the basis of their ethnic belonging (Wippman 1998: 230–41).

All of these problems are present in Bosnia. First, as Chapter 6 will show, the division of the country into ethnically defined regions greatly complicates the exercise of the right to return for those individuals who do not belong to the ethnic majority in a given area. Second, members of national minorities (Roma, Jews, Turks, etc. – labelled as 'others' in the constitution) are not eligible for a variety of administrative jobs and political offices because they do not belong to the three main ethnic groups. While this is an undeniable failing of the agreement, it is unlikely to be addressed by international agencies or domestic parties. The limited number of 'others' makes the matter marginal among the concerns of international agencies, while the three main ethnic groups are unlikely to protest against a condition of privilege. Third, the DPA gives priority to the three main ethnic groups, makes political representation dependent upon ethnic belonging, and thus discriminates against individuals who do not identify themselves ethnically or, even if they do, might not be able to exercise a variety of rights because they reside in an area where they constitute a minority.

The last problem is the one most directly related to the design of the institutions. Not only do consociational institutions demonstrate the difficulty of finding a balance between individual and group rights, but also they are internally contradictory. In its preamble, the state-wide constitution recognises 'three constituent peoples': 'Bosniak, Croat and Serb'. However, the Federation's constitution recognises only Bosniaks and Croats as 'constituent peoples', while the preamble of the RS constitution refers to the 'inalienable right of the Serb people to self-determination'. These clauses in the Entities' constitutions create the basis for discrimination of the Serbs in the Federation, and Bosniaks and Croats in the RS, and are in contradiction with the state-wide constitution recognising all three groups as 'constituent peoples'. This is a significant failure of the DPA, which originated from the fact that the Entity constitutions were created prior to the statewide constitution. The RS constitution came into force even before Bosnia had declared independence in spring 1992. The Federation constitution was created in 1994 as a result of the so-called 'Washington agreement'. The DPA created an overarching framework but did not harmonise the two Entity constitutions. Instead, it incorporated some discriminating aspects, for example in the election of the members of the tripartite presidency (see Chapter 4).

Given the inefficient and discriminatory nature of Bosnian institutions, it is hard to avoid the conclusion that 'clearly, there is a need to change the Constitution' (Tokić 2003: 45). However, despite the almost universal recognition that changes to the institutional structure are needed, reform is delicate. The debate on how to change the basic institutional formula established at Dayton (three peoples, two Entities, one state) has been part of the democratisation process since the beginning of international intervention. The different views held by local nationalist parties, civil society groups, and international agencies on the substance of reform and the legitimacy of the state complicates the possibility of meaningful changes. International agencies fear that the prospect of an extensive revision of the DPA could 'open a Pandora's box of competing claims' (Lyon 2000: 115). Consequently, they have repeatedly rejected proposals for a 'new Dayton', that is, a new all-encompassing agreement to move the peace process beyond the stalemate that has characterised most post-settlement international intervention.

Proposals for change

Four institutional options have been discussed: the elimination of the Entities to be replaced with a 'one man, one vote' democratic structure; the 'cantonisation' of the country; the creation of three Entities; and the process of internal reform of the DPA, as advocated by OHR and most international officials. Before turning to the last option, which prevailed, and its implications for institutional change, I will address the three alternatives and their rationale. Each of these proposals has been advanced by the former warring parties as a potential way to overcome the post-Dayton impasse. Each focused on the problem of institutional discrimination, but neglected the equally pressing question of institutional efficiency.

Particular attention is paid to the question of how to provide the Croats with a stake in Bosnian institutions. This question became especially urgent since in early 2001 the HDZ protested its exclusion from power in the Federation, which resulted from the formation of the ruling Alliance for Change, by proclaiming the 'restoration of Croat autonomy', creating a de facto third Entity and withdrawing its military officers from the Federation army. The resulting constitutional crisis was described, perhaps too emphatically, as 'the biggest challenge to the Dayton Peace Accords since they were signed in November 1995' (ICG 2001b: 1). The attempt was ultimately unsuccessful. In March 2001, the High Representative sacked Ante Jelavić, the Croat member of the presidency and HDZ leader, for his role in attempting to break away from Bosnia's common institutions.[6] Social Democratic Party (SDP) member Jozo Križanović replaced him and soldiers returned to their barracks. While the question of the Croats' position within the Bosnian state was dropped, at least for the time being, the crisis suggested that parallel administration and structures had existed all along, despite international agencies' timid attempts to dismantle them. The failed secession attempt further delegitimised these parallel structures, but also worsened relations between Croats and their Bosnian and international counterparts.

Proposal 1: abolishing the Entities

A view popular among European and Bosnian liberal commentators is that the elimination of the Entities and the creation of a majoritarian democracy based on individual human rights represents the solution to the domestic institutional deadlock. Manfred Nowak, Austrian member of the Bosnian Human Rights Chamber, contends that Bosnia should 'rid itself of its redundant and inefficient Entities'.[7] Similarly, Bosnian constitutional lawyer Zoran Pajić (2002) argues that, if Bosnia's future is one in which both society and political institutions are to be ethnically integrated, then there is no political and institutional space for any Entity. This view is often echoed by the Bosniak leadership, which has also called attention to the need to establish a more integrated country along the lines of 'one man, one vote' principle. However, in a context where individuals vote largely (but by no means exclusively) along ethnic lines, majoritarianism is likely to create a state disproportionately dominated by the largest voting group (the Bosniaks) and thus one rejected by both Serbs and Croats.

This is the reason why these two groups have always been suspicious of the Party for Bosnia's (SBiH) call for the elimination of the Entities. (This is not entirely correct. The Croats might actually agree on the prospect of abolishing the Entities, but hold different views about what should replace them – see below.) The party, whose electoral basis is almost exclusively Bosniak and was the brainchild of wartime prime minister Haris Silajdžić, campaigned for both the 2000 and 2006 elections with the slogan *Bosna bez entiteta*, or 'Bosnia without Entities' (Silajdžić 2000). The international agencies' ambivalent response to this slogan, which violated the DPA and therefore could have subjected the SBiH and its leadership to sanctions, made the Serbs nervous. While changes to the DPA have been regularly excluded, international officials erred by often reacting to the SBiH slogan quite favourably, hoping that the party would challenge the electoral support of the main Bosniak nationalist party, the Party for Democratic Action (SDA), and thus undermine a perceived obstacle to further democratisation. This ambiguous approach backfired. At the 2000 general elections Serb nationalists were able to raise the spectre of a Bosnia without Entities dominated by Bosniaks and rally support behind their national cause to defeat Milorad Dodik, the West's favourite moderate candidate (Perić 2000). In the 2006 election campaign Dodik employed electoral tactics which put him on par with the most radical Serb nationalists. In response to Silajdžić's call for the abolition of the Entity system, Dodik championed a nationalist reaction against reunification of the country. By threatening to conduct a referendum in the RS to secede from Bosnia, he gained Serb voters' support and became the uncontested winner of the elections.

Proposal 2: re-cantonisation

The abolition of the Entities is also one of the institutional solutions preferred by the Croat leadership. The Croat National Council, envisaged as a transitional structure that would operate as the Croat self-governing body before the substantial reorganisation of the state, has proposed 're-cantonisation' as a way to weaken the RS, while promoting Croats' interests throughout the country (Sinanović 2000). The idea of creating cantons as an alternative to the Entities is not new. The Vance–Owen Peace Plan (VOPP) first proposed the cantonisation of Bosnia in 1993. Ivo Komšić, former president of the Croatian National Assembly, presented a similar scheme in 1994, probably attempting to capitalise on the fact that the VOPP was particularly generous to the Croats. After the signing of the DPA the

Croat leadership has continued to toy with this idea. As Vitomir Miles Raguz, the former Bosnian Ambassador to the EU and NATO and prominent Croat politician contended, 'newly constituted cantons ... would provide each community with institutions that they consider their own, and that they will take into a common state each feeling that it has a part of a whole to defend in Sarajevo' (2001). These local institutions would be closer to local issues and problems and thus, theoretically, would be more democratic. The proposal found sponsors in Croatia proper where Drazen Budisa, the leader of the Croatian Social Liberal Party, put forward a plan envisaging the abolition of the Entities and the creation of a federal state made up of 12–14 cantons (Hedl 2001). The High Representative, however, summarily dismissed the proposal on the grounds that it would amount to the unravelling of Dayton (Petritsch 2002a: 344–45). International officials always feared that the re-cantonisation of the country could hide an agenda for further political and social dismemberment. The Serbs, who would lose their semi-independent republic, would probably oppose this solution (Ivanić 2005: 282), and even if they accepted it, there is no guarantee that ethno-nationalist elites would not abuse newly created cantons.

Proposal 3: establishing three Entities

As an alternative to re-cantonisation, Croat nationalists have championed the idea of changing the DPA to create a third Entity. Former defence minister Miroslav Prce (2001) has pointed out how Croat support for Bosnian institutions has been fading steadily since 1995, in stark contrast with the popular Serb attitude in the same period. The Serbs increased their support for a unified state from a mere 4 per cent in 1996, to almost 30 per cent in 2000. The Croats' support for the joint institutions declined dramatically after the signing of the DPA, from two-thirds to one-third within a few years. According to Prce, the reason for this difference lies in the fact that the Serbs (and the Bosniaks) have an institutional stake in a common state they can identify with, while the Croats do not. As a result, Prce emphasised the importance of changing the DPA to better represent Croat interests. While he did not openly call for a third Entity, he did suggest that only the creation of 'three smaller, multi-ethnic, citizen federal units' would produce a 'countrywide civil society'. When the Croats attempted to establish a self-governing authority in early 2001, Prce called for the Croat soldiers not to serve the 'illegitimate' Federation government and to remove Bosnian insignia from their uniforms. As mentioned above, the rebellion was defeated with the return of soldiers to the barracks and the sacking of Prce from the position of defence minister.[8] Since then, the HDZ has been officially in favour of strengthening common state institutions, while simultaneously balancing the presence of a stronger state with stronger municipalities.

Because the re-cantonisation of the country and the creation of a third Entity have been ruled out, there remains the possibility of internal reform of the institutions created at Dayton. Procedurally, however, the process of revising the constitution is burdensome, and likely to be easily stopped by any dissenting group. Under Article X of the constitution, a decision of the Parliamentary Assembly, including a two-thirds majority of those present and voting in the House of Representatives, is needed to amend the constitution. If any of the three constituent peoples consider a proposal of the presidency or Parliamentary Assembly destructive of its vital interests, the constitution contains detailed procedures to stop possible escalation (art. IV, 3e and f; art. V, 2d). Substantively, the problem of constitutional reform is made more acute by the fact that there is no agreement among local political actors, as the overview above clearly indicates. The failed attempt at constitutional reform in early 2006 demonstrates that the institutional solutions defended by the main nationalist parties reflect their efforts to gain advantage or benefit for themselves or their respective ethnic groups (see Chapter 7).

For fear of opening a can of worms of competing claims, international agencies have adopted a dual strategy. They have guaranteed the survival of the basic constitutional structure established at Dayton, while promoting piecemeal reforms with a view to making the two Entities as multinational as possible. A mechanism within the constitution (art. III, 5b) allowed for a transfer of competence from the Entities to the state, but only with the express consent of both Entities. This clause permitted the High Representative to argue that the DPA was both open to evolution and should not have been changed until fully implemented (Petritsch 2002a: 336–41). Because all main Bosnian nationalist parties found at least some reason to give support to the peace agreement, while maintaining different interpretations of what the DPA allows for and how it should be interpreted, the Dayton infrastructure was able to preserve stability. Paradoxically, however, the international agencies' position is a de facto alliance with the same nationalist parties these agencies have quite explicitly attempted to undermine. Attempts to promote multi-ethnic parties and enforce human rights norms clash with the international agencies' commitment to preserving discriminatory and exclusivist institutions that can be easily captured by the nationalist elites.

Since 1995, this approach has had two far-reaching negative consequences. First, the promotion of multi-ethnic politics within an institutional structure that does not particularly encourage inter-ethnic accommodation is comparable to the labour of Sisyphus – a merciless task with no obvious end-point. International agencies' attempt to promote ethnic diversity and compromise has increased in scope and assertiveness to overcompensate the failings of Bosnian institutions. Instead of changing the dysfunctional order established at Dayton, international agencies have increasingly reacted by removing from office those nationalist politicians who are the product of that order. Second, democratisation has increasingly become an international, not a domestic issue. Since the establishment of the Bonn powers, domestically generated political debate on institutional and social options has been almost totally absent. When, for example, two foreign analysts published a damning critique of OHR in summer 2003 suggesting that the Bonn powers should be terminated, the article was widely discussed in the international press, but largely ignored by the Bosnians (Belloni 2003). As Bosnian international law expert Szebor Dizdarević put it shortly after the publication of the article, 'it is their conversation, not ours'.[9] This comment illustrates the long-term dangers of the Bosnian quasi-protectorate: the Bonn powers do not mobilise elements of civil society indispensable to further democratic development. Instead, they appear to reinforce ethno-nationalist parties as the most significant political force in the country.

The constituent peoples case

The Constitutional Court's ruling on the constituent peoples case, issued in July 2000, allowed international agencies to pursue their dual strategy of ensuring stability while promoting piecemeal reforms. The ruling attempted to tackle the problem of discrimination, but did little to address the equally important issue of efficiency. Rather, as argued below, the post-ruling reforms further complicated domestic governance.

The case began as a result of a civil society initiative. The Serb Civic Council (SCC) was created on 27 March 1994 to represent, in the words of its founder, 'that part of the Bosnian Serb nation which had never accepted the policy of ethnic cleansing and ethnic division of Bosnia' (Pejanović 2002: 194). The SCC was founded in part as a response to the establishment in February 1994 of the Bosniak/Croat Federation. The failure to include the Serbs was a political blow for many of those Serbs who had endured years of fighting on the Federation side to demonstrate their attachment to the principle of a multi-ethnic Bosnia. Following the establishment of the Federation, many Serbs feared the possibility of being relegated to the status of second-rate citizens in a Bosniak/Croat-dominated political structure. As a result, some Serbs decided to leave Sarajevo while others organised around the SCC. Since its creation, the organisation struggled to preserve Bosnia as a united, decentralised, and democratic state constituted by equal citizens and peoples (SCC 1998). The SCC has been at the forefront in the attempt to make Bosnian institutions more inclusive and representative.

Changing the constitution

The initiative to change the constitution has been the organisation's defining political battle. On 4 April 1997, the SCC issued a 'Declaration on the Human Right to Political and National Equality', lobbying international agencies to terminate the legal discrimination of nationalities in the territory of Bosnia by extending the 'constitutive people' status, which grants a privileged status to Croats and Bosniaks in the Federation and to Serbs in the RS, throughout the entire territory of the country (SCC 1997). As we have seen, the constituent people status is important for at least two reasons. First, from a political point of view, the recognition of such status implies the equality of all groups. Second, legally such designation guarantees the ability to exercise a set of important rights, such as that of vetoing decisions that would directly affect the group's 'vital interests'. The SCC argued that the special status of Serbs in the RS, and Bosniaks and Croats in the Federation, is discriminatory and both politically and legally unwarranted. It is a 'typical example of ethnic apartheid, which harms all three peoples in a state that ought to be common'. Such institutional discrimination has a negative impact on one of the major clauses of the DPA, that is, Annex 7 on the right to return of the displaced population. As the SCC put it, within the discriminatory framework established at Dayton, 'one cannot expect the return of refugees and displaced persons to their homes ... they will not want to accept the position of second-class citizens or the impossibility of exercising their human rights'.

The SCC's declaration was addressed to all major international agencies and foreign embassies. On 25 April, the Association of Independent Intellectuals Circle 99, in addition to the Council of the Congress of Bosniak Intellectuals, publicly endorsed it (Circle 99 1997). Other declarations of support followed, including that of prominent international officials, most notably that of High Representative Carlos Westendorp. Yet no concrete steps were either discussed or taken until the SSC called upon Bosniak leader and member of the presidency, Aljia Izetbegović, to submit the issue to the Constitutional Court and thus place it on its agenda (Pejanović 2002: 235–36). In February 1998, Izetbegović instituted a challenge, *inter alia*, to Article 1 of the RS constitution, stating that 'Republika Srpska shall be the state of the Serb people and of all of its citizens', and Article 1 (1) of the Federation Constitution, declaring Bosniaks and Croats as constituent peoples. According to Izetbegović, closely following the original SCC's argument, these articles are in contravention of the final paragraph of the preamble of the BiH constitution, establishing a principle of collective political equality under which Bosniaks, Croats, and Serbs are all to be considered constituent peoples.

The court's decision

In July 2000, the court found that the challenged provisions were indeed in violation of the preamble of the BiH constitution where the principle of equality of all three constituent peoples throughout the Bosnian territory is asserted. As the court noted, the constitutional principle of collective equality of constituent peoples 'prohibits any special privilege for one or two of these peoples, any domination in governmental structures or any ethnic homogenisation through segregation based on territorial separation'

(Ustavni sud BiH 2000: para. 60). The decision of the Constitutional Court asserted that both Entities were not providing equal status for all their peoples, and ruled as unconstitutional twelve provisions of the RS constitution and four articles of the Federation's, including Article I of both constitutions and the preamble of the RS constitution. Among the most far-reaching elements of the court's decision was the order to remove from the preamble of the RS constitution any reference to that Entity as being the 'State of the Serb People'. As for the Federation, the court ordered that Bosniaks and Croats couldn't be considered as sole constituent peoples.

The three main ethnic groups are 'constituent peoples' of the Bosnian state and no one group can be discriminated against or have a second rate status. In justifying its decision, the court explained that there is no definition of 'constituent peoples' in the constitution (ibid.: para. 50). However, despite the lack of definition, 'it clearly designates all of them as constituent peoples, i.e. as peoples. Moreover ... the Constitution prohibits discrimination on any grounds such as, *inter alia*, association with a national minority and presupposes thereby the existence of groups conceived as national minorities' (ibid.: para. 52). The Court also noted that 'the text of the Constitution of BiH thus clearly distinguishes constituent peoples from national minorities with the intention to affirm the continuity of Bosnia and Herzegovina as a democratic multinational state' (ibid.: para. 53). Not only is discrimination based on being a 'national minority' unacceptable, but also none of 'constituent peoples' can rightfully be perceived as a national minority. The term 'constituent peoples' ensures that the status of minorities does not apply to Bosniaks, Croats and Serbs. The 'others' referred to in the constitution are national minorities, including the Roma, Jews, Turks, Czechs, Albanians and other minority groups.

The court's reasoning amounts to a direct indictment and unmistakable condemnation of ethnic exclusivism and the resulting violation of individual and group rights institutionalised in the Entities' structure. The court argued that

> the accommodation of cultures and ethnic groups prohibits not only their assimilation but also their segregation. Thus, *segregation is, in principle, not a legitimate aim in a democratic society* ... .Territorial delimitation thus must not serve as an instrument of ethnic segregation, but – quite contrary – must provide for ethnic accommodation through preserving linguistic pluralism and peace in order to contribute to the integration of state and society as such.
>
> (Ibid.: para. 57; emphasis added)

The court referred to the fate of the displaced population to justify its condemnation of ethnic segregation. According to the court's reasoning, the internal division of the Bosnian state between two Entities established on an ethnic basis has allowed the outcome of ethnic cleansing to be preserved (ibid.: para. 61). The court cited population figures for both the RS and the

Federation to substantiate its claim, thus confirming the original intuition of the SCC on the difficulty of ensuring refugee return in a context of institutionalised discrimination. In the RS, the Serb majority sharply increased from 54.3 per cent in 1991 to 96.8 per cent in 1997. Simultaneously, the Bosniak population decreased from 28.8 per cent to 2.2 per cent, while the Croats dropped from 9.39 per cent to 1.02 per cent (ibid.: para. 86). As for the Federation, the court noted that the proportion of Bosniaks in the territory of the Federation increased from 52.1 per cent to 72.6 per cent between 1991 and 1997, while the Serb population dropped from 17.6 per cent to 2.3 per cent (ibid.: para. 130).

These figures suggest that, two years after the end of the war, the DPA's main human rights component, the right of return, remained unimplemented, particularly in the RS. The court explicitly considered and rejected the claim of representatives of the RS National Assembly that the slow pace of post-war returns was due to complex social and economic conditions unrelated to local authorities' discrimination against non-Serb returnees. Rather, local authorities must take at least partial responsibility for this state of affairs. Bosnian authorities at all levels are required to repeal bureaucratic procedures and legislation which are discriminatory against refugees and displaced persons, and should 'create the necessary political, social and economic conditions for their harmonious reintegration' (ibid.: para. 81). These positive obligations require the parties to ensure freedom of movement, right to property and the right not to be discriminated against in the enjoyment of various civil, political, economic, social and cultural rights (Nowak 2001: 119). Thus, the court's analysis makes clear that the low level of minority returns in Bosnia cannot be attributed to minority preference. By condemning the delays in the return home of the displaced population, the court stated that the defence of group rights cannot be achieved through the violation of individual human rights.

In sum, the court recognised and legitimised collective group rights, but only to the extent that these rights did not hinder the individual's right to move freely and establish residence anywhere on Bosnian territory. Thus, the decision favours greater individual freedom and thereby loosens consociationalism's rigid group features. Political rights should not be granted on a group basis, but rather they should be attributes of individuals (Mansfield 2003: 2068). The Constitutional Court's decision contributed to the establishment of a framework more conducive to the implementation of Annex 7 of the DPA. As argued in Chapter 6, since the year 2000 minority return has accelerated considerably, although the pre-war level of ethnic intermixing is unlikely to ever be recreated.

Implementation and impact

The Constitutional Court's 2000 decision to guarantee legal equality to Serbs, Croats and Bosniaks throughout the Bosnian territory is the most significant development since the signing of the DPA. High Representative Wolfgang Petrisch defined the ruling in the constituent people's case as 'historic'(2002c). American ambassador Thomas Miller compared the importance of the decision for Bosnia to that of *Brown v. Board of Education* for racial integration in the United States.[10] The academic Anna Morawiec Mansfield defined it as 'a watershed moment for post-war reconciliation in this troubled country' (2003: 2053). Its impact on the possibility of recreating a multi-ethnic polity could indeed be far-reaching. However, while the court had laid down the general principle of the legal and political equality of the three constituent peoples throughout Bosnia, the practical implications of such a principle needed to be interpreted and agreed upon though a political process involving all major, interested local players. The court's decision opened the way for the long-awaited changes to the state's basic institutional set-up without, however, specifying which institutions and procedures would satisfy the principle of collective equality of Bosniaks, Serbs and Croats.

The Constitutional Court is comprised of four members from the Federation (two Bosniaks and two Croats), two from Republika Srpska, and three – who cannot be citizens of Bosnia or any neighbouring state – selected by the European Court of Human Rights (ECHR). Although the court is a Bosnian institution, its composition makes it similar to a 'shared sovereignty' entity (Krasner 2004) with sovereignty divided between international and domestic actors. Bosniak and foreign judges voted in favour, while Serb and Croat ones opposed the ruling. Elements of the Serb and Croat leadership argued that the ruling resulted from the Bosniak's manipulation of the court and therefore they challenged the legitimacy of the court's decision. This argument could have caused an acute constitutional crisis. According to Robert Hayden, because of the internally divided nature of the state, in the case of resistance to the implementation of the Constitutional Court's ruling, 'any attempt to enforce a decision … would have to take the form of aggressive military action by the army of at least one constituent people against the army of the other' (1999: 132). The fact that no military campaign took place highlighted two issues. First, it confirmed the court's legitimacy as an important statewide institution. The presence of foreign judges allowed the court to avoid the accusation of being an undemocratic instrument of Western neo-colonial control – a criticism often levelled at OHR. Rather, despite the objections of the dissenting judges opposed to the ruling (Bieber 2006b: 123–24), the court demonstrated itself to be a transparent and efficient *local* institution. Second, the ruling proved that consensus, which is the standard decision-making procedure of consociational institutions and often leads to deadlock, is not indispensable. Indeed, simple majority voting is a legitimate voting procedure in which the consequences apply to all representative ethnic blocs, even for such a prominent and far-reaching decision regarding constitutional reform.

Constitutional commissions

The process of transformation from the general principles established by the Constitutional Court into concrete constitutional and legislative changes showed the persistence of the local parties' disagreement over the nature of the Bosnian state and international agencies' impatience to overcompensate for domestic failures and impose a solution. Neither Entity showed much enthusiasm for discussing changes in line with the court's ruling. Petritsch waited for six months, until January 2001, before he intervened to establish constitutional commissions in each Entity charged with drafting amendments to the Entity constitutions. The commissions were asked to make proposals for the implementation of the court's decision. Petritsch appointed sixteen members to each commission, four from each constituent people, in addition to four 'others' (OHR 2001b). In protest at the internationally sponsored changes to electoral rules in autumn 2000 (see Chapter 4), the HDZ refused to nominate any members to the Federation's constitutional commission, although the party was nonetheless an active player in the process of determining the constitutional amendments. International agencies and the Alliance for Change portrayed the issue of implementation as the result of a new partnership between them. This partnership, it was hoped, would ensure the involvement of local actors and thus improve the range and impact of the reforms needed to implement the court's decision.

However, the discussion on what changes would be necessary to implement the Constitutional Court's ruling highlighted the presence of significant differences among the parties. At the heart of the difficulties were three issues that the DPA had left vague and unresolved: the definition of vital national interests and mechanisms for their protection; the practical implication of the principle of equal representation of all constituent peoples (and 'others') in the legislature, judiciary and executive; and the definition of the official language(s) and scripts of the Bosnian state and their use throughout the Bosnian territory (ESI 2002b: 6; Lindvall 2003: 75–78). By July 2001, the Federation Commission reached a consensus on a single set of constitutional amendments. Although the Commission was ready to submit these amendments to parliament, it decided to wait until the RS parliament voted on its own amendments. The members of the RS Commission, however, failed to agree on any change.

An important symbolic step was taken on 25 January 2002, when the eight major political parties from the Federation and the RS met in Mrakovica to discuss aspects of constitutional reform. This was the first post-Dayton meeting of political party leaders independent of international sponsors or pressures. Although little concrete progress was made at the meeting, the very fact that the parties had decided to meet carried enormous symbolic weight. Petritsch capitalised on this initiative and invited the parties to Sarajevo in the hope of reaching a compromise. On 27 March 2002, the Mrakovica–Sarajevo Agreement was reached and signed by some of the parties in the multi-ethnic Alliance for Change coalition (SDP, SBiH, NHI).[11] Four RS representatives, including prime minister Mladen Ivanić and SDS speaker of the National Assembly Dragan Kalinić, signed a document expressing their support, but with reservations about specific clauses. The HDZ protested the limits placed on minority veto and left the negotiations, followed by the SDA, which complained that the changes did not create two entirely symmetric Entities, but preserved significant differences between the RS institutional structure and the Federation (BiH Media Round-up, 28 March 2002). The Agreement recognised Bosniaks, Croats, and Serbs as constituent peoples in both Entities, and introduced the principle of 'fair representation' for all ethnic groups in the central and Entity institutions. The different ethnic groups in both Entities should hold legislative, executive, and judicial posts in proportion to their numbers. Furthermore, the agreement determined a list of vital interests and foresaw the creation of a weaker chamber in the RS to protect those interests (ICG 2002b).

The moderate parties' appraisal of these changes was positive. SDP leader and then foreign minister Zlatko Lagumdžija described the amendments as the biggest political change in Bosnia since Dayton (BCR 2002). Perhaps a good indication of the significance of the agreement in ensuring ethnic pluralism is the nationalists' condemnation, particularly in the RS. The Serb representatives of the constitutional commission refused to support the amendments. RS president and SDS leader Mirko Šarović argued that such measures achieved no less than the abolition of the RS through the back door. After the amendments had been presented to the RS parliament for ratification, but before voting started, the Serb members presented their own secretly drafted list of changes. These changes included provisions significantly distinct from those of the 27 March agreement, including a citizens' right to call referenda, a right that international agencies feared could be used for the RS to secede from Bosnia and join Serbia (ICG 2002b). In the Federation, the amendments were adopted in the House of Peoples but failed in the House of Representatives when both the SDA and the HDZ left the chamber before the vote, complaining that the newly created RS Council of Peoples had considerably less power than its counterpart in the Federation. The High Representative finally resolved to impose amendments to the constitutions of both Entities on 19 April 2002. In explaining the reasons for his decision to use the Bonn powers, High Representative Petritsch argued: 'I simply cannot accept the continuing obstruction on the side of these nationalistic dinosaurs. I cannot allow the prospect that these … parties could hold the citizens of this country hostage' (2002c). Because the imposition was grounded on earlier agreement by Bosnian parties, Petritsch argued that 'this is an imposition, but it does not look like the previous impositions. This time, the largest part of the job was done by the domestic authorities and I congratulate them for that' (BiH Media Round-up, 22 April 2002).

The High Representative's imposition of constitutional amendments was probably unwarranted. Constitutional design, as Daniel Elazar points out, is a 'preeminently political act' (1985). As such, it is a matter for political negotiations among the parties involved. The imposition prevented the necessary and long-overdue domestic political debate. The stated reasons for imposing constitutional amendments confirmed the less than compelling grounds for such action. The High Representative argued that his imposition was required in order to hold the October 2002 elections on time. The Entities were supposed to enact the amendments in time to allow for the elections to take place, which, according to the constitution, had to be announced in the state parliament 170 days before election day, that is, by 18 April. The amendments were necessary to complete the election law, taking into account the changes in the Entities' constitutions. The very fact that the High Representative's decision was one day after the 18 April deadline, and required amending the election law, highlighted the artificiality of the argument about the deadline.

Furthermore, the constitution provides that the articles of the Entities' constitutions that are inconsistent with its own should be amended within three months of the state constitutions coming into force, that is, by 14 March 1996. After six years had passed without any change in this direction, it is difficult to argue that the High Representative's imposition was a matter of 'urgency'. Both chairpersons of the Constitutional Commissions did not deem the imposition of the High Representative necessary.[12] As the European Stability Initiative concluded, while the Constitutional Court had asserted a principle of collective equality, 'the concrete implications of this general principle can only be interpreted through a political process. It is untenable to suggest that respect for the Court's authority requires this political process to be cut short, or replaced by an international decision' (ESI 2002b: 1).

Constitutional changes

The changes were far-reaching, involving the composition of both the RS and Federation governments, the representation of the three constituent peoples in all public institutions, the use of scripts and languages in both Entities, the creation of a new Council of Peoples (or Upper House) in the RS, and the definition of the 'vital interest' clause. All of these changes came into effect soon after the High Representative's imposition, with overall positive repercussions for the representativeness of domestic institutions but not for their efficiency.

The substance of the changes imposed by the High Representative built on the Mrakovica-Sarajevo agreement, so that the RS government would consist of sixteen ministers, eight of whom would be Serbs, five Bosniaks, and three Croats. The Federation's government would consist of eight Bosniaks, five Croats, and three Serbs. The three constituent peoples and the 'others' should be proportionally represented in public institutions – from the municipal to the Entity level – according to the 1991 census (thus avoiding the ratification of wartime ethnic cleansing by holding a new census and using it as the basis for allocating public office to the three constituent peoples). Only when Annex 7 on refugee return is declared fully implemented will a new census be carried out and new quotas determined. In practice, the use of the 1991 census meant that roughly 45 per cent of all ministerial jobs in the RS, the Entity potentially most affected by the implementation of this provision, became reserved for non-Serb employees. In the RS, both Cyrillic and Latin became the official scripts, and the languages of the Serbs, Bosniaks and Croats became the official languages. In the Federation, the High Representative imposed similar language requirements, in addition to changes in the composition of the legislature, where it was decided that a minimum of four representatives of each constituent people should be represented in the House of Representatives and that the House of Peoples of the Federation shall be composed of the same number of representatives from each constituent people. A second assembly in the RS, the Council of Peoples, was created, composed of an equal number of Serbs, Bosniaks and Croats and tasked with ensuring the protection of vital interests in that Entity, while the House of Peoples would perform the same task in the Federation.

Perhaps the most important change regarded constitutional amendments defining the 'vital national interests' of constituent peoples, a definition that is absent from the Entity constitutions. The definition of 'vital national interests' is a step towards reassuring the three constituent peoples about matters of particular concern to them. Unfortunately, not only is the list of acceptable vital interests long and broad, other issues can also be raised 'if so claimed by two thirds of one of the caucuses of the constituent peoples in the House of Peoples' (Amendment XXXVIII). This open-ended veto right opens the door to the possibility of perpetual stalemate. Other solutions could have been envisaged. In Germany, for example, a mediating commission is tasked with overcoming deadlock between the Federal Parliament and the Federal Council. Similarly, in Kosovo, in cases of deadlock a three-member panel made up of representatives of the two sides (Albanian and Serb) and a third member designated by international authorities takes decisions by majority. A similar procedure, along the lines of a shared sovereignty Entity as in Kosovo, would probably be useful in Bosnia to ensure governability.

Impact

The constitutional changes created a system of constitutional tri-communalism giving Bosnia's three main ethnic groups an equally privileged status throughout the Bosnian territory and ending systematic discrimination based on ethnic belonging. Because it embodied the rhetorical values international officials had embraced since the signing of the DPA, international agencies, think-tanks and most international observers gave a positive appraisal of the changes. Ian Campbell, head of the OHR legal department and the most influential international expert on constitutional reform, argued that the changes will 'contribute to the affirmation of multi-ethnic parties' and 'change the attitude of politicians towards their voters, because they will have to win over their followers among members of other peoples' (Campbell 2002). The OSCE commended it as a small revolution, which everybody who advocates a multi-ethnic Bosnia and Herzegovina should support (Stiglmayer 2002). According to the influential International Crisis Group, the 'constituent peoples decision represents an attempt to transform the existing Entities within the Dayton architecture and to move Bosnia' in a multi-national direction (ICG 2002b: 25). Accordingly, 'implementing the Constitutional Court's decision will be a big step toward reintegrating and reconciling Bosnia's peoples'. Optimistically, the changes were praised as 'a first step towards overcoming separatist tendencies and, ultimately, towards the abolition of the Entities' (Solioz 2005: 96).

Not all observers make a positive appraisal of the constitutional changes. Historical determinists condemn it as a 'remarkable attempt to rewrite the constitution by fiat' which will not improve the functionality of Bosnian institutions (Hayden 2005: 248). Autonomists see in the constitutional amendments an ineffective effort to impose multi-ethnicity from the outside. For these critics, the constitutional amendments represent an instance of a 'reality gap' between international and domestic actors. David Chandler, for example, argues that 'while the constitutional changes may produce governments which look good on paper, they institutionalise and perpetuate the problems which they seek to address' (2004: 317). Chandler claims that the international imposition of the 'rule of law' is 'in contradiction with self-government' and 'against the will of the people'. Although Bosnian people may have a legal framework guaranteeing and institutionalising a set of rights, 'these imposed rights appear as an oppressive, alien and artificial creation' (2004: 328). Instead of imposing reform through a top-down process, international agencies should respect local autonomy and self-government.

Autonomists such as Chandler, however, typically fail to identify the 'people' who are entitled to self-determination. After wartime ethnic cleansing, the compelling question is whether self-government applies to the present population or the pre-war population of a given area. Chandler suggests that the criterion for self-government is the demographic status quo. The use of the 1991 census to determine quotas for political representation allows DP leaders to be elected to their pre-war municipal councils even if they have been living away from their hometown for years. For Chandler, 'this has heightened political tensions and raised questions over the legitimacy of policy made by people who do not have to live with the consequences of their decisions' (2004: 317). Although this might be true, one cannot fail to notice that politicians often live in the other Entity because they were victims of ethnic cleansing – not as a result of free choice – and often are prevented from returning home by discrimination, intimidation and lack of employment. If only the demographic status quo were used to determine the 'will of the people', it would reflect and implicitly endorse previous transfers of population, and it would prevent individuals who were forcibly expelled from an area from expressing their will or being elected to office. Furthermore, the parties to the DPA have endorsed the principle of return of refugees and DPs and their full participation in the social and political life of the municipalities where they lived prior to the outbreak of war – thus subscribing to the principle that all original residents of an area should enjoy both passive and active political rights.

Instead of being an alien and undemocratic solution to ethnic disputes, the creation of inclusive institutions and the expectation that everyone will be treated in a reasonably fair manner increases the legitimacy of these institutions and provides a potential alternative to irreconcilable self-determination claims. The support of all three groups in favour of ending legalised discrimination throughout the Bosnian territory suggests that the groups accept the preservation of Bosnia as a multiethnic state, and supports the strategy of building an effective and representative state authority. The overwhelming majority of Bosniaks are in support of the constituency of all three nations across the Bosnian territory, an attitude reflecting traditional Bosniak support for strengthening the central state. Almost two thirds of all Serbs also supported the principle that all three groups should be constituent peoples everywhere on Bosnian territory. More importantly, however, most Croats welcomed the constitutional decision.[13] As a result, 'secession is now off the agenda' (Wheeler 2003: 12). The choice facing Bosnians of all groups, of 'whether to pull together or pull apart ... is no longer relevant' (UNDP 2002a: 7). Serb politicians increasingly acknowledge and accept the existence of the state, and Croats speak of strengthening it, instead of leaving it altogether.

The end of legalised ethnic discrimination also had a positive impact on the Bosnians' ability to freely choose their place of residence, particularly the Bosniaks' ability to return to the territory of the RS (see Chapter 6). As Amnesty International pointed out prior to the constituent peoples case, many Bosniak DPs would return home 'only if as Bosniaks they could be free and equal citizens in Republika Srpska' (AI 1998: section 2). The court's decision and its implementation helped reassure returnees that their interests were properly represented in local and Entity institutions. Furthermore, the use of the 1991 census showed the desire to contribute to reversing ethnic cleansing by creating jobs for the returnees – the missing element for sustainability in the return of the displaced population (MRGI 2003). In practice, the use of the 1991 census represented an affirmative action project for non-dominant groups in both Entities (Bieber 2006a: 150).

On balance, these constitutional changes greatly improved the representativeness of domestic institutions, but at the cost of entrenching ethnicity as the basis of representation. Instead of opening new opportunities for non-nationalist identities to emerge and consolidate themselves, the constitutional changes further define individual identity in ethnic rather than civic terms – despite the recognition of the importance of individual rights. By definition, this excludes both individuals who do not belong to any of the three major communities (e.g. Roma, Jews, Turks, etc.), and people whose predominant identity is 'Bosnian', that is, people of mixed ethnicity who do not wish to declare themselves as belonging to one dominant group, and those individuals whose primary identity is civic instead of ethnic. As a result, the structure of multi-ethnic consociationalism diminishes these individuals' eligibility for political representation and participation. Moreover, as the next chapter will argue, the electoral system rewards ethnic identity and electoral competition along opposing ethnic lines. Because inter-ethnic accommodation and the long-term survival of the Bosnian state require the presence of some form of Bosnian civic identity, the question becomes whether this goal can be achieved by further privileging ethnic identity.

Two issues highlight the problem with further entrenching ethnic principles into Bosnian politics. First, the experience of post-World War II Yugoslavia is not encouraging. Many of the consociational mechanisms included in the DPA and further developed by the process of constitutional revision were failures in the Yugoslav system (Andjelić 2003: 36–42). The degeneration of the Yugoslav multi-ethnic federalism throughout the 1970s and 1980s occurred with the progressive ethnicisation of the federal institutions and the squeezing out of a Yugoslav civic identity. Post-war Bosnia faces the additional challenge of creating some overarching Bosnian identity in a context of deep institutional and social fragmentation. The danger of increasingly subjecting individual identities to ethnic ones has motivated several individuals and groups to lobby for alternatives. A group of Bosnian intellectuals has called for the creation of a 'Third Republic' as a stepping stone towards human rights protection and integration into European institutions.[14] This initiative was followed in summer 2003 by the publication in a Bosnian newspaper of a 'Declaration' on the creation of a 'Federal Republic of Bosnia-Herzegovina', signed by seven prominent Bosnian pundits (*Oslobođenje* 2003). In December 2003, twenty-four European political officials, including former Polish premier and UN Human Rights Representative in Bosnia, Tadeusz Mazowiecki, issued a declaration on the need to reform the DPA. The think-tank European Stability Initiative put forward its proposal in early 2004 (ESI 2004a). This lobbying for alternative institutional arrangements culminated in the attempt at constitutional revision in early 2006. Although constitutional reform failed, the debate that surrounded it confirmed a growing awareness of the need to change the dysfunctional elements of the constitution (see Chapter 7).

Second, many practical changes in both the Federation and the RS have been largely cosmetic. Bosnia displays the character of a 'passive-aggressive

state' in which veto players at lower levels of governance block implementation of reforms agreed by the central government (Deets 2006). The
RS has retained the old definition of the RS as a 'state' of the Serb people,
as the RS government website proudly states. The Council of Peoples was
constituted in July 2003, but so far it has failed to pass a single decision.
According to Mirjiana Vehabović, a Croat member of the council, 'this
institution simply does not work. Its members are appointed by the main
nationalist parties, and do not represent the interests of returnees, as originally conceived.'[15] In the Federation, the authorities appointed 'docile
Serbs to the positions earmarked for them, thereby ensuring that there will
be as little alteration as possible in the pre-established practices of Bosniak-
Croat power-sharing' (ICG 2003b: 4). Similarly, the Croat vice-president of
the RS, for example, has only limited competencies. The de facto continuing
predominance of Croats and Bosniaks in the Federation and Serbs in the
RS explains why the Entities have been maintained despite the fact that they
provide protection to the three constituent peoples similar to that which
they enjoy in statewide institutions (Bieber 2006a: 133). These institutional
problems have been compounded by the October 2002 nationalists' victory
at the general elections. Following the elections and the creation of a
nationalist-dominated government, the spirit of inter-ethnic cooperation
that the constitutional changes were meant to foster was compromised. The
regular use of the 'emergency procedure', strongly encouraged by international agencies, and requiring legislators to either accept or reject laws but
not to propose amendments, is in itself a sign of the still limited functionality of Bosnian institutions.

Vital interest and state functionality

Since the 2000 constituent peoples case the Constitutional Court has
returned a number of later decisions on the issue of groups' vital interests
and non-discrimination. In February 2004, the court found the wartime
renaming of towns and municipalities in the RS by adding the suffix 'Serb'
to be unconstitutional. Not only was renaming discriminatory, but also the
designation of municipalities as 'Serb' would prevent the return of refugees
and displaced persons, and thus violate Article II, 5 of the constitution and
Annex 7 of the DPA (Ustavni sud BiH 2004b). In the absence of concrete
steps from RS authorities, in September 2004 the court renamed all of these
cities and municipalities (Ustavni sud BiH 2004c). In 2004 the court was
also asked for the first time whether a vital interest had correctly been
invoked during the parliamentary process. Under examination was the
Framework Law on Higher Education in Bosnia, which was contested by
the Croats on the grounds that it did not guarantee the establishment of a
university with instruction in the Croatian language. The framework law
was found destructive of the vital interest, but for reasons different from the
ones invoked by the Croats. The court argued that this law did not provide

for equality of all the three languages and thus it did not guarantee equal access to higher education. More interesting from the point of view of the functionality of state institutions, the court also argued that the effective participation of constituent peoples in public life – including the invocation of the 'vital interest' – must be evaluated in combination with the efficient working of the state (Ustavni sud BiH 2005).

In later decisions, not only did the court re-affirm the principle that the protection of vital interests must be balanced with ensuring the functionality of state institutions, but also it again touched upon the importance of eliminating discrimination to facilitate the return of refugees and displaced persons. In May 2004, the court found that the Draft Law on Amendments to the Law on Refugees and Displaced Persons was destructive of the vital interest of the Bosniak people (Ustavni sud BiH 2004a). In order to be restored their property, the Draft Law required citizens to demonstrate that they 'exchanged property under duress' during the 1992–95 war – a requirement placing an unacceptable burden of proof on returnees. In March 2006, the court addressed a number of issues related to the flag and coat of arms of both the Federation and the RS (Ustavni sud BiH 2006). In substance, the court found that the Entity's symbols in the Federation discriminate against the Serbs; conversely, the RS flag and coat of arms discriminates against Bosniaks and Croats. Moreover, the court established that references to the 'statehood of Republika Srpska' and to the 'moral norms of the Serb people' in the anthem *Bože Pravde* is also discriminatory, and an obstacle to the return of non-Serbs to their homes of origin in the RS. The court's decisions remain contested, and sometimes are exploited for narrow electoral purposes, particularly in the RS (Katana 2006). Nonetheless, with these decisions the Constitutional Court has been playing an important role in balancing ethnic representation and interests with the need to ensure both the respect of individual and group rights and the functionality of state institutions.

Conclusion

The July 2000 Constitutional Court decision on the constituent peoples set in motion a process of profound reform which has considerably improved the legal standing of the three constituent peoples. The reform has increased the multi-ethnic character of Bosnian institutions and has reduced Croats' dissatisfaction about their role within the Bosnian state. At the same time, however, the reforms added a degree of complexity that could render Bosnia ungovernable (Bieber 2006a: 144). Moreover, the constitutional reforms raise the question of the legitimacy of the Entities. If both the Entities and the state are meant to provide a similar degree of protection to all constituent peoples, then they are redundant institutions, which perhaps justifies the proposal to abolish the Entities, as advocated by some liberal observers and part of the Bosniak leadership.

Furthermore, the extension of the consociational institutional framework to all levels of governance cannot in itself solve the structural conditions perpetuating the appeal of ethno-nationalism and making the lack of inter-ethnic cooperation a rational political choice for nationalist elites. A fundamental problem with consociationalism is the underlying assumption that culture and identity are largely fixed and unchanging, and its tendency to entrench such identities in the political structure. Entrenching group rights favours the same nationalist parties that international intervention seeks to undermine and complicates the state building agenda. Not surprisingly, since the implementation of constitutional changes international agencies have continued to impose solutions on local parties even when they are downsizing their presence in the country and in principle favour the development of local policy-making and responsibility.

As a result, constitutional reform remains high on the agenda. A number of possible alternatives to the current institutional impasse are available, including the simplification of the institutional structure through the elimination of the Entities, the reform of the presidency and the House of Peoples and the streamlining of decision-making procedures (as discussed further in Chapter 7). Many rounds of elections in a consociational framework have proved that, without reform, both the current institutional structure and electoral legislation complicate the process of post-war democratisation. As the next chapter will show, the lack of electoral incentives for the domestic elite to appeal to voters other than those from their own ethnic group and the short-term approach of international intervention remain significant stumbling blocks in the post-settlement transition.

4   Elections and electoral engineering

International agencies organised and ran Bosnian elections until 2002. Most notably, they chose the rules for all elections (municipal, cantonal, Entity level and presidential) until the adoption of a permanent election law in August 2001. The consociational institutional structure, described in the previous chapter, set important constraints on successive election rules by prescribing a high degree of proportionality in the ratio of votes to seats in electoral outcomes. Proportional electoral rules allow for the representation of all major groups in society and the consolidation of strong party leadership (both key consociational prescriptions), but at the cost of favouring electoral competition along ethno-national lines and encouraging extreme party fragmentation. Both the resulting nationalist parties' predominance and party fragmentation hindered effective governance and led international agencies to intervene increasingly in the local political process. Paradoxically, instead of increasing politicians' accountability and responsibility vis-à-vis their constituencies, elections have entangled international agencies further in the complexities of Bosnian politics.

While the goal of the DPA was to provide the conditions for the creation of multi-ethnic party pluralism (consisting of countrywide parties sustained by more than one ethnic group), the early post-Dayton electoral process led to a situation of multi-party ethnic pluralism, dominated by uni-ethnic political organisations largely supported by a uni-ethnic voting base which thrived on the divisions perpetuated by the consociational system (Cohen 2002: 134). International agencies have responded by trying to persuade Bosnians to renounce their wartime leaders and vote for 'change'. They have attempted to design electoral rules that favour cooperation and compromise among the existing ethnic leadership and encourage voter support of moderate multi-ethnic parties. This electoral strategy, combined with the establishment of democratic institutions and processes, the emergence of a moderate leadership, the return home of refugees and DPs to their pre-war homes, and the growth of a tolerant and diverse civil society was expected to overcome mistrust and zero-sum conceptions of the political process.

As this chapter shows, the international agencies' strategy has had limited success. First, international agencies initially manufactured electoral rules that backfired. The adoption of a system of proportional representation (PR) with closed party lists (whereby voters choose a party and cannot express a preference for a specific candidate) contributed to the victory and consolidation of nationalist parties at the first few rounds of elections and greatly complicated later peace building efforts. Second, in order to limit centrifugal political competition along ethnic lines, third parties attempted to foster inter-ethnic accommodation through electoral engineering – an approach often known as 'integrationist' (Horowitz 2000; Reilly 2001). While sound in principle, these rules were unlikely to have a positive effect because they were adopted in a consociational system that reifies ethnic division and complicates compromise. Third, group-based features of the political system ran counter to individual human rights. All political offices are allocated on the basis of ethnic criteria, complicating the exercise of both passive electoral rights (the right to stand for election) and active electoral rights (the right to vote). Citizens who do not identify themselves as one of the three constituent peoples are barred from standing for the state and RS presidencies. Federation voters are limited in their choice of presidential candidate to either a Bosniak or a Croat, while RS voters can only elect a Serb for the RS presidency. These legal provisions are discriminatory and in violation of the Copenhagen Commitments and of Protocol 12 of the European Convention on Human Rights.

Despite justified criticism, however, the temptation to reject the electoral process altogether should be resisted. Elections enable positive steps forward and are likely to remain the preferred means to improve governance and conflict management in weak and failing states. In Bosnia, the existence of democratic institutions is a visible sign that the war has really terminated. Ballots have replaced bullets and decreased the temptation of political violence. Soldiers have demobilised. International financial organisations have legitimate local interlocutors to negotiate loans and grants, and bureaucratic services are provided daily to citizens. The question is not so much what non-democratic conflict management tools might be available to replace elections and state building, but rather how to put into place electoral rules that maximise the chances for inter-ethnic compromise. The bulk of this chapter focuses on the 2000 elections, when international agencies first attempted extensive electoral engineering, and the 2002 elections – the first ones organised according to the new permanent election law.

Consociational democracy and early elections

Post-settlement democratic elections are central to peace processes and state building efforts. Elections serve a variety of different purposes reflecting both domestic democratisation needs and the needs of the foreign powers and agencies that mediated the end of the conflict. At least three objectives were predominant in the decision to hold elections in Bosnia shortly after the end of the conflict: to provide legitimacy for the withdrawal of the international (particularly American) military presence, to create representative and democratic institutions, and to provide a tool to begin redressing the injustices of the war (Shoup 1997). Not surprisingly, the multiplicity of reasons complicated the electoral process and made the electoral results not always consistent with the plans of international interveners.

The first round of post-war elections (1996–98) helped to consolidate ethnic rule with little impact on the promotion of peace building and democratisation. The 1996 elections in particular exemplified how the range of different goals complicated the peace building process and risked undermining the possibility for reconciliation. The desire to create local institutions quickly in order to shift international responsibilities to the local parties predominated over other objectives. Despite the lack of acceptable local conditions, international agencies, under pressure from the United States, decided to hold elections nine months after the end of the war. Because NATO troops were scheduled to leave shortly after the elections, mutual fear and insecurity predominated and decisively influenced the choices of the voters (Bildt 1998: 270–1). Simultaneously, however, elections became intertwined with two other peace building goals. First, the elections were used as a mechanism to marginalise some of the Serb leadership most directly connected with the policy of ethnic cleansing and, in general, with the crimes committed during the conflict. In the summer of 1996, international pressure led to the resignation of Karadžić, both as president of the RS and head of the SDS. Soon thereafter Karadžić went underground. Second, peace builders hoped that elections could help the displaced population to return to their pre-war homes, thus encouraging heterogeneity and some degree of ethnic intermixing. The DPA (Annex 3, art. IV) allowed voters to cast their vote where they resided in 1991, a measure meant to offer Bosnians an incentive to return to areas from which they had been 'cleansed' because of their ethnicity. With evidently excessive optimism, the DPA foresaw that by election day the return of DPs would be underway, and Bosnians could cast their ballot in person. At the same time, however, by using the so-called 'P-2 form', citizens were also allowed to vote in a place of their own choosing, provided that the municipality chosen became the voter's permanent future residence. For this reason, Bosniak leader Alija Izetbegović condemned the P-2 form, which he considered 'a means of the continuation of ethnic cleansing as some sort of "final solution" to the ethnic question in Bosnia' (2003: 362).

Not surprisingly, the registration procedure became a contentious terrain for the three major ethnic parties, which attempted to use the registration process to solidify their political control (Bildt 1998: 262). RS voters were pressured to register in those towns where the SDS leadership saw the possibility of consolidating its territorial conquests achieved during the war. Similarly, in a mirror image of the Serbs' attempts at ethnic consolidation, the SDA used the voter registration process to consolidate its position within the Federation.[1] The HDZ put pressure on the Croats to register in towns where the party wanted to consolidate its electoral majority. In the end, instead of reversing ethnic cleansing, the electoral process helped consolidate territorial gains. Overall, in this as in later elections, ethnically heterogeneous municipalities showed more support for nationalist parties than ethnically homogeneous ones (Caspersen 2004b).[2]

Electoral rules contributed to both nationalist parties' early success in post-war elections and party fragmentation. Closed party lists (in which voters choose parties instead of candidates within the list) and proportional representation (PR) facilitated the victory of the main nationalist parties and thus contributed to the subsequent legitimisation of new social (dis)-order arising from the war. Consociationalists prefer PR with closed party lists because, by allowing a party leader greater control, it sustains conditions favourable to 'elite cooperation' against the disintegrative tendencies of their society. Furthermore, the system ensures that the ratio of votes to seats is observed closely. When the electorate is polarised along ethnic lines, this system guarantees representation to all major groups in society (Lijphart 1999: 144–50). PR systems can be distinguished further according to the formula used to translate votes into seats. All legislative mandates in Bosnia are allocated using the Sainte-Lague method, which tends to favour smaller parties.

In a post-settlement context, the need for inclusion and representation of all groups provides a strong theoretical justification for the desirability of PR over majoritarian or semi-proportional systems. The importance of maintaining PR is easily understood when one contrasts the electoral mechanisms of any Western democratic society that has no dramatic ethnic cleavages with those mechanisms likely to prevail in a deeply divided society such as Bosnia. In democratic systems there are usually numerous shifting and cross-cutting political and economic cleavages that allow for the possibility of broadening a political party's support, and create new coalitions and alliances. In such a context, an electoral defeat still permits the electoral losers to reorganise and possibly win the next elections. In deeply divided societies, on the contrary, where the political system is polarised into ethnic parties, the dominant ethnic cleavage prohibits coalitions across ethnic lines. Rather than casting their vote, citizens vote their caste. Parties then are relegated to organising within their own ethno-national bloc. In this case, the lack of numerical strength may result in permanent exclusion from political power (Horowitz 2000: 348–49).

Most Bosnian political parties are ethnic ones, a situation which favours electoral competition within, and not between, national communities. Since the end of the war the main moderate political party has been the Social Democratic Party (SDP), which has a multi-ethnic leadership but a voter base primarily concentrated in the Federation. In the Entities, there exist (relatively) moderate political parties. Haris Silajdžić's Party for Bosnia and Herzegovina (SBiH) advocates a moderate agenda alternative to that of the nationalist SDA, but its support comes almost exclusively from Bosniak voters. The party's aversion to the preservation of the Entities makes it suspect to most non-Bosniak citizens, in particular Serbs fearing for the survival of the RS. In Croat areas, small parties have attempted to undermine the domination of the nationalist hard line party HDZ. Former presidency member Krešimir Zubak broke with the HDZ in 1998 to create the

New Croatian Initiative, but attracted only a fraction of the Croat vote. In 2006 a serious challenge to the HDZ came from the New Croatian Democratic Union 1990 (HDZ 1990), created by some prominent HDZ defectors who wanted to uphold and protect the HDZ's founding principles, including ever-closer ties with Croatia, from continuing party scandals and infighting. At the October 2006 elections HDZ 1990 won two seats in the forty-two-member House of Representatives, one less than the HDZ, and even received the majority of votes in one of the traditionally HDZ-ruled cantons in the Federation. Similarly, in the Serb Republic the Alliance of Independent Social Democrats (SNSD) of Milorad Dodik, and since 2000 the Party of Democratic Progress of Mladen Ivanić, represent a moderate alternative to the electoral domination of the SDS – the hard line party of wartime leader Radovan Karadžić. However, neither party ever had significant support from other communities. Moreover, both Dodik and Ivanić have often been as intransigent in their stance towards Bosniaks as the SDS. In particular, Dodik's political programme has grown increasingly similar to that of the SDS. At the 2006 elections Dodik became the most important RS politician by reneging on RS commitments to police reform and by threatening to call an independence referendum.

In this context, polarised along ethnic lines, PR satisfies the need for inclusion of all main ethnic groups. At the same time, however, PR allows for the consolidation of hard line nationalist political parties, who can achieve electoral success by making narrow, sectarian appeals to their core ethno-political bases: 'the surest route to electoral victory under PR is to play the ethnic card – with disastrous consequences for the longer-term process of democratisation' (Reilly 2002: 132). As the election results demonstrated, in conditions of group insecurity and mutual distrust, with no incentive for politicians to appeal beyond their own ethnic constituencies, elections predictably turned into an ethnic census. The vast majority of Bosnians chose their incumbent ethnic bloc elites and war leaders, who in turn gained democratic legitimisation for their policies, and reinforced the grip on their constituencies. In the first post-war elections, all newly created institutions were filled with nationalists providing, as an observer argued, 'a pseudo-democratic legitimisation of the ruling parties' (Shoup 1997: 11). Female representation in the House of Representatives was a meagre 2 per cent – the result of the lack of any proactive measure to get women onto electoral lists. The lack of time for moderate alternative parties to organise also contributed to the nationalists' victory. In sum, as Gramsci (1971) noted in his early critique of liberal democracy, not only are elections a means to choose political leadership, but also they can be exploited by political elites as a tool to gain access to power and control the powerless through a legitimate and democratic mechanism.

These first post-war elections set the stage for the RS National Assembly and municipal elections in 1997 and general elections in 1998: democratic procedures gave the stamp of legitimacy to those leaders who led Bosnia into war, and whose behaviour during and after the conflict gave them the reputation of ethnic cleansers, thugs, and war criminals. The very frequency of the elections provided political parties with an opportunity to expound their nationalist rhetoric for narrow, short-term political goals.[3] Ultimately, elections empowered nationalist parties, made the reversal of ethnic cleansing more difficult, and complicated plans for the departure of international interveners from the country. This created the paradoxical situation whereby the implementation of the peace agreement depended on those most likely to sabotage it. Predictably, instead of promoting reconciliation, these parties inverted Clausewitz and promoted the continuation of war by (relatively) peaceful means. As a result, Bosnia has been characterised by constant tension among the three major ethnic groups, the decision-making process has been burdensome, and the institutional structures inefficient. In sum, the consociational prescription to ensure proportional representation of all major groups in society has been achieved at the expense of governability and efficient decision-making. Pure proportionality rewards divisions and divisiveness and in the long run may engender more consensus-breaking than consensus-making (Sartori 1997: 72).

International agencies have reacted to the nationalist parties' consolidation and lack of efficient domestic governance by progressively increasing their control of domestic political processes. The more elections legitimated unpalatable local nationalists and complicated governability, the more international agencies intervened, for example, using the Bonn powers to dismiss un-cooperative but democratically elected local officials. Ironically, elections have triggered a mechanism that, instead of favouring the creation of responsive and democratically accountable institutions, has led to the removal of power from local parties and undermined the autonomy and democratic self-government of local communities. Elections have drawn international agencies further into the intricacies of Bosnian politics and undermined the consolidation of Bosnian institutions whose accountability is directed to international agencies rather than local constituencies. As a result, voter preferences are not translated into policy changes, and local democratic institutions are failing to develop the necessary legitimacy and effectiveness. After a decade of international intervention, the gradual erosion and delegitimisation of democratic institutions has become as great a challenge to democracy and democratisation as the excesses of ethnic politics.

The rise of electoral engineering

Not only have international agencies begun to intervene assertively in domestic political life, but also they have attempted to devise electoral rules to promote non-nationalist parties, foster cooperation and compromise and increase politicians' accountability to their constituencies – an approach often labelled as 'integrative'. According to Donald Horowitz (2000: 601–52), the key to making moderation pay off is adopting electoral and governmental structures that give politicians incentives to accommodate their respective viewpoints. For Benjamin Reilly (2001), who builds on Horowitz's pioneering work, 'centripetal institutions' can be designed to encourage moderate, centrist forms of political competition. This approach is more promising in the long term for democratising states than consociational approaches that take the politicisation of ethnic groups as given. For both Horowitz and Reilly, the choice of electoral system can be particularly important in lessening the appeal of inter-ethnic confrontation. The central mechanism to foster inter-ethnic cooperation through electoral design is to make politicians reciprocally dependent on the votes of members of groups other than their own. Only if office-seekers recognise the need to seek second-preference votes from outside their own core constituencies will they opt for shared interests across groups over narrow parochialism. This system encourages legislators to consider their political adversaries as part of the same political and moral universe.

Rules that favour vote-pooling and preference-swapping, such as the alternative vote (AV), are the preferred integrationist approaches to fostering compromise. The AV system enables voters to rank candidates, with the assumption that the first choice will be given typically to a member of the ethnic group to which the voter belongs. If no candidate gains an absolute majority of first preferences, the candidate with the lowest number of preferences will be eliminated and their ballots redistributed to another candidate according to the second preference. The process continues until a candidate gains a majority. If there are enough moderate constituencies within a polarised society to make cross-ethnic voting possible, this type of electoral engineering can have a significant impact. If, however, voters are so polarised they either do not indicate a second preference or give that preference to another member of their own ethnic group, then the system loses its thrust.

By late 1998 the design of the electoral system had become the core of the international democratisation strategy. The PIC set specific integrationist requirements for the drafting of the Permanent Election Law, including the need to promote the multi-ethnic character of the state, favour political pluralism, encourage parties with broad support amongst all citizens, and uphold the right of refugees and DPs to vote in the municipalities of their pre-war homes. Several human rights and advocacy groups, institutions and individual experts contributed to the debate and advanced proposals to reform the system in a way that made moderation a more central feature of Bosnian politics. The International Crisis Group proposed a system that was essentially 'Horowitzian', recommending the adoption of a multiple-vote system in which voters of all ethnic groups have a say in the election of the leaders of each group (ICG 1998d). In a typical integrationist formula, ICG argued that, in seeking second choice votes, candidates would have to moderate their appeals to cross the ethnic divide.

International agencies have attempted to build moderation by electoral design while preserving the institutional consociational system. However, because this system is easily prey to nationalist parties, any positive effects of electoral engineering can occur only under the most unusual and unpredictable circumstances. Moderation and accommodation are also stifled when international agencies impose solutions on recalcitrant local parties, depriving them of the political breathing space to reach compromises and preventing the possibility of local institutions developing legitimacy and effectiveness. As the 2000 elections confirm, this does not invalidate integrationist designs, but calls into question the ad hoc and shortsighted use of electoral engineering in a system that can easily be exploited by nationalist parties.

The 2000 elections

The 2000 elections differed from the previous elections in several important aspects (OSCE 2000b). First, campaign financing was regulated for the first time, consisting of four key components: disclosure, donation limits, spending limits, and enforcement. Second, election rules made it compulsory that at least one third of party lists be reserved for women. Because of this regulation, the number of women in office has significantly increased, making Bosnia the most receptive to women's political participation among all European countries. And yet, interestingly, a public opinion poll found that 71 per cent of women surveyed believe that women's interests are represented only 'poorly' or 'not at all' (Freedom House 2001: 116). Perhaps the reason for this disappointing statistics lies in the fact that most women still do not hold high-profile positions. Successive Bosnian governments have perpetuated gender inequalities by appointing mostly men to senior positions in government and administrative bodies (Lithander 2001: 22). Of the nine ministries in the Council of Ministers of Bosnia, a woman is the minister of finance and treasury, while the remaining positions are held by men. Further, of 148 mayors in Bosnia, only three women were elected in Drvar, Oštra Luka, and Istočni Stari Grad.

In addition to these changes, three additional innovations were introduced specifically with a view to fostering inter-ethnic moderation. First, open lists and multi-member constituencies were introduced. Second, a preferential voting system was adopted for the election of the RS presidency. Third, new rules for the election of members of the House of Peoples in the Federation were introduced. However, these three changes did not have the intended impact. The first did not specifically foster inter-ethnic accommodation but rather disadvantaged multi-ethnic and civic parties; the second and the third, both inspired by an integrationist approach, backfired because of the timing and method of their adoption. The OSCE imposed new electoral rules a month before the elections, allowing Bosnian nationalist parties to exploit this circumstance in order to denounce a supposed bias against them and rally support among their respective communities.

Open list and multi-member constituencies

Until the 2000 elections, Bosnians could vote only for a party and not for a specific candidate. All elections were conducted using a closed list system, whereby the party fixed the order of candidates elected and voters were unable to express a preference for a particular candidate. This provision placed considerable power in the hands of political parties and their leaderships. In a context polarised along ethnic lines parties could present candidates with little concern for their personality traits. The Roman emperor Caligula made his horse a senator, and today's expression 'Caligula's horse' suggests that anybody can get himself elected (Sartori 1997: 17). Bosnians use the expression *foteljaši* (armchair politicians) when complaining bitterly about politicians from all national groups who sit in powerful and comfortable positions to work for their own personal welfare (Grandits 2007). Closed party lists in multi-member constituencies make both Caligula's horse and *foteljaši* more easily elected. By contrast, in an effort to mitigate the influence of the incumbent party elites and to forge a link of accountability between elected representatives and the electorate, the rules and regulations of 2000 provided for open lists, whereby voters could indicate either individual candidates, or party list, or both their favoured party and favoured candidate.

This system alleviates one of the major drawbacks of proportional representation, that is, the lack of direct accountability of representatives to voters (Bose 2002: 223–24). Indeed,

> the intention is to increase the level of accountability for elected officials at all levels by having them rely on the positive approval of the electorate rather than relying on influence within their party to be placed high on the party candidate list. By using open lists, voters have the option of selecting candidates whom they like irrespective of their order on the party list.
>
> (AEO 2001: 7)

Open lists were institutionalised in the final election law, with the aim of 'fostering a direct link between the voters and the candidates and offering an opportunity to the voters to get around parties' hierarchies by indicating the candidates of their own choice' (OSCE 2002b: 4). However, although open lists can increase accountability, they do not necessarily favour moderation and the affirmation of multi-ethnic parties – both explicit goals that the election law was supposed to achieve. When ethnic affiliation remains the primary basis of voter choice, multi-ethnic parties fail. Unsurprisingly, this provision was contested by the SDP – the most multi-ethnic party.

The creation of multi-member constituencies (MMCs) for the elections of the statewide and two Entity parliaments was implemented with a similar rationale, that is, the attempt to establish a direct relationship of accountability between voters and their representatives. The Entities were divided into smaller districts: five multi-member constituencies were created in the Federation and three in the RS. The official justification was that: 'The system will make legislative bodies more representative geographically. Candidates will run in local constituencies, and the voters will have a chance to know their elected representatives and their record in office' (AEO 2001: 9). When combined with alternative voting (see below), multi-member AV can lead to very skewed election results, making it inappropriate for ethnically divided societies. AV in multi-member districts displays overwhelming majoritarian features when party support in the electorate ensures that preferences flow from the first candidate on the party list to the next on their list (Reilly 2001: 153). To offset this possible flaw, compensatory mandates were created to make up for insufficient proportionality that could derive from adding up the results from the individual multi-member constituency races. Compensatory mandates not only ensure 'near-perfect proportionality between votes obtained and seats secured' (Bose 2002: 220) but also open greater opportunities to smaller parties or coalitions that may not have received enough votes in a given constituency race to win a seat, but have received enough votes in the overall electoral unit to win a mandate. Twenty-five per cent of mandates for all legislative bodies are allocated through compensatory seats. So, for example, twenty-one members of the House of Representatives of the State Parliament were elected in six MMCs from the Federation, while the remaining seven seats were assigned through compensatory mandates; nine seats were elected from MMCs from the RS, with five seats reserved for compensatory mandates.

The flaw with MMCs as constituted in Bosnia is similar to the problem with open lists. While sensible in theory, in that it improves accountability, in practice its impact on fostering inter-ethnic moderation is small. To begin with, the sheer complexity of the system was likely to be difficult for voters to understand, thus discouraging electoral participation. Furthermore, the way the MMCs were drawn up, preserving a clear ethnic majority within each constituency, made it unlikely that candidates would seek support across ethnic lines. In addition, the use of compensatory mandates guaranteed pure proportionality in the translation of votes into seats but did nothing to address the trade-off between representativeness and governability. In fact, compensatory mandates allocated to parties with less than 3 per cent of the votes could only increase the number of parties represented in parliament, encouraging political fragmentation at the expense of stable government.[4]

Preferential voting

The adoption of preferential voting for the election of the RS presidency was motivated by previous experience. At the 1998 presidential elections, 17.2 per cent of votes for the Serb member of the presidency were invalid, mainly unmarked ballots suggesting that Bosniak and Croats did not support any of the candidates, all Serbs with the exception of one Bosniak candidate running for a minor party (Keane 2001: 95). Had preferential voting been in place in 1998, allowing voters to express more than one preference, it is likely that Biljana Plavšić (then the West's preference) rather than ultra-nationalist Nikola Poplašen would have won. The adoption of preferential voting for the 2000 election was intended to promote the newly favoured candidate, the more moderate Milorad Dodik.

Alternative voting, or 'preferential voting' as international agencies defined it, is a pivotal integrationist feature aimed at fostering inter-ethnic accommodation. It was hoped, in keeping with Horowitz, that this would moderate Bosnian politics. According to the OSCE, which was in charge of the elections, preferential voting was 'the key change in the electoral system ... .Candidates who want to be elected will be encouraged to adopt more moderate programmes to attract these secondary preferences' (OSCE 2000c). Furthermore, 'when more than just the first-preference votes are taken into consideration, the moderate candidates stand a better chance of winning the elections, as they will have support from a large cross-section of the electorate' (AEO 2001: 8).

In practice, as Sumantra Bose (2002: 230–33) has convincingly argued, the preferential voting system has not worked as intended. To begin with, second preferences were almost superfluous, as the ultra-nationalist SDS all but gained an outright majority with 49.8 per cent of votes in the first round. More importantly, 60 per cent of Serb voters made the SDS their first choice in the RS presidential elections to defeat the absentee Bosniak vote. For the election of the RS parliament and for that of the RS members of the State Parliament (for which ethnic Serbs did not worry about the influence of a negligible number of Bosniak votes), only 44 per cent and 48 per cent respectively voted for the SDS. It is possible that Serb voters understood the intention to undermine the SDS and decided to support it more than they would have done otherwise. The system did not work even in convincing minorities to vote for a moderate candidate of another ethnic group; 98 per cent of Bosniak voters of the Federation-based Bosnian Party, which gained the least number of votes and therefore whose second preferences were counted first, gave their second preference to other Bosniak parties rather than to moderate Serb candidates.

Bose concludes that 'it is probably fortunate that the designers of Bosnia's Election Law eventually decided not to make the elections to the tripartite BiH state presidency dependent on an AV-type multiple/preferential voting system' (2002: 238). Nevertheless, preferential voting for the RS presidency was unlikely to be a reliable test for at least two reasons. First, this system is unlikely to produce conciliatory behaviour where ethnic groups are concentrated in particular geographic regions. In these instances, the politicians' incentive to seek support from various groups depends on the presence and size of minority groups. Because the RS electorate was not ethnically heterogeneous, only under the most unusual circumstances could AV have influenced the ethnic outcome of the results. Since 2000, however, an increasing number of minorities have returned to their pre-war homes, creating the possibility of ethnically mixed constituencies (see Chapter 6). Second, because the system itself was introduced (more or less openly) to support Dodik, it was likely to be recognised as such by Serb voters. When Richard Holbrooke (then US Ambassador at the United Nations) announced, just before election day, that the SDS should have been banned, voters were probably further galvanised to support the party. This reflected a broader shortcoming in the international agencies' strategies, that is, the attempt to manipulate short-term electoral results by manufacturing electoral rules to favour specific candidates, instead of strengthening local institutions and creating a stable and locally accepted electoral system. The constant changes in the electoral rules weaken voter capacity to understand the electoral system, thus diminishing its intended impact, and possibly provide an excuse for nationalist parties to rally constituency support.

Electing the Federation House of Peoples

In addition to creating open lists and multi-member constituencies, and introducing preferential voting for the RS presidency, the electoral rules changed the method of election of the Federation House of Peoples. This institution is elected indirectly. It is meant to represent the Bosnian ethnic groups rather than citizens, and is designed to uphold the 'vital interest' of each group. Until 2000, members of the cantonal parliaments belonging to the same community elected members to the House of Peoples. A month prior to the elections, the OSCE introduced new procedures, strongly desired and supported by OSCE ambassador Robert Barry – thus known as the 'Barry rule' (OSCE 2000a). The rule aimed at regulating the method cantonal assemblies used to elect members to the Federation House of Peoples. Under the previous rule, each national group in the cantonal assemblies selected its own representatives. The new rule decreed that all members vote for all candidates, so that Croats would vote for Bosniak representatives and vice versa. Quotas for each canton secured thirty seats for Croats in the Federation House of Peoples, thirty for Bosniaks and twenty for Others (including Serbs, Jews, Roma, and other minorities), thus respecting the principle of equitable representation of all communities.

The Barry rule was intended to foster moderation by making elected members rely on votes other than those of their own community. The HDZ objected vigorously. It argued that when all members of the cantonal assembly elected the delegates in one election, there would be an influence of the majority group, the Bosniaks, on the selection of the delegates from the smaller group – the Croats. The HDZ began its 2001 rebellion against international policy as a protest against the Barry rule, leading to a major confrontation between the party and international interveners (Bieber 2001). The quarrel terminated only with the High Representative's dismissal of the HDZ party leader, and the eventual decision to delete the rule from the Permanent Election Law.

The short-term impact of this rule, however, was the opposite of that intended. The HDZ – a party machine that thrived on the fear of Bosniak domination – was able, predictably, to rally the Croat community in support of its stand against unjust electoral rules. During its election campaign the HDZ made extensive use of the slogan 'Self-determination or extermination'. The way the Barry rule was adopted, less than a month before election day, confirmed in Croat eyes a bias against them. Even the International Crisis Group, usually willing to censure the Croat leadership for pursuing narrow self-interest, recognised how the Barry rule had: 'evoked genuine concern by Croats that they risk being marginalised in a state where Bosniaks and Serbs enjoy special advantages' (ICG 2001b: 6). In the run-up to the elections, the HDZ leadership increased its vocal campaign for the creation of a third Croat Entity. In October, it organised a referendum on the 'position of the Croat people', attempting in practice to recognise the existence of Herceg-Bosna. More than 70 per cent of registered Croats voters participated, with 98.96 per cent voting in favour. Despite its lack of legal force, the referendum had the result of legitimising and therefore mobilising greater support for the HDZ, which won the Croat vote overwhelmingly at the November elections.

The 2000 election results proved disappointing for international agencies, despite a few hopeful signs of an erosion of nationalist control over political institutions. In the Federation, the HDZ was able to garner enough seats in the cantonal assemblies to win a majority of the Croat representatives to the House of Peoples. In the RS, the SDS was the clear winner. Only the main Bosniak nationalist party, the SDA, lost votes to the moderate anti-nationalist Social Democratic Party (SDP). This party was able to gain the majority of Bosniak votes, and gained power in several important municipalities, including Sarajevo, Zenica, Tuzla, and Bihać. The number of municipalities controlled by nationalist parties fell from 124 to 76 (Gall 2000). The 40 per cent of votes received by moderate parties such as the SDP highlights the existence of cross-cutting interests and a body of the electorate potentially amenable to integrative devices. Despite the SDP's performance, dissatisfaction with the peace process became increasingly evident. Western governments announced new cuts in the international military presence, while Petritsch publicly blamed the United States for insisting on holding frequent elections on the simplistic assumption that elections equate with democracy (Smith 2000).

Despite the less than satisfying results, the energetic lobbying of the American and British ambassadors was nonetheless instrumental in helping the SDP and SBiH to form a coalition of ten moderate parties and create the Alliance for Change. This coalition replaced the rule of the ethno-nationalist parties and assumed power in 2001.[5] The Alliance formed a government led by Croat Božidar Matić until June 2001 when, following the failed attempt to adopt the permanent election law (see below), SDP leader Zlatko Lagumdžija replaced him. The Alliance also elected SDP Karlo Filipović, a Croat, to the presidency of the Federation, and SBiH Safet Halilović, a Bosniak, to the vice presidency, and established a working arrangement with pragmatic and moderate parties from the RS – the Party of Democratic Progress (PDP), the Party of Independent Social Democrats (SNSD), the Socialist Party of the RS (SPRS) and the Serb People's Alliance (SNS). In the RS, international pressure on the presence of hard-line nationalists in government positions proved too strong for the SDS. Despite the fact that the party emerged as a clear winner from the elections, obtaining the Entity presidency and vice presidency, and thirty-one of the eighty-three seats in the National Assembly, the SDS could not form a government. Instead, Mladen Ivanić (PDP) created a government of 'independent experts' in which SDS members participated as individuals, leaving their party affiliations during their term in office. This compromise allowed for the formal exclusion of the SDS from power, and thus for the continuation of the disbursement of much needed foreign aid.

In sum, electoral engineering at the 2000 elections did not work as intended. It is likely that the introduction of open lists damaged multi-ethnic parties. Preferential voting in the RS was introduced to support a politician with little grassroots support, triggering instead voters' support for the SDS. The Barry rule raised fears among Croats that electoral mechanisms would undermine their interests under the guise of forging cross-ethnic moderation. Eventually, the creation of the Alliance for Change was able to sideline the three main ethnic nationalist parties. However, as the 2002 election would show, this development had shallow roots, demonstrating the futility of promoting non-nationalist and moderate political parties in a context where politicians can get re-elected by making narrow nationalist appeals.

The difficulty in sustaining the development of multi-ethnic and civic political parties in Bosnia is hardly surprising. Since the early twentieth century Bosnians have often voted along ethno-nationalist lines when given the opportunity, and it is not startling that they continue to do so in the aftermath of the 1992–95 war, particularly given that constitutional and electoral norms favour ethnic voting. Confronted by continuing voter support for nationalist parties, international agencies misread the reasons for such apparently puzzling behaviour and began to grow weary of Bosnian citizens' presumed lack of maturity. Unlike the situation in other democratic states, elections have become less a test of governing policies than a test of the maturity and reliability of voters, and their capacity to grasp the complexities of the electoral process. One is reminded of Bertolt Brecht's mocking of the communist government's attitude in East Germany during the Cold War: if the people did not do better, the government would have to fire the people and elect a new one. Similarly, international agencies have often been tempted to 'fire the Bosnian people' instead of using their power and influence to reform the constitutional structure and the electoral law to support the growth of a civic political alternative. In fact, the permanent electoral law adopted in 2001 by the Bosnian parliament and greeted with international approval preserved the discriminatory aspects penalising non-nationalist political parties.

The permanent election law and the 2002 elections

The July 2000 Constitutional Court decision on constituent peoples demanded that the Entity constitutions be amended consistently with the principle of equality of Bosniaks, Serbs, and Croats (Chapter 3). The decision provided an opportunity to draft the permanent election law to overcome some of the most negative characteristics of the political system. The electoral reform was supposed to create incentives for moderation and cross-ethnic appeals, to support the creation of pre-electoral coalitions and to elect moderate candidates. Instead, the permanent election law, adopted in August 2001, further entrenched the discriminatory features of the political system. The moderate coalition in power between 2001–2 was internally divided and unable to pass a law that would have better served the interests of their members. As mentioned above, the election law failure even led to the resignation of moderate prime minister Božidar Matić, the first politician holding this position who did not belong to any of the three main nationalist parties.

Electing the three-member presidency

Confirming the choice made for the previous elections in 2000, the permanent election law adopted open lists and multi-member constitiuencies. For the election of the three-member presidency and the president and vice-president of the RS, the first-past-the-post system was chosen. Furthermore, with regard to the election of the members of the presidency, the law maintained the principle that the Croat and Bosniak members be elected directly from the Federation, while the Serb member was still to be elected by voters registered in the RS. This stipulation has at least two important shortcomings.

First, it is questionable according to international human rights standards. The European Commission for Democracy Through Law (Venice Commission), which periodically is tasked by the Council of Europe to express opinions on a specific issue, noted how the provisions regulating elections to the presidency and the House of Peoples are incompatible with democratic principles (Venice Commission 2001). Citizens who do not identify themselves as Bosniak, Serb or Croat are effectively barred from the state presidency and other offices. Moreover, because about 30 per cent of the electorate are estimated to live in an area where they constitute a minority, such electors are constrained in their choices to vote for a candidate from an ethnic group other than their own. Federation voters can choose either a Bosniak or a Croat as presidential candidate, while RS voters can only elect a Serb for the RS seat. These provisions violate the Copenhagen Commitments and Protocol 12 of the European Convention on Human Rights, which according to the DPA applies directly to Bosnia and takes precedence over any other law.

Furthermore, the Bosnian Constitutional Court had explicitly criticised the ethnic character of Bosnian institutions. In the constituent peoples case the court noted that, in the case of the election of the Serb member of the presidency, he or she is elected by all RS citizens, thus representing 'neither Republika Srpska as an Entity nor the Serb people only, but all citizens of the electoral unit Republika Srpska' (Ustavni sud BiH 2000: para. 65). Similarly, the Bosniak and Croat members represent all Federation citizens, not simply Bosniak and Croat voters. The Venice Commission (2001: para. 17) expanded on this issue. Since members of the presidency represent all citizens residing in the Entity which elected them, then they should not identify themselves as belonging to a specific group. Thus, it is not true that only Serbs can defend the interests of the RS, and only Croats and Bosniaks can defend the interests of the Federation. In sum, the ethnic character of Bosnian institutions violates citizens' voting rights, excludes minorities, and does not satisfy international standards for democratic elections.

Second, in addition to being discriminatory, the rules for the election of the tri-partite presidency preserved the rigid consociational structure that reified ethno-national rule and complicated the emergence of moderate political alternatives. In conditions of ethnic insecurity and as long as leaders can rely only on their ethnic constituencies, nationalists can be easily voted into office and moderate politicians are disadvantaged. Ethnic parties are not 'dinosaurs' doomed to extinction, as the High Representative called them (see Chapter 3), but they are rational political actors who thrive by playing the ethnic card while presenting themselves as the only solution to ethnic insecurity. In this context, civic-minded parties are likely to continue to lose out to ethnic ones.

In response to the charge of short-sightness, international electoral engineers argued that the election law could not contradict the constitution and that group-based features should be respected. For these reasons, the range of options available to foster political moderation via electoral rules was severely limited.[6] The fact that electoral rules should be compatible with constitutional norms is undeniable, and suggests that electoral reform can only be achieved in the context of a broader constitutional overhaul. However, international agencies' defence of discriminatory rules ignored the criticism of both the Bosnian Constitutional Court and that of the Venice Commission. Moreover, it misrepresented and failed to learn from the experience of other deeply divided states. International officials erroneously cited the case of Belgium to justify the electoral rule supporting discrimination in the election of the three-member presidency. OSCE ambassador Robert Barry grossly misrepresented the election law in Belgium when he argued that in this country an individual of French origin can vote only for a French candidate, while a Flemish can only vote for a Flemish candidate (Selimbegović 2001). Instead, voters can choose any candidate. An elected candidate must then take an oath in French and then join the French-speaking group in the House of Representatives, or else must take an oath in Flemish and belong to the Flemish group. In practice, a French speaker could belong to the Flemish group by taking the oath in Flemish, but would lose their status as a French speaker, with important political consequences, not least for the French voters who elected them. In the mid-1980s, the Belgian case was brought to the European Court of Human Rights, which ruled that the system did not violate the European Convention and that the principle of equal treatment of all citizens in the exercise of their right to vote and their right to stand for election was respected.[7] It is hard to see, however, how this case could constitute a precedent to justify electoral discrimination in Bosnia. What the Strasbourg ruling did determine was that states can have some discretion in applying the principle of non-discrimination, not that citizens can only vote for their respective ethnic constituencies.

There were both legal and political reasons to reconsider the creation of a statewide electoral base – a key move in an integrationist direction. First, the July 2000 Constitutional Court decision provided a legal justification for the statewide option. The ruling stated unambiguously that 'all provisions reserving a certain public office in the executive or judiciary exclusively' for one group 'without possibility for "others" to be elected ... seriously violate Article 5 of the Racial Discrimination Convention and the constitutional principle of equality of the constituent peoples' (Ustavni sud BiH 2000: para. 116). More specifically, the court had openly criticised the rigidity of the ethnic structure of the presidency, and explicitly rejected the principle that the method used for electing this body could be compared to the Belgian system. Supporters of electoral change in the direction of a statewide electoral base argued that the opinion of the court could have been incorporated into the electoral law, while international agencies argued that such changes were possible only after the conclusion of the work by constitutional commissions created in January 2001 to harmonise the Entity constitutions with the court decision. In retrospect, the international argument was a self-defeating one, since the High Representative eventually decided to impose constitutional changes.

Second, the Council of Ministers, at the time backed by moderate parties, advocated that Bosniaks and Croats outside the Federation and Serbs outside the RS should be able to run for the presidency. Furthermore, a poll, conducted in April 2001 shortly before the adoption of the law, showed that in addition to the predictable support of Bosniaks (80.4 per cent), 49.3 per cent of Croats and 47.6 per cent of Serbs supported the idea of every voter being able to vote for every member of the collective presidency (UNDP 2001b: 12). This local institutional and popular backing for change would have provided political support for a different approach. Instead, international electoral experts chose the preservation of the discriminatory aspects of the electoral law, and failed to propose or encourage alternative integrationist solutions.

Displaced persons and their voting rights

The voting rights of displaced persons provided an additional hurdle to international electoral engineers. For all post-war elections, this problem has been the crux of political debate and outright manipulation by the nationalist parties. As explained at the beginning of this chapter, at the first post-war elections international agencies expected that most Bosnians would vote at their pre-war residence, either in person or with an absentee ballot. An exception was made, however, for those who wished to live in a new municipality. Although all groups took advantage of this regulation, the Serbs fraudulently arranged absentee Serb majorities in key strategic towns that previously had a Bosniak or Croat majority (ICG 1996a). Because of this the first municipal elections had to be postponed several times, and were only held in September 1997. International organisations revised the electoral rules to make manipulation less likely. Voters displaced within Bosnia were required to provide proof of residence in a new municipality in order to be permitted to vote there. Refugees outside Bosnia had to provide a 'pre-existing, legitimate, and non-transitory nexus with the future municipality', such as an offer of employment or a property title. Because refugees had to show their documentation in the municipality where they intended to live, few actually took advantage of this option.

The voting rights of displaced persons continued to be a point of contention when the permanent election law was being discussed. The draft limited passive electoral rights in cases of illegal occupancy by making it impossible for an individual to stand for election if living illegally in someone else's apartment. Under pressure from Bosniak nationalist parties, the draft law was also amended to restrict the active electoral right, that is, the citizens' constitutionally guaranteed right to vote. The SDA in particular argued that citizens should not have been allowed to vote in the communities where they lived as displaced persons. Instead, they should have voted where they lived before the war, an idea opposed by Serb and Croat parties. As a compromise the OSCE initially offered to give voters a choice.[8] Eventually, the election law prescribed that illegal occupants of property were allowed to vote in the municipalities of their pre-war residency only, not in the place of their current illegal residency.

Thus, in the effort to defend and promote the individual rights of the displaced population, the law violated internationally accepted human rights standards, which prohibit linking voting rights to property rights.

Moreover, in addition to being debatable in principle, the mechanism to demonstrate illegal residency proved unworkable in practice. The electoral register and the housing register were not compatible: while the former is centralised, the latter is decentralised at the municipal level and equal standards are not applied. The law did not clarify from which moment illegal occupancy was considered, whether at the moment of registration or at the moment of actually going to the polls. The law also failed to identify exactly who was an illegal occupant, and did not clearly spell out which type of executive decision would determine someone's legal status. Moreover, even in the presence of a legally binding decision, there remained the question of whether the status of illegal occupant is to be extended to the family of the person identified as such. Ultimately, the decision to leave local authorities with the politically sensitive responsibility to determine claims of legality ensured that very few cases were reported to the Election Commission.[9]

In the case of both the presidential election and of the voting rights of displaced persons, international agencies declared themselves in favour of fostering inter-ethnic moderation and respect for human rights through electoral design. In practice they endorsed legislation that complicated the affirmation of multi-ethnic parties and violated the rights of citizens, either by disenfranchising them or by permitting the adoption of questionable and unenforceable provisions that infringed the voting rights of the displaced population.

The election test

The October 2002 elections marked a decisive transition in the country's post-war experience. After seven years of internationally organised and supervised elections, Bosnian officials were for the first time fully responsible for running the electoral exercise. An Election Commission composed of four Bosnians and three international civil servants (two from the OSCE and one from OHR) replaced the Provisional Election Commission, which was created by the DPA and was composed of and controlled by members of the OSCE. Technically, the elections were a success, reflecting the achievement of 'free and fair' standards. Substantively, however, the results disappointed most international interveners and observers. The adoption of PR favoured extreme fragmentation and proliferation of political parties (fifty-seven parties, nine coalitions and three independent candidates ran). The provision of compensatory seats to parties that failed to pass the 3 per cent threshold produced further fragmentation. Fourteen additional parties were given seats in the Federation assembly, whereas in the absence of these rules only four parties would have been represented. In the RS assembly, ten parties were granted seats in addition to the six that passed the threshold.

The parties often competed on similar platforms, making it more difficult for voters to distinguish between them, and thus discouraged participation. Only 54 per cent of eligible voters went to the polls, compared with 104 per cent in 1996, when party fraud and voter mobilisation ensured that virtually all voters cast their ballot, some more than once. Absenteeism was particularly high in urban areas, traditionally more supportive of non-nationalist and civic alternatives. Among the explanations for decline in voter turnout, one should include: the frequency of elections since 1996 (in combination with little visible political change following each electoral round); the complexity of the electoral system; the failure of the Alliance for Change in the 2001–2 period; and the perception that the overwhelming role played by international agencies made the election of local politicians redundant. As predicted, the much-debated provision upholding the rights of the displaced persons proved difficult to enforce. The rule was applied to just 200 people out of the many thousands of registered voters who may have been illegal occupants (IEOM 2002: 4).

The same nationalist parties responsible for the war and perceived as an obstruction to successful peace building defeated their more moderate rivals and won the elections. The collective presidency was filled with nationalist politicians. Sulejman Tihić (SDA) was elected to the Bosniak seat, Mirko Šarović (SDS) won the Serb one, and Dragan Čović (HDZ) obtained the Croat mandate. The civic-minded parties supported by international agencies were penalised most. Their experience in government following the 2000 elections had proven disappointing to many voters who, instead of voting for the main nationalist parties, often chose to abstain. In the Federation, the biggest loser was the SDP – which lost even its traditional strongholds of canton Tuzla and canton Sarajevo, both relatively moderate and multiethnic areas. In the RS, pragmatic premier Mladen Ivanić was the biggest loser. In this context dominated by the nationalist parties, Dodik's party (SNSD) did surprisingly well, obtaining only a handful of seats less than the SDS, but not enough to provide grounds for optimism among domestic non-nationalist observers and foreign analysts. Rather, the local independent press featured editorials entitled 'Back to the Future' or 'Forward to the Past', suggesting disillusion with the peace building process and particularly with the elections as a means of promoting democratisation and peace. Some foreign observers went as far as defining the elections as 'a disaster from the standpoint of international peacebuilding efforts' (Caplan 2005: 182). Others raised doubts about the long-term survival of the state within its currently recognised international borders (Pfaff 2002; Waters 2004).

The post-election period was marked by a complex coalition-building attempt in an effort to create a government for both Entities. The victorious nationalist parties not only complained that the compensatory seats skewed the election results but also argued that the fragmentation of the political system complicated the formation of a government. Whether or not this was true (it took three months to form a government), it is undeniable that compensatory seats further complicated an already complex electoral system and arguably antagonised ordinary electors. Furthermore, party fragmentation increased the influence of small parties in policy-making, while diminishing the government's responsiveness to citizens. The government is often more accountable to the potential blackmail tactics of small parties than to the voters. Both large and small parties are ultimately more accountable to international agencies, who can dismiss Bosnian politicians, than to local constituencies who cannot.

The nationalists' return to power was marked by a rise in ethnic tension, ethnically related episodes of violence and corruption scandals. In April 2003, Šarović resigned following two scandals, one involving illegal military exports to Iraq, and the other related to espionage. SFOR had discovered in March that the RS military intelligence had been spying on international officials, opposition leaders, Federation politicians and Croatian institutions, and sharing information with Serb authorities in Belgrade. Šarović was replaced by SDS member Borislav Paravać. His wartime role as mayor of the ethnically cleansed town of Doboj has fuelled speculation about his possible indictment for war crimes (Katana 2003).

Faced by continuing obstructions to the implementation of the DPA, on 30 June 2004 the High Representative dismissed sixty democratically elected politicians. Fifty-nine of them were Serbs allegedly involved in the criminal network of a silence of complicity that keeps wartime leader Radovan Karadžić safe from arrest and transfer to the ICTY in The Hague (Belloni 2004). In December, the High Representative dismissed nine police commissioners and local government chiefs in the RS after Bosnia failed to join NATO's Partnership for Peace Programme for the second time because of the Serb Entity's lack of cooperation with The Hague. In the ensuing political crisis, RS president Čavić appointed the SDS's Pero Bukejlovićas as prime minister in January 2005, a choice signalling a continued lack of cooperation with international agencies' demands (Katana 2005).

Overall, elections and institution building have had a contradictory effect on democratic consolidation. The excessive emphasis on elections – BiH has had nineteen electoral races between 1996 and 2006 – has been counterproductive. Politicians in constant campaign mode are more interested in being re-elected than adopting policies requiring moderation and compromise. Furthermore, the existing electoral system allows them to be elected on an ethnic platform, further reducing the incentive for accommodation. Finally, the frequent elections and changes of electoral rules make it more complicated for voters fully to understand the complexity of the system and to vote strategically. As experience from other cases confirms, a gradual process of political learning only occurs if successive elections are held under the same rules (Reilly 2001). Perhaps better than anyone else, Paddy Ashdown captured the international agencies' disillusionment with the electoral process:

> we thought that democracy was the highest priority, and we measured it by the number of elections we could organise. The result ... is that the people of Bosnia have grown weary of voting. In addition, the focus on

elections slowed our effort to tackle organised crime and corruption,
which have jeopardised quality of life and scared off foreign investment.

(Ashdown 2002b)

International agencies are slowly becoming aware of the limitations of the
current system and the need to improve the legitimacy and efficiency of
local institutions.

After the 2002 election, the choice of an election law for Brčko District provided another opportunity to discuss the relative merits of different electoral
options. The initial draft law presented in June 2003 embodied a clear integrationist philosophy. The draft foresaw Brčko District as one electoral unit in
which office-seekers competed against each other and were selected by a process
of proportional representation. The assembly would then elect the mayor from
among the assembly councillors. A 3 per cent threshold was proposed to limit
fragmentation. In order to overcome the deadlock common to consociational
institutions, the draft law did not envisage the protection of 'vital national
interests', or the right for any national group to veto legislation. As Brčko
supervisor, ambassador Henry Clarke, explained, the vital national interest
clause 'could make the Assembly incapable of acting on anything controversial,
especially since there is no way to define a "vital national interest" intelligently –
it is inevitably an emotional position, not a rational one' (OHR 2003).

The draft electoral law for Brčko thus quite explicitly rejected the underlying principles of years of international intervention. Instead of guaranteeing ethnic representation, the law assumed that each of the three national
groups would have enough votes to ensure representation in the assembly.
The 'one man, one vote' principle was adopted as the main innovation from
previous electoral rules at all levels. Furthermore, instead of granting the
right to each group to invoke compelling national interests to block legislation, the draft law envisioned a situation in which each group, party and
even individual councillor had to build support, probably across ethnic
boundaries, instead of exclusively relying on their own ethnic constituencies.

The debate resulting from the draft law highlighted the familiar positions
of the three main ethnic groups. Bosniaks, who were a clear majority in the
district prior to the war, expressed concern that the law could legitimate
ethnic cleansing by virtue of proportional representation of the current
residents. Croats also had reason to oppose the law. Because they are the
smaller group in the district, they are likely to obtain only a few seats
through proportional representation. For this reason, they lobbied in favour
of a proposition that would give each national group a minimum number of
seats in the assembly. The law was finally approved in September 2003. The
Bosniak and especially Croat opposition to the draft led to a reversal of some
of its most important innovations. In particular, the law provided guarantees
for a minimum representation of all ethnic groups, although these guarantees
fell short of satisfying everyone. Instead of the guaranteed six seats the
Croats had demanded (out of twenty-nine), they were granted only three.

Conclusion

The post-settlement electoral experience in Bosnia has had a contradictory impact on democratisation and peace building. On the one hand, elections and the slow creation of domestic institutions are visible signs of a movement away from the trauma of the war and a necessary step towards the development and consolidation of democratic institutions and practices. On the other hand, elections and related electoral rules have permitted a consolidation of the power of the same nationalist parties that conducted the war and who are perceived as the main obstacle to successful peace building. Furthermore, the continuing voter support for nationalist parties has reinforced the feeling among international organisations that Bosnians do not do well enough on their own and need additional external regulation and direction.

International agencies have reacted by using the Bonn powers extensively in order to remove obstructive politicians, while at the same time manipulating electoral rules to favour inter-ethnic compromise. This effort has been partially successful. In an institutional context where nationalist politicians can easily be elected by playing the ethnic card, the effectiveness of electoral engineering in favouring cooperation is destined to be extremely difficult. Furthermore, the ad hoc, short-term approach adopted has played into the hands of local nationalists and disadvantaged the few multi-ethnic constituencies that intervention meant to make more politically visible and influential. Elections, electoral engineering, and the related growth in external regulation have alienated many voters who increasingly feel they have a very limited impact in the policy-making process. At the October 2004 local elections, turnout fell to 46.8 per cent, with less than 15 per cent of Bosnians under thirty deciding to go to the polls (HCHR 2005). At the October 2006 general elections turnout was less than 54 per cent, despite the introduction of 'passive registration' that increased the electoral base by more than 400,000 people.

In sum, the post-war building of political institutions has been a slow and frustrating process. The 'stateness problem' remains to plague Bosnia's democratic consolidation. The continuing difficulties at institutional level prompted the search among international interveners for alternative ways to overcome local divisions and make Bosnia a functioning and self-sustaining political entity. The reform of the current constitution, which would which make the elimination of the discriminatory aspects of the election law easier to accomplish, has taken centre stage in debates about the future of Bosnia (see Chapter 7). Meanwhile, since its early disappointing years, international intervention has attempted to address the social dimension of stateness by working to develop a tolerant and robust civil society and to recreate some degree of ethnic inter-mixing by returning the population displaced by the war to their homes. As the following two chapters will confirm, some positive results have been achieved in both areas, but questions about sustainability qualify this success.

5   The limits and virtues of civil society

Since 1998 civil society building has become an integral component of international intervention. This timing reflects two developments. First, US president Bill Clinton announced in June 1998 that the mandate of SFOR peacekeepers would be extended indefinitely. In principle, this decision allowed for the development of a long-term strategy for the consolidation of a civil society pillar, instead of a short-term, crisis-driven approach. Second, after more than two years since the signing of the DPA, a profound disappointment with top-down political strategies had emerged, suggesting the need for a new approach. As seen in the last two chapters, Bosnia's political structure is highly fragmented and easy prey for nationalist parties. International agencies have responded to continuing domestic deadlock by imposing solutions and removing recalcitrant politicians. Although this assertive approach has guaranteed short-term efficiency, it has also raised fundamental questions about the sustainability of a democratisation process characterised by limited domestic ownership. Civil society provided international agencies with a promising avenue to complement institution building, sidestep domestic political leaders, soften and possibly overcome domestic divisions, and promote reconciliation. Accordingly, growing amounts of financial and human resources have been allocated to civil society building programmes.

This chapter examines the impact of the two main bottom-up, societal intervention strategies. First, the influence of economic incentives for reconciliation and reintegration is addressed. International interveners believe that a stable market economy will help overcome inter-ethnic divisions. The enlightened economic self-interest of individuals and groups is expected to rebuild bridges between communities and contribute to overcoming Bosnia's stateness problem. Second, the contribution to democratisation and peace building of domestic voluntary organisations such as non-governmental organisations (NGOs) is scrutinised. At least rhetorically, international agencies value these organisations because they pursue a broad public policy agenda that is often explicitly committed to multi-ethnicity, political compromise and reconciliation.

Correctly, international agencies have reasoned that strengthening civil society is an indispensable component of a broader strategy aimed at addressing Bosnia's stateness problem, improving state–society relations and providing better domestic foundations for the post-war transition. In practice, however, international civil society strategies have had a limited impact. As this chapter argues, although economic aid and market reforms have been touted as important post-war democratisation tools, they have exacerbated divisions and contributed to the ethnicisation of the economy and society. Instead of providing incentives for inter-ethnic cooperation, foreign monies and market-oriented reforms gave further opportunities to ethnic elites to enrich themselves – while doing little to generate sustainable economic development and lift Bosnians out of poverty. International agencies have responded by attempting to sidestep local elites and provide funding directly to local NGOs, but even this strategy has had limited success. Bosnian NGOs depend too heavily on foreign resources and, for this reason, they often implement the priorities of their donors instead of articulating and addressing the needs of local communities. In addition, short-term and changing international priorities complicate the work of NGOs and the affirmation of domestically engrained conflict management practices. In particular, the American-led 'war on terror' had visible negative repercussions in Bosnia, where at least in some instances human rights have been subordinated to American interests.

Strengthening civil society was destined to be a difficult undertaking. Bosnian civil society organisations are frequently divided along ethnic, religious and national lines. Although most of these groups and associations may openly reject violence, they often endorse and promote a world-view that considers groups' relations in zero-sum terms, and resist compromise and cooperation. When civil society organisations are not civic, multi-ethnic and multi-religious their contribution to democracy and peace might be spurious. Sectarian organisations perpetuate the divisions within society and can contribute to political polarisation and continuing confrontation between groups. Although these divisions complicate the task of international agencies, they do not make it impossible, but it requires a judicious assessment of the local reality and careful support to those groups which strive to promote civic politics instead of ethnic politics, and social and political spaces of dialogue instead of ethnic or national segregation. This chapter ends with a brief description of how civil society can have a significant impact in furthering democratisation and peace. Although international interveners have often considered Bosnia as a blank slate, there exist the human and social resources necessary to implement an effective bottom-up peace building strategy. At the same time, civil society is not a panacea. The Bosnian experience shows that effective institutions have an indispensable role in ensuring the conditions for economic development and civic participation.

The political economy of peace

The DPA divided Bosnia into two politically weak Entities kept together by inefficient central consociational institutions – as Chapter 3 showed. It has achieved a similar result at the level of society by dividing the country into economically unviable regions. This is not necessarily a failure of the peace agreement, but one condition that was created by design and could have had significant positive consequences by inducing former enemies to re-establish ties because of economy necessity.[1] In fact, while the DPA is often credited for having stopped the war, its main consequence is perhaps that it divided the country in an unsustainable way, as neither Entity is economically self-reliant. The sociologist Jasminka Udovički cites the Sarajevo independent paper *Free Bosnia*, which in 1996 ran an article asking whether Bosnia, having survived the war, will be able to survive the peace. The article's focus was on the country's natural resources. It is worth quoting this article at some length:

> Lead, zinc and three quarters of the coal deposits ... are located in the territory belonging to the Federation, but almost all deposits of fuel necessary to operate the power plants are in the Republika Srpska. Republika Srpska sits on two thirds of all the iron deposits, but the entire iron-production industrial plant is situated in the region owned by the Federation. Three quarters of the bauxite deposits are in the mines of Republika Srpska, but the centre of the industrial processing is in Mostar. Banja Luka, the self-proclaimed capital of Republika Srpska, is potentially a strong industrial, cultural, and educational centre but is completely cut off from the sources of electrical energy, which are under the control of Croats. The forests, finally, are divided roughly fifty-fifty. Most of the lumber industries, however, are in the Federation.
>
> (Udovički 1997: 279)

The presence of natural resources scattered throughout the Bosnian territory is an incentive for inter-ethnic cooperation. Not surprisingly, individuals and businesses operate daily across the separation line. Over the long term, economic needs might have a stronger impact in leading reintegration than any other internationally driven programmes. The DPA implicitly recognised this possibility. While dividing Bosnia into two Entities, several of its provisions suggest the preference for an integrated economy. The constitution guarantees freedom of movement for goods, services, capital and people; a single currency and monetary policy; and a centralised foreign trade policy, custom policy and balance of payments system. Since 1996, economic needs led to the creation of statewide institutions aimed at creating a framework for a national economy, including a state border service and an indirect tax administration to replace the two Entities' customs administrations.

From war to peace economy

The international intervention template includes a neo-liberal economic agenda aimed at increasing the quantity and quality of economic links between the three main Bosnian groups. Starkly put, international agencies expect that economic interdependence will provide all sides with an interest in refraining from violence. As Immanuel Kant argued over two centuries ago, the 'commercial spirit' cannot coexist with war. When individuals and groups are busy improving their economic position, they are less concerned about ethnic, religious, or other differences. As ethnic issues are replaced by questions of material welfare, ethnic identification may become a less significant factor because citizens are likely to think of themselves as either mobile individuals or members of a socio-economic class. Class differences gradually overcome other distinctions, leading individuals to organise along class lines instead of ethnic ones. To some extent, this is already happening in Bosnia. The limited instances where Bosnians mix across ethnic lines in the workplace demonstrate that opportunities for repeated, horizontal interaction support positive inter-ethnic relationships (Pickering 2006).

Moreover, years of privation and uncertainty about the future have led the majority of Bosnians to reconsider their list of priorities. Bosnians attribute much more importance to economic and social issues than ethnic ones. An opinion poll conducted by the National Democratic Institute found that only 13 per cent of Bosnian citizens consider their 'national interests' among their top two concerns. They worry about unemployment (officially standing at 40 per cent, but much less when the 'shadow economy' is taken into account), corruption, poverty and crime (NDI 2002). The increasing number of strikes protesting overdue wages or contributions to pensions and health insurance schemes confirms both the dire straits of Bosnia's economy and the new priorities of Bosnian citizens (Jelacić and Ahmetasević 2003).

At the same time, however, one should be careful not to place unlimited trust in economic self-interest and the impact of market forces. The break-up of Yugoslavia was also the break-up of an integrated market, leaving all republics (with the limited exception of Slovenia) less economically viable than was the case previously. Furthermore, peace and trade do not always reinforce each other. Rather, intensive inter-ethnic economic cooperation occurred during the 1992–95 war, when smuggling and black marketeering across front lines was all too common. The proliferation of clandestine inter-ethnic trading might even have sustained and prolonged the war, instead of ending it (Andreas 2004). In Bosnia as in other war zones, conflict provides thugs with an opportunity for quick enrichment (Mueller 2000).

In the post-Dayton period cross-ethnic economic matters have emerged alongside national ones, instead of replacing them. After the disappointing experience of the reformist and multi-ethnic Alliance for Change, at the October 2002 elections Bosnians chose national parties instead of those parties rhetorically committed to economic and social reforms extending across inter-ethnic lines. While many reasons determined this choice (see Chapter 4), it is quite certain that many Bosnians were disillusioned with how international aid and market reforms had failed to improve their lives. As a consequence, they could hardly trust the international agencies' pre-electoral suggestion that voting for the reformist parties would facilitate the disbursement of further international aid, and lead to economic development and widespread prosperity. As the next two sections show, the post-war delivery of aid combined with the privatisation of the economy had reinforced ethnic divisions instead of undermining them, while leaving most Bosnians in a state of dire poverty.

International aid

International economic investment has been colossal relative to the size of the country. For most of the 1990s, the cost of intervention amounted to about $US9 billion annually, $7 billion of which was spent to maintain the NATO-led Stabilization Force. The overall amount spent since 1992 is estimated between $81 and 91 billion (Papić 2001: 18). The funds allocated for the reconstruction programme and economic rehabilitation, although less than the resources spent to maintain a military presence, are very significant. In May 1999 the last donors' conference for Bosnia was held, meeting the commitment of providing the country with $US 5.1 billion in aid. On average, about $1,400 per person has been made available for the Bosnian reconstruction programme, several times more than the Marshall Plan's $200 at today's prices (Dobbins 2003–4: 96). Spending privileged infrastructure over other political aspects of the transition such as the need to create jobs for demobilised soldiers. The reconstruction programme was virtually completed by 2000, and widely considered successful. Among the macro-economic successes is the fact that the GDP is back to about 80 per cent of what it was before the war, while inflation was almost non-existent for most of the post-Dayton period – until the introduction of a value added tax on 1 January 2006 led to a short-term price rise.

A closer look at the allocation and impact of international aid reveals a more nuanced picture. To begin with, the actual amount of money spent is difficult to determine with precision. Donor obfuscation, that is, lack of transparency in the actual delivery of monies, makes the assessment of donors' performance difficult. Such performance was further influenced by a dispute between the World Bank and the United States about the role of conditionality in the disbursement of aid. Washington argued that aid should be coordinated by OHR and made conditional on the parties' implementation of the terms of the DPA (Hertić *et al.* 2001). The World Bank objected to the principle of subordinating the delivery of aid to political criteria. While the World Bank had to concede to American pressures, conditionality remained inconsistently applied and enforced. As a result, much time and resources have been squandered on poorly coordinated projects (Simpson 2003). Since May 1999, when the last donors' meeting was held, no consultative-type meeting has even been held, with aid coordination operating on an ad hoc basis.

Conditionality proved to be a weak tool in ensuring compliance to the various clauses of the peace agreement and contributed to undermining other intervention goals – in particular the re-establishment of economic ties between former enemies (Donais 2005). In Mostar, a symbol of the Bosniak/Croat conflict in the Federation and of the general difficulties in the implementation of the DPA, the EU alone has spent 200 million euros, yet the city still remains almost completely divided (ICG 2003a). A 2004 re-unification plan established joint institutions, but their functioning has been hampered by continued wrangling among the parties. Furthermore, the distribution of reconstruction money reinforced the division between the two Entities, instead of overcoming it. In the first two years of the post-settlement transition, only 2 per cent of international aid was delivered to the RS. Charles Boyd referred to this disparity as 'righteous retribution directed against the Serbs, reminiscent of the Allied approach to Germany after the First World War' (1998: 46). While the Serb leadership's resistance to abiding by the commitments subscribed at Dayton justified this choice, in practice it worked at cross-purposes with the goal of economic reintegration. If the lesson of Germany has any meaning for Bosnia, then Boyd's analogy can be taken further. The harsh economic and political conditions applied to Germany after World War I were a direct cause of Hitler's rise to power. The similarly harsh conditions imposed on the RS neither undermined the influence of the ethno-nationalist elite, nor did they convince Serb citizens to embrace liberal norms and practices.

Beyond preserving ethnic division, post-war international aid had four further negative consequences. First, aid has reached Bosnia through the Entities' incumbent leaders and, in so doing, it buttressed the state-like qualities of these semi-independent and autonomous territories and fed corruption and mismanagement. The central state institutions have been largely sidestepped and the municipal governments were slowly sworn in only after the elections of September 1997. In some cases, the implementation of municipal elections took as long as a year, complicating the municipalities' role in managing reconstruction and assistance funds. In general, the focus on the rapid disbursement of funds consolidated the political predominance of the elites that emerged from the war.

Second, international assistance and the presence of hundreds of humanitarian and development organisations have had negative effects on socio-economic development. The international humanitarian aid industry largely replaced the local public sector and hindered the development of the local labour markets and skills. Particularly in the early post-war phase, the presence of a large number of international agencies obstructed the development of governmental responsibility in the fields of social regulation, redistribution and provision. In addition, by recruiting the few remaining local professionals for well paid jobs outside their field of expertise, international agencies undermined the long-term ability to develop a sustainable local economy and social structure (Deacon and Stubbs 1998).[2]

Third, international assistance gave the politico-economic elite a further post-war opportunity for enrichment. Criminal groups, in connection with part of the political class, could extend their illegal practices from war to peacetime while taking advantage of the influx of foreign monies. Shortly after the signing of the DPA the nationalist parties successfully lobbied international agencies to extend post-war amnesty for draft dodgers to economic crimes. Tellingly, the period covered by the amnesty did not simply include wartime, but went back to January 1991 – when the three main nationalist parties were voted into office (Andreas 2004: 44). Then, insulated from prosecution by a sweeping amnesty, well connected mafia-like groups continued to be involved in both legal and illegal activities. An 'unholy alliance' between nationalist parties, sections of the socialist-era nomenklatura, and ethnically segregated mafias perpetuated Bosnia's economic woes (Donais 2005: 40). Only after ethnic nationalist elites were charged in 1999 with having diverted up to $US1 billion from international aid, did corruption and mismanagement become a reason for concern and international funds come to be better scrutinised (Hedges 1999). However, the independent corruption watchdog group Transparency International continues to rank Bosnia among the 'most corrupt countries' in the world (TI 2006).

Fourth, international aid gave Bosnian politicians an additional resource for economic patronage. Even moderate politicians could use international monies to bolster their position – while paying lip service to implementing the DPA. For example, after his 1998 election as RS prime minister, moderate politician Milorad Dodik first promised to return all Bosniak and Croat DPs and refugees to the RS if his government was given $US1 billion for reconstruction. When the money was allocated, however, he directed it towards his own constituency and only a few thousand minority returns occurred to the RS under his tenure. In sum, international aid increased the local nationalists' grip on power while entrusting political change to their dubious goodwill.

Growth and the ethnicisation of the economy

Economic development is an indispensable component of peace building. Cross-country evidence suggests that the likelihood of conflict is directly related to poverty and underdevelopment. Conversely, there is much evidence that economic prosperity is a necessary (albeit not sufficient) condition for peace (World Bank 2003). Accordingly, economic development has been publicised as a possible path to a sustainable peace and the reintegration of Bosnia into a viable political and social space.[3] The international agencies' recipe for economic development is encapsulated in the neo-liberal template mentioned in Chapter 2: economic liberalisation and macro-economic stability are expected to create the conditions for private sector development and economic growth (Paris 2004). The World Bank has developed a 'Bosnian path' to privatisation and deregulation which does not differ from the recipe adopted in any other developing country with a weak economy unsuited for global economic competition: 'in many respects the government must "get out of the way"' (1997: 43).

Privatisation and foreign direct investment

The recipe for getting the government 'out of the way' is twofold. First, Bosnia's central bank operates as a currency board under the direction of an IMF-appointed governor who, according to the DPA, 'shall not be a citizen of Bosnia-Herzegovina or any neighbouring state'.[4] The DPA foresaw that the bank would operate as a currency board for the first six postwar years. Contrary to the functions typically performed by a central bank, currency boards set a fixed exchange rate between the local currency and a stable foreign currency (in the Bosnian case, the German mark, until the introduction of the Euro in January 1999). The domestic currency is fully backed with convertible foreign assets. This arrangement is essential to generate confidence in a weak currency, and it effectively contains inflation. In Bosnia, it also fulfils another purpose: it prevents the Federation from taking loans, while imposing inflation on the RS (and vice versa). The decision in mid-2003 to extend this monetary regime for another six years suggests that political concerns still predominate over the country's need to assume full monetary sovereignty. Because of the central bank's functioning as a currency board, the active role of the state in economic recovery, regeneration and development is precluded. This leaves private economic actors with the lion's share of responsibility for making economic growth possible.

Accordingly, the second fundamental aspect of the programme of economic development is the selling of state assets to private actors in order to establish the condition for a free market economy sustained by private investment. In theory, where state institutions do not control productive activities the ethnically blind market can allocate resources in an economically viable way. Eventually, production and hiring decisions will not be taken on the basis of ethnic or other political concerns, but simply to meet market demands. The post-communist experience in East Central Europe suggests that there is no single model of transition which can be applied everywhere. In the Czech Republic, for example, the voucher privatisation initially dispersed ownership among thousand of citizens, in the hope that later transactions in the market would lead to a concentration of ownership in efficient mid-level enterprises. In Hungary, by contrast, a decentralised reorganisation of property rights gave managers of public enterprises an opportunity to consolidate their control. In these and other similar cases, institutions of coordination (often known as 'networks') between public and private actors were the most significant elements in the transition process (Stark and Bruszt 1998).

Bosnia underwent a transition process which could be described as a hybrid of the Czech and the Hungarian experience. The creation of a market economy went hand-in-hand with the survival of corporatism and clientelism. A reckless programme of privatisation placed economic resources not in the hands of economic entrepreneurs, but in those of politically/ ethnically connected elites (Singer 2000; Bojičić-Dželilovic *et al.* 2004). Instead of improving the underlying economic situation and creating the conditions for the establishment of a free market economy, the process of privatisation 'turned into a costly charade' (ESI 2004b: 17). Citizens of each Entity were given certificates enabling them to invest in small/medium size companies. At the same time, the managers of these companies forced down their value, while criminals, war profiteers and well connected private businessmen bought the certificates at bargain basement prices. Not unlike East European cases, including Russia, privatisation often enriched the 'wrong people' instead of empowering economic entrepreneurs. Furthermore, since the state's assets were sold to members of the dominant political/ethnic group in each area, the initial impact of the privatisation programme was to reinforce ethnic cleansing, and to perpetuate the nationalist grip on power (AFP 1999; Papić 1999). The ethnicisation of the economy further contributed to the failure to create a single economic market. The RS maintains close economic ties with Serbia, and Herzegovina trades heavily with Croatia, but internally separate rules and regulations for the two Entities make it difficult for businessmen to buy and sell goods across the country.

The process of privatisation occurred with the blessing and active engagement of international agencies. The United States Agency for International Development (USAID) designed the privatisation scheme – envisioning it would rapidly be completed within two years. Too optimistically, USAID believed that even if the initial allocation of resources was suboptimal, over time the market mechanism would adjust the distortion by either turning ethnic nationalists into economic entrepreneurs, or by a process of ownership transfer from the former to the latter. International agencies also assumed that the restructuring of uncompetitive enterprises would be easier after the completion of the privatisation process. These expectations failed to materialise. While in the long term private ownership might foster economic growth and development, in the meantime privatisation has been a disappointing process: '[t]he effect of mass privatisation has been ... negligible as far as providing the economy with fresh funding, expertise, know how and markets' (Bojičić-Dželilovic *et al.* 2004: 15). Perhaps even more importantly, privatisation cemented the control of a class of ethnic oligarchs over both the political process and the economy. As a result, 'the process has done more to date to entrench the economic positions of country's nationalists and reduce the prospects of ethnic reintegration than to establish the foundations for sustained economic growth and recovery' (Donais 2005: 119).

The much publicised case of Aluminij Mostar, Bosnia's most profitable industry, is perhaps the best example of how private property is not a panacea for combating ethnic and political arrogance. The company is a stronghold of the HDZ, which took over its management board in 1996 and turned it into a tool of economic support for its political agenda. A dubious process of partial privatisation has transferred ownership from institutions controlled by the HDZ, to managers still HDZ-affiliated. Despite the fact that Aluminij had suffered little damage during the war, its management board devalued the company from the pre-war value of $US620 million to $84 million. International auditors found evidence of irregularities, but the ownership structure was not changed (Pugh 2006). Its clear political and ethnic colour does not exactly make it an instrument for reconciliation. Aluminij, as well as the vast majority of other Croat-run industries, does not employ non-Croat workers, effectively preserving a major obstacle to the sustainable return of minorities (ICG 2001a: 25). The proportion of the company's employees who were Croat increased from 44 per cent in 1992 to 93 per cent in 2003 (AI 2006a). Because Aluminij is economically profitable, it is an exception instead of the rule. In most other cases, the main purpose of privatisation was to favour economic restructuring and improve corporate governance, but neither goal was achieved. Even the World Bank was forced to admit two major failings of the privatisation process: the voucher-privatised industries have not restructured and become more productive, and the broader business environment has not improved significantly, making Bosnia one of the more unfriendly regimes in the region (WBOED 2004: 23).

The gradual withdrawal of international agencies and foreign aid taking place since 2000 has exposed the economic woes of the country. In presenting the results of a thorough research project on Bosnia's competitiveness, the director of the World Bank in Bosnia noticed that Bosnia's economic indicators show an 'alarming' picture and warned that the state is not in a position to 'make the shift from reliance on public capital flows, or aid dependency, to private flows attracted by investment climate' (Ingram 2001). While international agencies considered the selling of public assets as an indispensable step to attract foreign direct investment (FDI), in practice this did not occur as expected. Bosnia's international divisions contribute to delays and inefficiencies, making it an unattractive destination for investment. The parliament adopted a Law on Foreign Direct Investment in mid-1998, but the Federation and the RS adjusted their legal frameworks accordingly only three and four years later – in 2001 and 2002 respectively. Moreover, foreign investors must deal with five different levels of bureaucracy to obtain the necessary documentation legally to set up a company, increasing considerably the time required and the costs involved. The absence of a single internal market with common and enforceable rules also complicates the work of companies across Entities. Unsurprisingly, FDI remains extremely low, at around $US250 million per annum.

The creation in 2002 of a Bulldozer Initiative to remove obstacles to investment, economic growth, and job creation slightly improved the general business climate. The Bulldozer Initiative mobilised the business community to bulldoze barriers and red tape procedures by identifying concrete legislative changes in a brief period of time – fifty reforms in 150 days (Herzberg 2004). One of the most innovative and productive features of this initiative was its attempt to engage important segments of the population – the business community – and turn it into an active constituency for reform and development. The initiative can only improperly be defined as truly 'bottom-up', since the process was initiated by international agencies. However, it quickly transformed itself into a locally owned initiative, demonstrating that local interest was present and just needed to be encouraged.

The initiative's modest objectives granted it widespread support or, at least, benevolent neglect. By amending some legal obstacles to investment, instead of demanding a radical overhaul of the law, the initiative did not change the underlying liberal approach based on privatisation, the retreat of the state, and the trust in FDI as engines of growth, and it minimised the possibility of opposition. Parliaments of both Entities effectively supported it by adopting many amendments to existing laws under the fast track procedure. Over time, however, because no major issues were tackled or spectacular results achieved, the local business community began to lose interest. In the end, the initiative's most significant impact resides not in the number of laws amended, but in the changed outlook among the business community – which began to realise that the private sector has a legitimate right to demand reform from the government, and that such demands can be channelled publicly through institutional avenues (Omanović 2005: 6).

Despite this belated attempt at reform, the Bosnian economy remains in a dire state. The pre-war GDP is not expected to be achieved before 2015. Per capita GDP is estimated at $US1,800 – one of the lowest in Europe. About 20 per cent of Bosnians live below the poverty line, and another 30 per cent are just above. Most of those in poverty are Serbs living in the RS. According to one study, the poverty rate in the Federation is 21.5 per cent, while it reaches 51.9 per cent in the RS (Bisogno and Chong 2002: 64). Women are poorer than men, with young people also generally worse off than older people. Unemployment is estimated at approximately 45 per cent of the workforce (Hadžiahmetović 2006). Half of all young unemployed people are so disillusioned that they are not even registered as seeking work. The external and internal total debt is considerable – and growing. The value of what Bosnia exports is roughly 25 per cent of what it imports. FDI remains at a very low level, and is not expected to grow in the near future. Black marketeering, the 'shadow economy' and widespread corruption dominate economic activities. In sum, a decade of economic restructuring left Bosnia dependent on foreign monies and structurally uncompetitive (Tzifakis and Tsardanidis 2006).

Perhaps unsurprisingly, international financial institutions absolve themselves from any responsibility. The World Bank argues that 'the lagging reform efforts and the disappointing economic performance since 2000 must be largely attributed to the reluctance or inability of the political leadership of BiH to implement effectively the reform agenda'. The overall intervention effort 'was truly the Bank at its best' (WBOED 2004: 33, 35). However, attributing the failures of economic restructuring entirely to the local political class obscures the role played by international agencies in the process. The international agencies' obsession with diminishing public economic space merged with the local nationalists' attempt to retain control of that space by taking advantage of the privatisation process. Privatisation represents an instance of an unholy (and surely unintended) implicit alliance between international agencies and the ethno-nationalist elites these agencies attempt to undermine. Moreover, the focus on speed prevented the establishment of much-needed monitoring mechanisms. The odd coalition between international interveners and the domestic elites that emerged from the war created a kind of 'anti-state', a weak entity unable to regulate the economy and easily prey to special and often illegal interests (Pugh 2006). Overall, the relationship between international and local actors can be described as a mix of 'collision and collusion' (Wedel 1998): international agencies often clash with nationalist parties because of their opposite worldviews and visions of Bosnia's future. At the same time, they guarantee the existence of a political, economic and social system vulnerable to parochial and often illegal interests.

The shadow economy

Perhaps the defining feature of the Bosnian economy is its illegality. Since the outbreak of the war in 1992 criminal activities have flourished. The war itself provided an opportunity for criminal groups to take advantage of favourable conditions for smuggling, pillage and aid diversion. According to Susan Woodward (1995: 319), for example, as much as half of all aid to the former Yugoslavia was misappropriated. In some cases, aid did not simply fall into the wrong hands, but even fostered the birth of local mafia groups arising to exploit the influx of resources. The end of the conflict did not halt criminal activities. Other peacetime opportunities have arisen while the underground economy continued to flourish. The 'bottom-up' dynamics of the clandestine political economy not only explain the length of the war, but also important dynamics of peace (Andreas 2004).

The general impoverishment of the population and the absence of safety nets accounts for Bosnians' reliance on petty crime and mafia-like networks. Illegal economic activities give many ordinary Bosnians an opportunity to survive. In the absence of social safety nets, and with the lack of an active role of the state in the economy, the poor are often left to rely on the black market. Bosnia's informal sector represents an estimated 40 per cent of the economy, allowing many impoverished Bosnians to survive. For all its fail-ings, the shadow economy has a positive impact on productivity and employment (Hadžiahmetović 2006; Pugh 2006). At the same time, however, this type of economy perpetuates patrimonial and patriarchical relationships – a considerable obstacle to broader socio-economic development, and in particular the empowerment of women (Pupavac 2006).

The shadow economy hinders economic development and peace con-solidation. It is a source of patronage and enrichment for local elites, and allows collusion between political power and illegal criminal networks. Particularly in the RS, the lines between legal and illegal business are very unclear and the collusion between political and economic life is extensive. Political and criminal groups coalesce in a system of mutual protection. The fact that a significant part of the economic and political elite benefits from its control over illegal networks of distribution means that the last thing it wants is a functioning state, even if that condemns the rest of the popula-tion to poverty.[5] As Timothy Donais puts it, 'nationalist parties and their allies also share a common interest in preventing fundamental structural reforms, since such reforms directly threaten their source of economic wealth and political power' (2005: 86). In short, the illegal economy forms a 'political economy of abnormality' that maintains the material basis for corruption, parochialism, clientelism, and ethnic nationalism (Bojičić-Dželilovic and Kaldor 1999). While this situation could be debilitating for developed Western democracies, it is even more so for a weak state such as Bosnia. The presence of widespread illegality and a political-criminal connection complicates the consolidation of democratic institutions.

The answer to creating and sustaining economic development lies in undermining the basis of this economy that feeds corruption and misman-agement through the building of state institutions. The problem of customs revenues exemplifies how economic and political corruption can only be effectively fought via state-building measures. Until 2000 border control was in the hands of lower-level authorities in competition with each other for revenue. Rates were not harmonised and import procedures were subject to abuse. The absence of a functioning border service gave free rein to eco-nomic corruption and criminal activities. Black marketeering could flourish, transforming Bosnia into a major route for illegal trade. Smuggled goods made their way through about 400 illegal border crossings, costing the state budget hundreds of millions of dollars each year and benefiting illegal and criminal elements, who were often politically connected. It is estimated that Bosnia lost approximately one and a half times its GDP in 1995–2000, or some US$6 billion (Bojičić-Dželilovic *et al.* 2004: 24). A state border service (in addition to a professional state customs service) was needed to fight illegality and ensure that the collected revenues were directed to the state (thus also giving state-level bodies a sound financial basis).

In 2000 the High Representative imposed customs policy and created a statewide border control agency. As a result, not only was an important revenue source for criminal interests undermined, but also the state was strengthened. Although border control remains weak, customs revenues lost to smuggling have dropped considerably. Two lessons are learnt from this example. First, the lack of a functioning state goes hand-in-hand with mismanagement and illegality. Second, international intervention can successfully overcome this state of affairs. International intervention to bolster the state's capacity has important positive repercussions on the economy. In addition to strengthening border controls, other structural policies could be considered, including an increased involvement of the state in job creation and public and social services.

The rise of NGO development

Economic development and regeneration and the reliance on the economic self-interest of individuals and groups as a vehicle to create peaceful cross-ethnic ties are only one component of the internationally led civil society strategy. A second and equally important way in which civil society can contribute to addressing Bosnia's stateness problem is by advancing public and altruistic agendas.

Beginning in 1998, 'civil society' began appearing in the official PIC documents, in which it was praised as an essential arena for deepening the peace process and overcoming uncertainties about the economic/political international intervention strategies. Following the lead from the main peace implementation body, other agencies have demonstrated a similar conceptual interest and practical commitment to developing Bosnian civil society, focusing in particular on NGOs (UNDP 1999: 12; MSI 2000: 6). By investing in civil society development, international agencies hoped to contribute to the idea of 'ownership' of the peace process and the related need for local groups and organisations to take on an ever-expanding role in the process of democratisation and peace building. In 2001, the High Representative set up a consultative Partnership Forum to discuss urgent issues related to the peace process and to support state institutions, as well as a Civic Forum in order to facilitate discussions with Bosnian citizens.

This interest in civil society/NGO development stems from disillusionment with the impact of economic aid and privatisation. Bosnian NGOs have been idealised as the alternative avenue to achieve success in those areas where Bosnia's post-war transition has been more difficult, such as minority return, the establishment of the rule of law, and the struggle against corruption and cronyism. Repeatedly, when international agencies proved unable to overcome a problem, local NGOs have been presented as the solution. When, for example, corruption entered the political discourse as the result of the mismanagement of humanitarian and reconstruction funds and the irregularities connected to the privatisation process, international agencies hoped that local civil society would address and solve this problem as well (SPAI 2002). As a result, civil society building has become an integral component of international intervention, the indispensable complement to failing top-down strategies.

The quantitative results of the international effort at civil society building have been remarkable, with over 7,000 local NGOs legally registered (Bricker 2005). However, the actual picture behind the numerical strength of the sector is more complex. To begin with, local organisations are not necessarily more progressive, democratic, and non-nationalist than the governments they are expected to challenge. There is evidence that some organisations have learned how to talk the language of multi-ethnicity, dialogue, and compromise necessary to obtain foreign funding, but do not always follow through, especially organisations in the RS (Katana 1999). As several cases confirm, from Nazi Germany to Hutu-dominated Rwanda, civic groups, not unlike political parties and independent media, are as susceptible to being mobilised in support of extremists as they are in support of democratic politics (Belloni 2008). Moreover, even when NGOs are genuinely committed to social change and reconciliation, they often struggle to survive on a tight budget, and have organisational imperatives which negatively affect their performance.

Research on NGO development in Bosnia has highlighted at least three major limitations with civil society building strategies (Evans-Kent and Bleiker 2003; Stubbs 2000). First, the donor–local NGOs relationship has shown the dangers inherent to the financial dependency of civil society on outside donors. Civil society building has been conceived as an externally driven process that is dependent upon international resources – which have been considerably reduced since 2000 and even more so following the events of 11 September 2001. Instead of being an efficient alternative to the delivery of aid through local elites, economic aid to local organisations raises new problems. Aid dependency often skews the priorities of local organisations away from local needs. In order to be funded, local NGOs have to operate according to the (frequently changing) preferences of the donors, instead of the needs of communities local NGOs are supposed to serve. As Smillie and Todorović point out, 'despite much talk of participation and consultation, donors especially ignore Bosnian NGOs in preparing their projects and programmes, focusing instead on their own priorities and agendas' (2001: 45). This approach leaves NGOs in an inherently weak and subordinated position, negatively affecting the implementation of their stated mission. Local NGOs tend to treat every project they are offered simply as a source of funds, regardless of whether the project fulfils the organisation's mission (TWST 2002: 12–13).

Second, this problem is compounded by the fact that competition for foreign funding discourages cooperation and long-term planning among local organisations. Forced by donor requirements, local NGOs must adopt a short-term and pragmatic approach unsuited to overcoming both the antipathy of local politicians, who often consider NGOs as foreign agents and carriers of anti-nationalist values, and the diffidence of ordinary Bosnians, who resent the top-down approach to social change. Donors often issue short-term, renewable contracts for discrete aid projects, and insist that local contractors bid competitively. As one study found, 'virtually all donor grant mechanisms had a time frame of one year or less. Some were for six months or even three' (Smillie and Todorović 2001: 31). Donors' focus on short-term results undermines structural goals requiring long-term strategies and slow and patient work. It is perhaps unsurprising that the uncertainty, competition, and insecurity experienced by all local organisations makes cooperation among them difficult and the promotion of broad public agendas unlikely.

Third, many Bosnians show antipathy towards a kind of international intervention that centres on international experts and trainers who often do not speak the local language, and have limited direct knowledge of local customs and culture (Evans-Kent and Bleiker 2003). Often the training itself is not so much in developing skills to increase local activism but more pragmatically on how to successfully write a project proposal and be funded. Once domestic NGOs are socialised in the language and expectations of international donors, aid delivery creates a hierarchy. There is a great discrepancy between the most developed NGOs that work in the bigger cities and take advantage of their contacts and exchanges with international agencies and the larger number of small NGOs and civic groups that strive for visibility and funding (Sterland 2003). As Ian Smillie (1996) has noted in an influential report, this situation has been visible since the beginning of the peace process, and has hampered the strengthening of local civil society. By contrast, the few international agencies that invest time and resources in developing already existing local knowledge and capacity are much more effective and their impact more lasting (Gagnon 2002).

At its core, the problem with the international approach lies in failing to recognise the existence of local resources while making local development dependent on the international presence. The 'Neglected Areas' strategy provides a good example of this failure. According to the OSCE, these areas are 'municipalities neglected by the international community because of their physical isolation, domination by nationalist hard-liners or failure to comply with the GFPA' (OSCE 1998). Areas such as eastern RS do not enjoy the presence of any type of civil society because of 'international neglect'. Accordingly, it is by directing resources and funding to these municipalities that civil society can grow. Paradoxically, while NGOs are usually praised and valued for their connections with local and grassroots communities, decisions about who can participate and be empowered are made through a top-down approach, where local communities lie at the receiving end of the process. Civil society comes into existence when international agencies redirect their efforts to areas previously unattended to.

This is essentially a top-down discourse embellished by a rhetoric of bottom-up empowerment that might lead to the unintended consequence of hindering rather than fostering participation. If one participates in an initiative the donor decides to implement in order to redress a previously unjustified policy of imposed isolation, it is doubtful that people will feel empowered, for at least two reasons. First, the community may see civil society development as an unpredictable and fortuitous process beyond their control and agency. After having been previously 'neglected', they are now back on the development agenda with no guarantees about how long the international care will last. Second, if citizens do not perceive themselves as a source of development or as actively shaping their community by adopting their goals and strategies, they might see no value in participating in an exogenously driven development project.

In sum, the international approach treated Bosnian society as a blank slate upon which to build civil society. Instead of favouring forms of partnership between international and domestic actors and the gradual local ownership of the peace process, civil society building tends to reinforce a form of foreign colonisation (Stubbs 2000; Sampson 2002). Pragmatically, NGOs tend towards a market mechanism that focuses on the provision of services at the expense of genuine political and social participation. Accountability is redirected towards the donor and away from the organisation's social base, and the idea of participation and empowerment is diminished by the reality of an externally driven process. As a result, a World Bank (2002: viii) study concluded that there is no straightforward correlation between the degree of affiliation with voluntary associations and the local consolidation of civic and democratic politics. Bosnian NGOs have been dismissed as representing a 'virtual civil society' with very limited impact on the process of political and social change (Papić 2001: 53; Sinanović 2003).

The limited impact of civil society building strategies, combined with the decreasing availability of international funding, has led international agencies to revise their approach. Over the last few years, international intervention has placed less emphasis on externally directed projects, and more on NGO sustainability. International agencies have begun pressuring local NGOs and Bosnia's various governmental levels to establish partnerships and avoid exclusive reliance on foreign support. Critics point out that this change of international policy creates the possibility that local NGOs will become extensions of the state, legitimising rather than transforming the status quo (Fagan 2006). While this is a possibility, it is the role and impact of international intervention that remains contentious. The next two sections – the first on the attempt to improve the legal framework for domestic organisations, and the second on the impact of the 'war on terror' – show how the still preponderant role of international agencies and their changing and sometimes conflicting priorities can hinder the development and consolidation of local capacities.

Improving the legal framework

One of civil society's main tasks is to use advocacy as a tool of sociopolitical change. International agencies understand civil society as a 'middle ground' between the individual and the state, a space that can limit the excesses of the state, and allow the individual's capacities to be expressed and developed. Accordingly, they have focused on supporting local advocacy and human rights groups pursuing a broad public interest agenda. These groups are deemed essential for their strategic role in guaranteeing a more balanced state/society relation.

Although this might be true in theory, in practice the social and political reality where local NGOs operate must be considered. From the social point of view, the creation of high-visibility, public-interest NGOs might not be the most productive tool to bring about change. In a country where many are still plagued by basic subsistence problems it is more difficult to mobilise citizens in the name of the public good rather than their immediate self-interest. More crucially, the advocacy role of NGOs is hindered by both the assertive role of international agencies and the nature of Bosnian politics and institutions. The process of adoption of the Law on Associations and Foundations shows how two problems hinder local civil society development. First, internationally driven projects are likely to keep civil society divided instead of uniting it. Second, the fact that most of the major decisions affecting domestic governance are made by exogenous actors rather than local institutions complicates the advocacy role of local civic groups.

Starting in 1997, several major international organisations, in cooperation with local NGOs and lawyers, embarked on the technical task of improving the legal environment in which local NGOs function.[6] The legal framework in place at the time of the signing of the DPA was not conducive to developing and strengthening the civil society sector. In the Federation three laws were in place to regulate this sector, with obvious contradictions and complications: the Law on Civic Associations, the Law on Humanitarian Organisations, and the Law on Foundations. In the RS an existing law inherited from the previous Yugoslav system was preserved after the end of the war. Because these laws required local organisations to register at the the Entity level, they also limited the organisations' capacity to operate throughout the entire territory of the country irrespective of the place of registration. These terms violated the realisation of citizens' right to associate freely and consequently contravened the constitutional provision requiring Bosnia to ensure 'the highest level of internationally recognised human rights and fundamental freedoms'.

The LEA/LINK project combined Law, Education, Advocacy, and Networking to develop a sound legal framework that was intended to allow NGOs not only to operate effectively but also to strengthen the mechanisms for their collaboration and collective advocacy. The major objective of the project was to draft a Law on Associations and Foundations and to advocate its adoption by the relevant local authorities. In June 1998, a draft law was completed and made public for discussion (HRCC 1998). In December 1998 a leading international organisation conducted a training session in advocacy and media relations to provide local NGOs with the necessary technical tools to launch an advocacy campaign in support of its adoption (OSCE 1999a). However, local NGOs never expressed widespread support for the law, nor did they visibly campaign for its adoption. Bosnian citizen groups either assumed that international agencies were better placed to lobby at the political level for the adoption of the law, or did not recognise it as reflecting their own preferences.

According to Sevima Sali-Terzić (2001), the local NGOs supporting the process of drafting the law were all linked to international donors and dependent upon them for their financial survival. Some benefited from DemNet, a programme created and funded by USAID, and designed to strengthen a core group of strong NGOs to ensure that they and the citizens they represented participate more actively and effectively in political life. Other NGOs involved in the project were those gathered within the Bosnian NGO Council, an umbrella organisation which has enjoyed the support of several international donors. Combined, these NGOs supporting the LEA/ LINK project numbered around seventy, that is, only about 4 per cent of the country's entire non-governmental sector, and therefore only a minor segment of that sector. The broader NGO community did not necessarily recognise ownership of the law, nor did it consider the law as a priority.

In light of the difficulties to create momentum in favour of the law, and despite the international rhetoric on local ownership, international agencies took the lead. OHR first gathered 'substantive comments' from the Council of Europe and the International Centre for Not-for-Profit Law and then 'finalised efforts' to present draft legislation on Associations and Foundations to local legislators (OHR 1999: para. 78). After substantial pressure from international authorities, the law was adopted by the parliament in December 2001, leaving the preparation of the by-laws to later legislation. Only in 2004 did the Ministry of Justice adopt complicated and time-consuming by-laws setting additional hurdles for the registration process at the state level, and frustrating citizens' aspirations to associate across Entity boundaries (HCHR 2005: 12). At the Entity level, the 'law on associations and foundations' was adopted by the Federation on 20 September 2002, while the RS still has not taken any step in this direction.

The NGO law underscored the structural difficulties of creating a favourable framework for civil society development in the context of two semi-independent Entities and a weak central government. The law did not provide for the mandatory re-registration of associations and foundations at the state level, but permitted it if organisations chose so. There are two reasons why local organisations may decide to take advantage of this opportunity. First, registration may be a prerequisite for membership in international umbrella organisations. Second, registration at the state level could be helpful to access foreign grants. Interestingly, however, there are very few local incentives for NGOs to register at the state level and work in the territory of both Entities. In fact, the central government/parliament does not have jurisdiction over tax matters, and therefore it is unlikely that these organisations will be granted any tax benefits. In the end, the lack of mandatory registration at the state level leaves the Entities with the same discretionary powers that the LEA/LINK project was supposed to overcome, and undermines the utility of state-level lobbying.

The experience with the drafting and adoption of the law underscores the difficulties inherent in promoting civil society in the context of weak state structures and of an assertive international presence. Instead of increasing the visibility and influence of local organisations, the interventionist role assumed by international agencies has greatly complicated the role that civil society should supposedly play in advocacy and democratisation, and has made a mockery of civil society's advocacy role. Since the adoption of the Bonn powers, the High Representative has decisively intervened in local political life by removing mayors and imposing legislation. Even if these measures were often helpful in breaking political deadlock among local ethnic authorities, they have further diminished the citizens' and NGOs' capacity to affect political processes and decisions. For the first decade of post-Dayton transition, formal political power has not simply been in the hands of local elites, but has become even more alien and inaccessible, removed from those local officials whose accountability has been increasingly directed upwards to international agencies rather than downwards to civil society. Thus, in the context of an assertive international presence and a weak state authority with limited competencies, the expectation that local organisations will hold political leaders accountable is a fundamental illusion. The advocacy role of civil society is better exercised by pressuring international civil servants rather than local political leaders.

The fight against terrorism: the 'Algerian case'

The multiple priorities of international agencies and foreign governments, particularly those with significant political and economic clout such as the United States, further complicate the advocacy role of NGOs. The 'Algerian case' highlights the dangers of prioritising foreign interests vis-à-vis the domestic interests of the rule of law, and the strengthening of local institutions.

In January 2002 Bosnian authorities handed over six Bosnian citizens of Algerian origin to the United States, which promptly transferred them to the US military prison at Guantanamo Bay, Cuba. Their plight began in October 2001 when SFOR first arrested them under suspicion of planning to blow up the American and British embassies in Sarajevo (Hećimović and Selimbegović 2002). SFOR effectively put itself at the service of the United States, despite the fact that the Americans did not provide any concrete evidence, claiming only that the main suspect, Bansayah Belkacem, was a prominent member of al-Qaeda and a close associate of Bin Laden. The Federation Supreme Court ruled that the six men should be released for lack of evidence after the United States refused to hand over recordings of intercepted telephone conversations supposedly incriminating them. The tapes, even if they did exist, had been made by one of the US intelligence agencies with no authority to tap telephones in Bosnia. On 17 January 2002, on the same day of the court ruling, the Human Rights Chamber ordered a temporary moratorium on the extradition of the six men in order to allow the chamber to discuss the matter during its next session. The chamber further established that the Federation and the state of Bosnia had violated the rights of these individuals by unlawfully stripping them of their citizenship. Bosnian authorities, however, decided to hand over the suspects to US officials, making the chamber's decision moot (Simić 2002). The Bosnian government was eager to appear as a strong ally of the United States and avoid any suspicion that Bosnia could provide a safe haven for Islamic terrorists.

The decision to hand over the six Algerian men to the United States against the ruling of the competent domestic legal authorities attracted much criticism. Madeleine Rees, head of the UN Commission on Human Rights in Sarajevo, argued that human rights abuses had been committed against the six men, and held the United States ultimately responsible (Rees 2002). According to Muhamed Džemidžić of the Helsinki Committee for Human Rights, this episode undermined Bosnian institutions and the country's progress towards respect for international human rights standards.[7] Bosnian institutions attempted to assert their authority but with limited success. In October, the Human Rights Chamber concluded that the treatment of the Algerian men was in violation of their rights, including the right to liberty and security and the right not to be arbitrarily expelled in the absence of a fair procedure, and restored their citizenship. The chamber ordered both the state and Federation authorities to use all diplomatic channels in order to protect the rights of the applicants. Amnesty International immediately called upon Bosnian authorities to implement these orders as a matter of urgency (AI 2002). Bosnia's Human Rights Chamber ruled again in April 2003 that the government of Bosnia was in violation of a number of articles of the European Human Rights Convention, which had direct applicability in the country (AFP 2003). The EHRC bans extradition to countries that operate the death penalty, except when guarantees have been issued that no such penalty will be used in a particular case.

In the case of the Algerian men, however, no such guarantees were obtained from the United States. Because of the lack of any initiative aimed at protecting the rights of the six detainees, AI intervened again in mid-2003 and called on US authorities to 'either release the six men or charge them with a recognizable criminal offense and try them in independent and impartial courts' (AI 2003a: 6). In December 2003 the Bosnian government agreed to pay a total of 20,000 euros to the families of the detainees to compensate them for their pain and suffering (Alić 2003a). In the summer of 2004 the UN High Commissioner for Human Rights in Bosnia pressured local authorities to request from the United States the return to Bosnia of the detainees.[8] In the autumn the Bosnian government was said to be actively seeking the six men's repatriation (Wood 2004). To date, the attempt has been unsuccessful, leaving the six men detained at Guantanamo Bay.

The immediate impact of the 'Algerian case' was to weaken the main human rights/advocacy organisation operating in Bosnia – the Helsinki Committee for Human Rights. Several members of the organisation openly defended the rights of the six Algerians to a fair legal treatment in the name of the rule of law. They were criticised and condemned by an odd coalition of domestic and foreign actors. Bosnian politicians were eager to accommodate the wishes of the United States, even at the cost of compromising the rule of law. Many international agencies and foreign embassies resented what they considered unjustified criticism. Neither OHR, nor any European country expressed support for the Helsinki Committee – which was effectively left alone in denouncing the case.[9] Moreover, the episode exacerbated divisions within the organisation. Slavko Kukić and Branko Todorović, Serb members of the Steering Board, distanced themselves from the Helsinki Committee's official position in defence of the six Algerians and terminated their tenure amid tensions and polemics. In its annual report, the organisation denounced the unsuccessful 'attempt to break up the Committee' and announced reduced international funding (HCHR 2003a).

In addition to weakening the leading Bosnian human rights/advocacy organisation, the Algerian case had important broader consequences for the much-needed strengthening of the rule of law and compliance with human rights norms. The fact that the ruling of the Human Rights Chamber was ignored in the case of the six Algerian men created a bad precedent for strengthening the legitimacy and reach of this important institution. An example can illustrate how ignoring domestic institutions can have far-reaching consequences. For years, international agencies have demanded that RS authorities respect the chamber's ruling on a rebuilding permit for the Ferhadija mosque in Banja Luka – an architectural masterpiece built in 1579 and razed to the ground by the Serbs in 1993. On two separate occasions a ceremony was scheduled for the laying of the foundation stone to rebuild the mosque, but each time Serb politicians obstructed the initiative. An apparently well organised mob of angry men throwing stones terminated the ceremonies (Bose 2002: 154–61). While it does not justify Serb resistance to the Human Rights Chamber ruling that the mosque be rebuilt, the Algerian case makes it much easier for RS politicians to pinpoint the selectivity of international commitments to the rule of law.

Unsurprisingly, the Human Rights Chamber emerged discredited by this episode. In mid-2003, the High Representative proposed to disband the institution by the end of the year, and transfer its caseload to the Constitutional Court. The chamber's existence was terminated on 31 December 2003, with more than 10,000 cases still pending, and with an average of 200 new cases being received each month. Human rights organisations described the HRC's closing as a 'serious blow to human rights protection' (AI 2003a). It is certainly a serious setback to the process of institution building in the field of human rights.

Civil society that works

Internationally led civil society building strategies assume that Bosnia does not have any civil society because of the realities of the Yugoslav totalitarian system that discouraged participation along the lines found in Western democratic systems, and because the 1992–95 war halted the development of the incipient post-communist civic and democratic politics. However, while the war certainly damaged the prospects for civic activism and grassroots democracy, it is also the case that the former Yugoslavia was never a totalitarian system in the same mould as Eastern European regimes.

The perception of pre-war Bosnia as civil society-free does not do justice to the subtleties of the Yugoslav political system under Tito, which was much more open and participatory than many Eastern European states run by nominally similar systems. While civil society in its liberal form was not part of Titoist Yugoslavia, civil society understood as an arena for communal and public activity was a defining feature of Yugoslav socialism. The presence of a variety of social organisations and small citizens' associations (*udreženja građjana*) providing material and social services to citizens distinguished Yugoslav self-management from other Eastern European systems. A World Bank (2002) survey documented how membership in these small associations was more common and diffuse than membership in the new NGOs that sprang up during and after the war. The same survey also considered the role of the *mjesna zajednica* (MZ) – a unique institution established in both rural and urban areas by the 1963 Yugoslav constitution. These administrative units below the municipal level allowed citizens to organise collectively and address many of the local day-to-day governance issues that directly affected their lives. Although in many municipalities MZs lost their legal standing and resource base after the war, Bosnian citizens still contributed to the work of MZ boards and were more likely to volunteer and provide funds to MZs than other organisations. In an interesting and rare study of economic development at the local level, it was found that effective development requires the mobilisation of local institutions and capacities such as the MZs (ESI 2002a). In the municipality of Kalesija, MZ presidents effectively involved citizens in the planning and financing of local infrastructure. Citizens responded by mobilising significant local resources to develop local communications and road networks. Kalesija became a 'success story' in post-Dayton Bosnia, demonstrating how considerable initiative and local resources exist even under the most difficult circumstances.

Not only do Bosnians organise around these local and largely self-governing institutions, but they also creatively and efficiently run Western-style NGOs. Women's groups created an economic network – BiH ZEM – with the primary task of strengthening the economic position of women in Bosnia. In 2004 the BiH Women's Initiative was established. The organisation provides support for women to start small business enterprises (HCHR 2005: 19). Furthermore, there are at least a few broad-based public policy organisations whose resourcefulness has been considerably effective in influencing the course of the peace process. Three of these initiatives are particularly worthy of note.

The first initiative is the Serb Civic Council's attempt to change the Entities' constitutions in order that they should conform to the statewide constitution proclaiming the equality of Bosniaks, Serbs and Croats throughout the entire territory of the country. Chapter 3 dealt at length with the content of this initiative and its impact on the institutional structure, and will not be repeated here. The Serb Civic Council initiated a process of change of local institutions by exposing the contradiction of preserving a multi-national state through largely mono-ethnic Entities. Despite the formal support offered by the High Representative, the initiative was carried out *against* international agencies' role as custodians of the (dis)order established at Dayton. While these agencies feel constrained by the structure agreed upon at Dayton, and have explicitly committed themselves to preserving it, parts of local civil society find this structure discriminatory and so have organised themselves to change it.

The second case of successful civil society work is the Igman Initiative. Initially created in 1995, when thirty-eight intellectuals from all over Yugoslavia visited Sarajevo under siege as a sign of solidarity with its citizens, it was launched again in November 2000 with financial support from Freedom House. A conference in Zagreb provided the opportunity for the decision to revive the process of regional cooperation by focusing on the Dayton Triangle, that is, the signatories of the DPA. More than one hundred local NGOs from these countries pledged to work towards normalizing relations and creating an atmosphere of trust between Bosnia, Croatia, and Yugoslavia (later Serbia and Montenegro and, since May 2006, Serbia – following a referendum on independence in Montenegro). These organisations have been working to reinforce political, cultural and economic relations among the states belonging to the Dayton Triangle with a view to creating a free trade and demilitarised area. The initiative was coordinated by three NGOs: the Forum for Democratic Alternatives, from Sarajevo; the Civic Council for Human Rights from Zagreb; and the Centre for Regionalism based in Novi Sad. By 'softening the borders' in the region and allowing the free circulation of individuals and goods, the NGOs involved believed that co-existence and toleration would be more likely to be consolidated. To this end, they drafted several proposals for changes in legislation that would facilitate and encourage cross-border cooperation. This approach is bottom-up, focusing on the municipal level as a stepping stone for cooperation at higher levels. As a result of this initiative, the mayors of Osijek-Tuzla-Novi Sad signed a wide-ranging agreement early in 2002. The municipalities of Dubrovnik-Trebinje and Herzeg Novi have been singled out for a similar development.

International agencies have also tried to encourage regional initiatives, but with limited success. There are at least eight such initiatives, the most well known being the Stability Pact for Southeastern Europe, often improperly heralded as the new Marshall Plan. However, while the Stability Pact has been criticised widely because its projects, resources, and impact were limited, the Igman Initiative is an indigenous project that successfully built cooperation from the bottom up.[10] In March 2002, representatives of the Igman Initiative visited the heads of state and ministries of foreign affairs to propose recommendations on a set of concrete projects, including an agreement on the establishment of a free trade zone, and a 'mini-Schengen' for the liberalisation of the visa regime, with a view to abolishing visas completely. This lobbying culminated in a meeting in July 2002 between the Yugoslav president, his Croatian counterpart, and the Bosnian tripartite presidency. The meeting was the first one organised without any help from international agencies, and led the Yugoslav and Croatian presidents to solemnly promise to honour the inviolability of Bosnia's borders.[11] In yet another example of the new attitude slowly developing in the region, in late 2003 the president of Serbia and Montenegro, Svetozar Marović, surprised his audience when, during his first official visit to Sarajevo, he apologised to the citizens of Bosnia for the suffering caused by the 1992–95 war. While his visit was not within the framework of the Igman Initiative, it is a further positive development reflecting the presence of the type of pragmatic relationship between the two countries that the Igman Initiative has been advocating (Alić 2003b). The success of this initiative was also demonstrated by the fact that international organisations have begun to model their own projects along the lines of the Igman Initiative.[12] In the summer of 2004 this new approach led to the OSCE's involvement in the creation of an Association of Multi-Ethnic Cities of Southeastern Europe. Representatives of some forty cities and local NGOs from the whole region subscribed to the Protocol on Inter-ethnic Tolerance, establishing the Association.

The third case of successful civic involvement in domestic politics involves the attempt to create a commission for truth and reconciliation. In February 2000 more than a hundred Bosnian citizens from throughout Bosnia met to consider how such a commission might work. They decided to model it along the lines of the one created in South Africa following the end of apartheid, and envisioned that the commission's tasks could be accomplished in thirty months. Four Bosnian NGOs organised the meeting. The initiative also has the support of various religious leaders, victims' families, and internationally of the US Institute of Peace, the Inter-Church Council of the Netherlands, and the International Federation of Human Rights, among others. But not all the major international players favour the creation of such a commission. The ICTY opposes the idea, fearing that testimony given before such a body would compromise prosecutions at The Hague.[13]

After the draft law languished for years in the Bosnian parliament, a new initiative gave the issue a renewed momentum. At the tenth anniversary of the DPA in November 2005, a working group composed of eight leading political parties was formed. Chaired by the Dayton Project (a local NGO which is the brainchild of American diplomat and former Deputy High Representative Donald Hays), the group was tasked with drafting a new law on the creation of a 'Truth Commission', its mandate and composition. The existence of this group and its composition (including a former member of the wartime 'Crisis Committee' in Prijedor – see Chapter 6 on the role of this committee during the war), sparked a much needed debate. Predictably, some political parties attempted to water down the commission's provisions. For example, article 5 of the draft law suggested that the commission's final report 'will not identify individuals who committed crimes' (Jelacić and Ahmetasević 2006), potentially diminishing the role and impact of the commission's work. Victims' groups have also voiced concern, claiming that they have not been sufficiently involved in the initiative. Eventually, in May 2006 the Council of Ministers established a six-member commission tasked with investigating 'the suffering of Serbs, Croats, Bosniaks, Jews and others' but only in the capital Sarajevo. This decision reflected a compromise between the Serb MPs' demands for determining the truth concerning the wartime fate of Serbs in Sarajevo and the Bosniak preference for a commission working on a national level. In late 2006 the commission completed a report defining its objectives and methodology, and foresaw 15 months' work.

What do these examples of bottom-up civil society building have in common? These initiatives have arisen from organisations present and active in the country before civil society became a fashionable aspect of Western assistance. The model that emerges is consistent across the three cases: ownership belongs squarely to Bosnians, who asked for international support but rejected the idea that decisions should be imposed by the High Representative; local actors have had full decision-making authority in devising the form of and strategy to bring about change; international agencies have publicly and repeatedly stated their backing without taking over the process. In substance, this small group of committed organisations had an impact on the peace process that went well beyond what their limited resources would seem to permit.

Conclusion

The hope that Bosnian citizens, individually or associated to NGOs, can deepen the post-war democratisation process and help address Bosnia's 'stateness problem' proved difficult to realise. International agencies reasoned that by following their enlightened self-interest citizens could re-establish economic ties across ethnic lines. At the same time, NGOs pursuing an altruistic public policy agenda could provide a counter-balance to the power of the state and an arena for the development of individual and collective capacities. However, to date, neither in its 'selfish' nor in its 'altruistic' version has civil society contributed to democratisation and peace building as expected. The initial flow of economic aid into the country, followed by a policy of macroeconomic stability, privatisation, and asset transfer to private ownership, reinforced the nationalist control of the local economy, and contributed to solidifying the country's social and spatial divisions. As a result, most civil society/NGO development programmes have developed in the most unfavourable conditions. Local NGOs often took over the state's responsibility in the field of service provision, but left untouched the structural conditions of separation.

International agencies have colonised the Bosnian social space, mistakenly assuming it to be an environment resembling a tabula rasa with little or no human and political resources to contribute to the process of reintegration. However, the examples of Kalesija, the constituent peoples case, the Igman Initiative, and the Truth and Reconciliation Commission confirm that there exist effective social and political resources working towards developing inclusive and democratic politics. The next chapter will show how refugees and displaced persons (DPs) can also positively contribute to post-war democratisation and peace building. Thus, the weakness of Bosnian civil society does not result from a lack of domestic human resources, but rather from the prevailing international approach based on top-down interaction that makes international/national cooperation unequal and places international agencies squarely at the centre of the post-war transition process. In addition, the context in which local groups operate is hardly conducive to helping them become effective agents of political and social change. The divided political structure of Bosnia greatly complicates the role of civil society. Not only are political divisions a constraint on policy-making, but also they prevent consistent implementation of reform through the state. The experience of Bosnia confirms that a vibrant civil society can only be a sign of a well functioning state, not its source (Belloni 2008).

In sum, the weakness of civil society is a reflection of the weakness and divisiveness of the political framework. The best way to promote civil society is to build viable state institutions – an agenda further developed in Chapter 7. Unfortunately, despite the rhetoric about state-building, international agencies have contributed to the state's weakness by dubious policy choices. They pushed through a privatisation process that undermined the ability of the state to play an active role in the economy and enriched the same local nationalists who were profiting from weak institutions. Furthermore, they have shown little regard for the authority of local institutions – thus undercutting their credibility and effectiveness. The weak and internally divided nature of the Bosnian state also complicates the post-war process of the return of DPs and refugees. As the next chapter will argue, Bosnia's internal divisions hinder the effective exercise and implementation of individual human rights – a cornerstone of the peace agreement which ended the war.

6 The antinomies of refugee return

The primary objective of international refugee policy is to return refugees to their country of origin. Return and repatriation relieve Western states from granting asylum to individuals escaping war. At the same time, return and repatriation can be used instrumentally to meet broader intervention goals, such as reversing ethnic cleansing. A number of recent peace agreements include provisions for refugees and displaced persons to return to their original homes, rather than simply being repatriated, only to face internal displacement. In addition to the DPA, peace settlements in Kosovo, Guatemala, Mozambique, Cambodia, Ethiopia and Eritrea all recognised the right to return home. A right to housing and property restitution is slowly supplanting the age-old idea that displacement from one's own home of origin is a permanent condition.[1]

In Bosnia as in similar other cases, 'home of origin' has been interpreted to mean the physical structure in which one lived before the war. Because that physical infrastructure is often under the control of an ethnic group other than the one to which the returnee belongs, return is a difficult process involving individuals who have been defined as ethnic or national 'minorities'.[2] At Dayton, international mediators endorsed the right to return both as an antidote to the forces that promoted ethnic cleansing and as a concession to the Bosniaks – many of whom had been expelled from their homes during the war. Since the signing of the DPA, UNHCR registered more than 1 million returns – about half a million of them minorities. The actual number may be even higher. Many returnees do not in fact register or signal their presence because they want to maintain health benefits or pensions awarded from their previous location. The overall success of this policy has led Paddy Ashdown – who became the fourth High Representative in May 2002 – to claim that international agencies invented a new human right in Bosnia: the right to return after a war (Glover 2002).

As this chapter makes clear, this success needs to be qualified, since often a lack of economic opportunities and/or continuing discrimination forces returnees to sell their houses and leave again. Nonetheless, post-war refugee policy demonstrates three important points, two concerning Bosnian social reality, and the other concerning international intervention. First, post-war return challenges the historical determinist notion that Bosnia is destined to break up into homogeneous nation-states. Instead, when given a choice, Bosnians of all ethnic groups have taken the opportunity to return home instead of relocating. Second, the active and resourceful involvement of Bosnians in the return process shows the importance of a 'bottom-up' peace building strategy, i.e. one based on the engagement and wishes of the local population instead of the choices of international officials. Third, the process of return highlights important contradictions in the intervention template. On the one hand, the return and reintegration of refugees and DPs is one of the principal benchmarks that the international administration of war-torn territories is measured against (Caplan 2005: 68). As international intervention in Bosnia confirms, considerable resources have been invested in attempting to reverse the homogenising effects of the war. On the other hand, ensuring the sustainability of return requires highly intrusive social and economic policies that fit uneasily with the broader intervention template based on political and economic liberalisation. As a result, international intervention has been successful in 'inventing a new human right', as claimed by Ashdown, but much less so in creating the conditions for its effective long-term enjoyment.

This chapter analyses the process which made return possible on a substantial scale. First, it begins with an overview of the pattern of displacement at the end of the war and the obstacles to implementing the right to return. Second, it shows how the post-Dayton forced repatriation of unwanted Bosnian refugees from Western Europe created an explosive situation. The vast majority of those repatriated were not allowed to return to areas where they constituted an ethnic minority. At the same time, international agencies could not permanently relocate them because of the fear of legitimising the wartime policy of ethnic cleansing. Thus, international policy created a potentially explosive mix, in which an army of dispossessed and dissatisfied DPs became increasingly amenable to ethnic polarisation. Third, the chapter highlights how the key to successful return was a change in international policy from a focus on minority returns – which created a strong resistance among the majority population – to a policy of property repossession for all Bosnian citizens regardless of their ethnic background. Finally, the impact and sustainability of minority returns are evaluated. Contrary to the historical determinists' argument that minority return and the enforcement of human rights augment ethnic tensions, the evidence suggests the opposite, that is, return has contributed to calming ethnic and political tensions. Although the ultimate success of minority returns avoided degeneration into widespread violence, the long-term demographic outcome remains unclear. Lack of employment opportunities and a scarcity of social and economic services for returnees are seriously hampering the sustainability of returns.

This chapter focuses on the region between Sanski Most (in the Federation) and Prijedor (in the RS) to illustrate the dynamics of return. While Bosnia is made up of many different localised realities that escape generalisations, the choice of this area is justified for two reasons. First, Prijedor/Sanski Most constitute a 'least-likely case' or tough test of intervention. Brutal wartime ethnic cleansing in Prijedor made this region an unlikely candidate for minority return. It is remarkable that many of those Bosniaks who were expelled during the war returned after the signing of the DPA. Second, the evolution of the situation in the Sanki Most/Prijedor region is a good example of how to make return happen even in extremely difficult cases. The process of return to Prijedor demonstrates that effective international intervention needs the support and participation of people on the ground to turn international policy declarations into achievable ends.

Displacement and the problem of minority return

The term 'ethnic cleansing' has its origin in the wars of Yugoslav dissolution and indeed it is a literal translation of the Serbo/Croatian/Bosnian *etničko čišćenje*. The expression refers to the practice of removing specific groups from a given area, exclusively based upon ethnic criteria. Its more general synonym is forced population transfer. Mary Kaldor (1999) argues that this practice is one of the aspects that sets the post-Cold War age apart from previous historical periods. The 'new wars' are different from previous warfare because they are driven by identity politics, are waged mostly against civilians and are financed through channels and methods that take advantage of the globalised war economy. According to Kaldor, Bosnia is the prototype of a 'new war' where the distinction between war, organised crime, and large-scale violations of human rights blur, and where civilians bear most of the costs of political instability.

While there exist undeniable differences between old and new wars, these can also be overstated. To the extent that 'new wars' involve population transfers and national homogenisation, these are not particularly new phenomena. The practice of ethnic cleansing or population transfer has been very widespread in the twentieth century, and was often endorsed by the great powers in the name of stability, self-determination, and democracy (Mann 2004). What has changed in the 1990s is not the practice of population transfer but the international perception that such practice is unlawful and inhumane. The international community strongly condemned ethnically motivated violence in the former Yugoslavia, in Rwanda, and in Cambodia, among other cases. In 1999 NATO intervened militarily in Kosovo on the behalf of the Albanian population with a bombing campaign that effectively ended Serb rule over the province. In Bosnia intervention occurred only after three and a half years of war, but was then followed by ever-increasing international assertiveness to ensure the right of return of the population displaced by the war.

Displaced persons, refugees and the right to return

Approximately 2.3 million people left their homes during and in the immediate aftermath of the conflict, from an original population of 4.4 million (according to the 1991 census). Out of this total number, more than a million became internal DPs. The majority of them were Bosniaks, reflecting their numerical preponderance in the country, the vicissitudes of the war, and its impact on the civilian population. In addition, 1.2 million became refugees, that is, they crossed an international border and became eligible for the protection and rights granted by the 1951 Geneva Convention on Refugees. Estimates show that 570,000 refugees came from the territory of the Federation and 630,000 from the territory of the RS (Rosand 1998). Furthermore, some 80 per cent of Serb refugees went to the Federal Republic of Yugoslavia, 55 per cent of Croat refugees went to Croatia, and 95 per cent of Bosniak refugees left the former Yugoslavia altogether, and dispersed themselves throughout twenty-five host countries.

Evidence from other conflict areas warns of the possibility that a large refugee population could undermine the peace process and suggests that return is necessary to ensure long-term stability. Where there is no solution to the plight of refugees, there is a possibility that they can be mobilised, militarised and develop into 'warriors', resorting to violence against their former enemies and/or the government that keeps them in exile (Lischer-Kenyon 2003). As confirmed by the problem of Palestinian refugees, who were expelled to neighbouring states following the 1948 war and the creation of Israel, individuals with little or no hope of return can become increasingly prone to violence. In the Bosnian case, a similar radicalisation has always been unlikely. Croat refugees in neighbouring Croatia have shown little interest to returning to Bosnia, preferring to permanently resettle in what many of them consider their homeland. Only 8 per cent of those Croats who became refugees in Croatia proper expressed any intention to return, while 71 per cent of them claim they have decided never to return (HCHR 2005: 10). Serbs, however, have considered return as a viable and realistic option. Since 2000 more than 35,000 of them registered with UNHCR to return to canton 1 and canton 10 in the Federation.[3] The Serbs' wish to return never became a security threat, both because of the relatively small numbers involved, and because of the presence of legal and accepted avenues to take repossession of their properties and return to the areas they had to leave during the war.

While many refugees in Croatia and Serbia were allowed to remain in their place of exile, if they so chose, this option was not available in the case of those refugees, mostly Bosniaks, who fled the region during the war to find safety in Western Europe. These refugees were in most cases accorded 'temporary protection', which included admission to the country of refuge, respect for human rights, treatment in accordance with internationally recognised standards of human rights, and protection against *refoulement*, whereby individuals cannot be forced to return to a potentially dangerous situation in their country of origin. The use of 'temporary protection' allowed Bosnians to avoid the normal, lengthy asylum procedures, while its temporary nature built domestic support in Western countries at a time of economic and political uncertainty. By 1996, the European Union accomodated about 584,000 refugees from Bosnia (Black *et al.* 1998: 7). More than 340,000 of them were in Germany.

International mediators at Dayton made the fate of Bosnian refugees and DPs a central part of the agreement. The DPA contains many provisions to remedy and potentially reverse wartime ethnic cleansing. Annex 7 is entirely devoted to the process of return. As chapter 1 of article I reads:

> All refugees and displaced persons have the right freely to return to their home of origin. They shall have the right to have restored to them property of which they were deprived in the course of hostilities since 1991 and to be compensated for any property that cannot be restored to them. The early return of refugees and displaced persons is an important objective of the settlement of the conflict in Bosnia and Herzegovina. The parties confirm that they will accept the return of such persons who have left their territory, including those who have been accorded temporary protection by third countries.
>
> (DPA, Annex 7, art. I)

All the parties (the state of BiH, the Federation and the RS) committed themselves to 'ensure that refugees and displaced persons are permitted to return in safety, without risk of harassment, intimidation, persecution or discrimination, particularly on account of their ethnic origin, religious belief, or political opinion' (art. I, 2).[4] A number of other articles within the annexes emphasise the right of refugees and DPs to return to their *home of origin* under conditions of safety and dignity. Accordingly, no part of the DPA foresaw explicitly the possibility of relocation.

Why return is difficult

While the right to return is compelling from the point of view of the displaced population, which was forcibly expelled and deprived of its property during the war, there are important obstacles to successful return. At the beginning of the peace process, neither Bosnian ethno-national politicians nor international agencies appeared fully committed to this goal. Minority return was hard to accept for both Serb and Croat political elites. The very premise of permanent return was intolerable to them, since one of the major reasons behind the war was to establish ethnically pure states. For the Serbs, large-scale return would have undermined the demographic nature of the semi-autonomous Serb Entity they fought for and were granted by the peace agreement. A Western official explained the Serb attitude well when he argued that it was like persuading Hitler to take the Jews back (Hockstader 1997). Croats were similarly opposed to permitting the return of the Bosniaks and Serbs in municipalities under their control. Because they are numerically the smaller of the constituent peoples, it is hardly surprising that many Croats have always feared for their survival as a group, particularly if a significant number of other ethnicities return to areas now predominantly populated by them. As discussed in Chapter 4, this feeling of being in a relatively weak position vis-à-vis the other ethnic groups explains the appeal the HDZ has had among many ordinary Croats, but it also explains why Croat hard liners have considered the return of DPs as a threat to their control. The very existence of the HDZ has been predicated upon the continuation of a siege mentality that sees the creation of a multi-ethnic society as a threat to Croat interests. Consequently, the HDZ has consistently blocked the return of Serbs and Bosniaks to those municipalities that (particularly in Herzegovina) it has controlled almost exclusively. At the same time, it has discouraged the return of Croats to any other region.

For all three main Bosnian groups, minority return could assume broader political and military implications. From a security point of view the large-scale return of former enemies presents a potential threat. Young males of military age belonging to a different ethnic group could be the foundation for a possible fighting force able to inflict considerable damage in the case of a new war (ICG 1999: 36). As Susan Woodward (1999: 96) points out, the return of minorities to communities where they would weaken the control of the majority group creates a potential 'Trojan horse' that could have devastating consequences, should NATO troops leave and a new war break out (I shall return to this point later in this chapter).

In addition to the reluctance of Bosnian ethno-nationalists, Bosnia's post-war structural conditions have further complicated the implementation of the right to return. The obstruction of local politicians is a symptom of an ethnically divided polity, rather than its cause. The DPA attempted a difficult balancing act between collective and individual rights, guaranteeing both the rights of groups to exclusive self-government and the rights of individuals to return to the places from which they were expelled. In practice, the simultaneous presence of the collective right to exclusive self-government and the individual right to return can be incompatible. The flight of about 60,000 Serbs from the suburbs of Sarajevo in March 1996 highlighted the difficult balance between these different rights. Weeks before the scheduled transfer of power to the Federation, pressure on Serbs to leave escalated. The SDS leadership ordered the Serbs to leave and burn down everything they could not bring to the RS. Thugs terrorised those who wanted to remain while IFOR and the IPTF stood by. The Federation authorities also showed little interest in preserving the multi-ethnic character of Sarajevo, thus increasing the pressure on the Sarajevo Serbs to flee (Bildt 1998: 196).

The failure to prevent the departure of Serbs showed the difficulty of preserving ethnic diversity and guaranteeing individual human rights within an institutional context structured along group lines. For some commentators, the DPA provides an unsuitable framework to preserve multi-ethnicity: 'trying to keep Serbs in Sarajevo went against the basic structure of the Dayton Agreement, which had ... divided Bosnia into three distinct ethnic areas' (Sell 2000: 199). At the same time, however, human rights provisions cast in individual terms are also an integral part of the Dayton Agreement.

There was nothing inherently insurmountable in the DPA that prevented the preservation of the multi-ethnic character of Sarajevo. Instead, the weak international military and police presence did not reassure those citizens who were willing to defy nationalist pressures and remain in areas where they would constitute an ethnic minority. Bosnians of all ethnic groups saw in IFOR's passive stance evidence that international agencies would not encourage multi-ethnic cooperation, and that unsavoury ethnic entrepreneurs preaching ethnic division would neither be constrained nor punished (Holbrooke 1998: 337).

Not only did the flight of Sarajevo Serbs highlight the problems with the enforcement gap created at Dayton, but also it gave an early demonstration of the international ambivalence towards preserving and restoring ethnic diversity in Bosnia. International agencies have frequently accused domestic politicians of obstructing the return process (Phuong 2000a). However, at least during the first four post-Dayton years, international policy was never fully committed to ensuring the right to return. Instead, international agencies have often feared the possibility that large-scale returns could create a backlash. The Commission on Real Property Claims (CRPC) – an international agency created to certify property rights – has captured the essence of this problem better than any other international body:

> The ethnic reintegration of BiH through the return of displaced persons and refugees to their pre-war homes continues to be the foundational principle of the peace process, both as an overwhelming moral imperative in the face of ethnic cleansing, and as a political requisite for peace and stability in the region. At the same time, such stability as BiH now enjoys has been achieved through the division of its territory and almost every aspect of civic life long ethnic lines.
>
> (CRPC and UNHCR 1997: 22)

Better than any other statement, this comment reflects the international agencies' ambiguity towards minority return. Their less than absolute commitment to return is perhaps justified. However, it is ironic that international agencies blame local politicians for obstructing the process, when in fact they take a similarly half-hearted approach.

Faced with the opposition of ethno-nationalist politicians, Bosnia's institutional divisions and the dubious commitment of international agencies, Bosnian refugees and DPs found themselves in a most unfavourable position. Particularly in the immediate aftermath of war, concerns about personal security were high – especially among women DPs (UNHCR 2000). Because the victims of the war were mostly men, many women were left without male support or protection, making them even more reluctant to return to their pre-war homes. While the issue of personal security affects all returnees, the lack of a male presence and the uncertain attitude of international security agencies heightened women's worries. Post-war initial reluctance to prosecute indicted war criminals and the lack of gender and ethnic balance of local police forces created additional hurdles for women's return. Furthermore, many women were traumatised by their experiences of rape, detention, and forced displacement, and needed specific help (ibid.). However, despite the gendered character of displacement, the right to return included in the DPA did not explicitly mention women and their needs – a significant failure of the peace agreement.

The problem of return was further compounded by Bosnia's dire housing conditions at the end of the war and by general socio-economic under-development. Bosnia's housing opportunities made the organisation and implementation of return a logistical nightmare. During the course of the conflict, about two thirds of the housing stock had been destroyed. The extent and nature of destruction and displacement created a scenario of 'musical chairs' whereby those displaced from one Entity or area occupied the houses and apartments of those similarly displaced or of those who became refugees abroad. Moreover, to additionally complicate the return *problématique*, many DPs were not willing to go back to where they had been forcibly expelled. Thousands of DPs in Bosnia's bigger towns (Sarajevo, Banja Luka, Tuzla, Mostar, Zenica) could access social and economic services unavailable in many rural communities. Urban life was originally not a choice but a necessity for those rural citizens escaping the brutality of ethnic cleansing. Over time, however, for many Bosnians it became a preference due to the better standard of living and safety nets that urban centres offered. As one international practitioner pointed out, urbanisation, and not ethnic insecurity, 'has become the strongest barrier to return' (Hovey 2000: 10). Many DPs and minority returnees have prioritised economic and social issues over ethnic ones, and made their decisions accordingly (World Bank 2002: 26).

Not surprisingly, return has been particularly difficult in eastern RS, the most underdeveloped area of the country with very little economic opportunities. Many municipalities and villages in this region witnessed a process of migration from the countryside to Sarajevo that began prior to the 1992–95 conflict. Urbanisation and industrialisation were in fact the most important post-World War II social and economic trends in the region. While in 1948 about 72 per cent of the Bosnian population were engaged in agriculture, by 1971 this number had fallen to 36.6 per cent (Andjelić 2003: 29). Families went to look for work in Sarajevo, sometimes keeping a summer house in their town or village of origin, sometimes relocating altogether. Thus, the war acted as a 'social accelerator' of an existing process, causing the urbanisation of tens of thousands of citizens. In Sarajevo alone, there are an estimated 60,000 DPs.

The urban/rural cleavage was exacerbated after the war, with Sarajevo receiving much of the reconstruction assistance and the eastern RS almost none. It is not surprising that minority return to eastern RS was difficult *both* because of the resistance of local hard line politicians and the resistance of the DPs themselves. Only after 2000 have return projects been implemented in this area and some minority return has occurred (Fischel de Andrade and Delaney 2001). However, the economic situation continued to discourage potential returnees. In the summer of 2002, municipalities in eastern RS around Sarajevo (in particular Sokolac, Rogatica, and Višegrad) had about 600 apartments and houses rebuilt that remained empty because the owners had decided not to go back.[5] In short, at the beginning of the peace process neither Bosnian politicians nor displaced persons nor international agencies seemed fully committed to the right to return. As the next section demonstrates, international policy exacerbated the very problem it attempted to resolve, that is, the presence of a threatening mass of DPs amenable to political radicalisation.

Forced repatriation and the creation of 'displaced warriors'

After the signing of the DPA, many European states effectively offered permanent residence to about 100,000 Bosnians who were accepted during the war under the 'temporary protection' clause (Black *et al.* 1998). However, not all European governments were open to this option. By 1996, several governments began considering repatriation. European states had vested interests in promoting return to Bosnia. Return serves the interests of the states hosting refugees by getting rid of an economic and social liability. Germany, in particular, was concerned about the welfare costs of maintaining a sizeable refugee population and desired more than any other European state to avoid turning 'temporary protection' into a tool for permanent immigration for Bosnian refugees. Soon after the signing of the DPA, Germany placed considerable pressure on UNHCR to devise a repatriation plan. The plan foresaw the lifting of the temporary protection clause and the return of refugees on the basis of the fulfilment of specific benchmarks, including the implementation of the military provisions of the DPA, the proclamation of an amnesty for crimes other than serious violations of international humanitarian law, and the establishment and effective functioning of mechanisms for human rights protection (Bagshaw 1997).

UNHCR's official view at the time was consistent with that of European states such as Germany. UNHCR believed there were four mutually reinforcing ways in which return contributes to peace building. First, return clearly signals the end of a conflict and the capacity of a state to protect its citizens. Second, it legitimises the post-settlement political order, by providing validation to subsequent elections and democratic processes. Third, return deprives duplicitous leaders of the ability to manipulate refugees politically and militarily to undermine the newly established peace. Finally, return (particularly that of professionals and skilled workers) contributes decisively to the economic recovery of war-torn societies. However, as the experience of Bosnian returnees would show, in practice return has a contradictory impact on political and social stability (Bagshaw 1997: 159–64).

Forced repatriation and its impact

Neither the German government nor international agencies working in Bosnia harboured the illusion that refugees could return to those areas where just a few months earlier they were forced to leave because they belonged to the 'wrong' ethnic group. The decision to begin mandatory repatriation of Bosnian refugees as of 1 October 1996, including the repatriation of those 'who presently cannot return to their areas of origin', both contravened the principle of safe return to the pre-war homes declared in the DPA and increased the problem of internal displacement. Between 1996 and 1998, about 150,000 refugees returned under pressure from Germany.[6] Many human rights organisations protested against forced return, believing that at least the third benchmark, the presence of 'mechanisms for human rights protection', had not been fulfilled.[7] Swiss foreign minister and OSCE chairperson Flavio Cotti took the same point further and openly linked repatriation to complicity with ethnic cleansing: 'Forcibly repatriating people to an area that is not where they come from in a region where they make up the ethnic majority means actively supporting ethnic cleansing and contradicting Dayton, the UNHCR and the community of nations' (Reuters 1997).

It is unclear whether or not the German decision to repatriate refugees was illegal.[8] On the one hand, the 1951 Geneva Convention on Refugees does not require that refugees be granted permanent admission to a new political community. If such admission was granted, it would undermine immigration controls and therefore reinforce the reluctance of host states to accept refugees during future crises. Moreover, the protection granted to Bosnian refugees during the war was explicitly 'temporary'. On the other hand, the Geneva Convention maintains that refugees should be granted protection against *refoulement*. The temporary protection clause explicitly stated the applicability of this principle. Episodes of violence against returnees suggest that at least in some cases forcible repatriation was not safe. A few of those returnees who ventured to areas under the control of another ethnic group did so at great personal risk. In the first few months following the signing of the DPA, the homes of returnees in the RS had been mined expressly to prevent their return (ICG 1996b: 14). In the Federation too, minorities have not always been welcome. In a much publicised case, in May 1997 hard line Croats destroyed Serb homes in villages near Drvar, when twenty-five houses were burnt and twice as many more were prepared for arson attacks (ICG 1997). The OSCE and the IPTF later directly implicated Drvar's mayor and deputy mayor (both HDZ members) and the local police. As late as summer 2003, UNHCR continued to express concern with the designation of Bosnia as a 'safe country' (UNHCR 2003). An additional concern is the legal status of those who were forcibly repatriated: refugees who were sent back but were unable to return to their place of origin remain de facto displaced persons, but they are not formally granted this status and thus are unable to access the rights and entitlements of DPs.

In addition to being legally and politically questionable, forced repatriation produced two negative results. First, instead of contributing to economic development, one of the outcomes UNHCR hoped to achieve by encouraging repatriation, the return of tens of thousands exacerbated the difficult economic situation. Even prior to the war, many Bosnians had found their main source of income in Western Europe. In 1981 there were 133,000 Bosnians working abroad (Andjelić 2003: 35). The 1992–95 war, by forcing more people to move abroad, added to a previous pattern of migration that allowed many Bosnian families to sustain themselves economically through foreign remittances. The repatriation of refugees undermined a much-needed source of income (BiH 2004; Black 2001: 195). Moreover, return posed an enormous strain on the scarce housing resources, a challenge that international agencies were not ready to face. UNHCR estimated that the return of 200,000 refugees required the reconstruction of 50,000–60,000 houses. However, the World Bank had not given priority to this area of intervention, probably because its major member states were not so inclined. As Carl Bildt recalled with frustration and disappointment, a US congressional committee decided that funds could not be used to repair houses. As long as states in the southern region of the United States maintained sub-standard housing, taxpayers' money could not be used to build houses in 'remote European countries' (1998: 315). Because of the lack of housing, many of those repatriated were accommodated in so-called Collective Centres, temporary accommodation that soon turned into long-term shelters (UNHCR 2001). A decade after the end of the war, there are still thirty-three collective centres in the Federation, nine collective settlements, and three transit centres (HCHR 2005: 10).

Moreover, in addition to complicating the economic and housing situation, the forcible repatriation of refugees further contributed to ethnic homogenisation and injected an element of instability into the country. Ethnic politicians in Bosnian municipalities both attempted to consolidate their political power by attracting additional individuals from their own ethnic group and resisted the return of individuals of other ethnic backgrounds. Whether for Bosniak, Serb or Croat returnees, international authorities did little to facilitate their return home. The High Representative believed that minority return could have been politically destabilising, and therefore was not ready to make it a central part of international intervention. The lack of enforcement of the right to return highlighted international agencies' ambivalence over the implementation of Annex 7 of the DPA. For the first two years of the post-Dayton transition, NATO commanders insisted that they had no mandate to assist returnees to go home and ensure their safety. As a result, it is estimated that at least 100,000 people, for the most part Bosniaks, went to join their ethnic group, becoming internal DPs and enlarging the ranks of frustrated and powerless individuals vulnerable to nationalist manipulation (ICG 1998c: 11–15; Black 2001: 188).

Not only did international agencies lack the political will to enforce the right to return, but they also did not want permanently to relocate Bosnian DPs for fear of legitimising ethnic cleansing. As a result, the increase in the already substantial number of DPs created a socially and politically explosive situation by exacerbating the domestic variant of the 'refugee warrior' phenomenon: the social, economic and political conditions of most DPs make them open to radicalisation, which in turn constitutes a real threat to the peace process. DPs vote consistently for the same ethnic parties responsible for the war, and deeply resent being prevented from excercising their right to return. As Amnesty International (AI 1998) warned, 'as long as territories within Bosnia-Herzegovina remain ethnically exclusive, the region will remain unstable, since victims of the war who were forcibly expelled from their homes, [sic] are likely to dwell upon that injustice'.

In sum, forced repatriation increased the presence of a mass of DPs who could not return to their pre-war homes, nor be permanently relocated because of international concerns about legitimising ethnic cleansing. The proclamation of the right to return with weak or limited enforcement to make it a safe and realistic option for the population, coupled with international resistance to relocation due to the human rights rhetoric, produced the worst possible outcome: it undermined the DPA's goal of reversing ethnic cleansing, while leaving many of those Bosnians who had lost their houses in an indeterminate and potentially unsustainable state of internal displacement.

Change of policy

The presence of a mass of DPs for whom there was no durable solution increased the possibility that they might develop into a new army at the disposal of Bosniak leaders dissatisfied with the territorial settlement established at Dayton. Many thousands of Bosniaks who were repatriated settled in the northwestern town of Sanski Most. The city's mayor and former Bosnian army general, Muhammed Alagić, welcomed the returnees in order to consolidate his own political power as well as the military victory that had retaken the town from the Serbs at the end of the war. By mid-1997, about 40,000 refugees had moved to Sanski Most, raising the total population to its pre-war level of 61,000. Faced with poor living conditions, these DPs constituted a menacing presence just across the IEBL, only a few miles away from their town of origin – Prijedor. A journalist described them at the time in these terms: 'these people are disenfranchised, unemployed, and miserable. Many of them want to return home, support themselves, and not spend the next couple of generations as the new Bosnian underclass' (Lippman 1999).

Faced with a potentially explosive situation, international agencies refocused on the problem of displacement. First, UNHCR began distinguishing between different types of relocation and decided that 'voluntary relocation', after the exchange or sale of property by consent, was acceptable. Voluntary relocation occurs with the consent of both the individual who is relocating to a new property and the original owner of that property. 'Passive relocation' occurs when displacement becomes a permanent condition not based on free will. 'Hostile relocation' is the deliberate placement of groups of people in housing belonging to individuals of other ethnic groups in order to secure control over territory and prevent minority return. UNHCR opposed these last two forms of relocation, and approved of voluntary relocation (CRPC and UNHCR 1997: 23). In practice, by early 1998 these distinctions were merely conceptual and did not reflect the presence of real options for the DPs. Voluntary relocation presupposed a degree of freedom of choice that DPs almost never have, either because they can't prove their property rights, or because this choice is conditioned by a hostile environment which severely narrows their options.

Second, international agencies declared 1998 as the Year of Return, underlining the fact that return was a core but dangerously ignored provision of the DPA. UNHCR hoped that more than 50,000 people would go back to their pre-war communities by the end of that year. International economic assistance to Bosnia became increasingly tied to local politicians' cooperation with minority return plans. In particular, the UNHCR-sponsored Open Cities programme provided that cities fulfilling certain criteria conducive to minority return would receive additional financial assistance from international agencies. This initiative reversed the earlier policy by using positive instead of negative incentives as a form of aid conditionality. High-profile conferences were also held, leading to a Sarajevo Declaration, which called for the return of 20,000 non-Bosniaks to that city, and a similar Banja Luka Declaration, which called for the return of non-Serbs to the RS.

This attempt at fostering return achieved very limited success. Authorities in many of the recognised Open Cities made only cosmetic changes, while paying lip service to the principle of minority return (ICG 1998b). The very idea of positive conditionality exacerbated resistance and opposition among the general population, and because the priority given by donors to minorities explicitly discriminate against the local majority (who might be as much in need as the returnees), positive conditionality quickly became counter-productive and reproduced the very same cleavages that emerged from the war (World Bank 2002: 31). By addressing the problem of displacement as a political problem (demanding that majorities accept the return of minorities) instead of a human rights problem (applying to everyone regardless of ethnic belonging), international agencies embraced the same ethnic divisions that nationalist elites were working to preserve. Furthermore, this policy placed too much confidence in the unlikely cooperation of local elites, the group most likely to boycott the return process. Despite the expectation that 1998 would bring about a significant number of minority returnees, only a few went back. Even in the high-profile cases of Sarajevo and Banja Luka, the numbers were negligible. Only 4,400 minorities came back to Sarajevo in 1998 and an insignificant number of DPs returned to Banja Luka (Slatina 1999).

While international officials blamed obstruction at the municipal level, they were not yet entirely committed to making minority return a priority. When minority return conflicted with other broader political goals, international agencies chose to give return a lower preference. The return strategy suffered from cognitive dissonance, whereby international agencies demanded from local politicians an absolute commitment to the rights of the returnees, but were themselves willing to sacrifice this commitment. The uncertain attitude towards Milorad Dodik, who was elected prime minister of the RS in 1998, shows how both Bosnian politicians and international agencies bear responsibility for policy failures. International agencies hoped that the election of Dodik would facilitate the process of return of about 70,000 DPs. Dodik first promised to return all Bosniak and Croat DPs and refugees to the RS if his government was given \$1 billion for reconstruction. When the money was allocated, however, he directed it towards his own constituency (Ćurak 1998). Eventually, international agencies decided to ease pressure on Dodik and RS authorities to accept minority return for fear that pushing for return would undermine the position of the new prime minister, one of the few Serb politicians who at least paid lip service to implementing the DPA (Partos 1999). As a result, during Dodik's tenure only 3,700 minority returns to the RS took place. The failure was additionally compounded by Dodik's loss of the 2000 elections, and further delays in the return process (Cvijanović 2000).

On the whole, there are two lessons to be learnt from this episode. First, when faced with a choice between guaranteeing group rights and pushing for the respect of individual rights, international agencies choose the former over the latter. Asserting that local politicians would not adopt the very same stance is not only naive, but also counter-productive. Second, this episode confirmed to Bosnian politicians that one can break one's commitments and still remain favoured by international interveners. Predictably, local politicians became increasingly inclined to speak the language of multi-ethnicity and reconciliation, as Dodik did, while preserving their practical uncompromising stance. By the end of 1999, the overall failure of the international policy was evident: four years after the signing of the DPA, approximately 830,000 persons were still internally displaced (Cousens and Cater 2001: 75).

Breaking the population logjam

The sheer magnitude of the DPs' problem led international agencies to further refocus intervention on the need for return. The process that led to a breakthrough in the number of minority returnees had been slow and frustrating. Eventually, return started to become possible because of two conditions: first, the active presence of NATO troops; and second, the initiative of organised groups of DPs who worked hard to make return a reality – sometimes even against the advice of international agencies.

Prijedor/Sanski Most

Prijedor, a hard line municipality that was never recognised as an Open City because of the local politicians' obstruction to minority return, was given to the Serbs by the DPA (Wesselingh and Valeurin 2003). In the summer of 1995, US mediator Richard Holbrooke stopped the Bosniak advance against the retreating Serb Army, reserved the region for Serb control, and thus implicitly legitimised their later rejection of a significant number of Bosniak returnees. Since the end of the war, the US Congress' Lautenberg Amendment, which prohibits the United States government from providing assistance to communities suspected of harbouring war criminals, placed Prijedor under an aid embargo.[9] Accordingly, international return schemes neglected this municipality. Hard line politics, international isolation and lack of reconstruction funding all made Prijedor a very difficult and unlikely case for successful minority return. Yet, international interveners today almost unanimously point to this region to highlight the achievements of foreign intervention. How could Prijedor be transformed from a hopeless case of domestic obstruction to a shining example of successful international policy?

Part of the answer lies in the stronger international commitment to implementing the DPA. In May 1997, the PIC met at Sintra, Portugal, and endorsed a more vigorous peace building approach proposed by the American administration. The Steering Board issued a political declaration that confirmed the international commitment to the peace process, and emphasised it would not 'tolerate any attempts at partition, *de facto* or *de iure*, by anyone' (PIC 1997b). The declaration reflected the strategic position of OHR, which wanted to replace the previous approach of high rhetoric and ambitious deadlines with a limited set of concrete demands on Bosnian authorities, with specific sanctions attached to them. Furthermore, the declaration set the stage for a more assertive foreign military presence. SFOR became increasingly active in the implementation of the civilian aspects of the peace operation. The first military action against an indicted war criminal came on 10 June 1997, when British troops in Prijedor captured one Serb and killed another who had been named by the ICTY in a sealed indictment. American soldiers arrested their first war crimes suspect on 22 January 1998: Goran Jelisić, a Serb known as the 'Serbian Adolf'.[10]

The July 1997 events had a profound impact. Following SFOR's overdue activism, the mayor of Prijedor and SDS hard-liner Milomir Stakić, fearing the possibility that ICTY had issued a secret indictment for his arrest, went 'on permanent vacation'.[11] Instead of the feared backlash against international peacekeepers, local authorities switched allegiance from the hard line wartime leader Radovan Karadžić to the more moderate leadership of Biljana Plavšić – and later that of Milorad Dodik. These changes gave Bosniak potential returnees a sufficient sense of security seriously to consider returning. They began the type of return that came to be known as 'spontaneous', that is, made possible because of the determination of the DPs themselves, rather than the international agencies' planning and direction. The term 'spontaneous return' can be a misnomer because it does not reflect the considerable amount of organised work by DP associations that preceded return. There is nothing spontaneous in organising DP associations, lobbying local authorities and international organisations, participating in municipal elections, organising assessment visits and repairing destroyed houses (ICG 2002a). In essence, the term underlines the importance of local initiatives and demonstrates the existence of domestic capacities and resources that can be mobilised to turn the rhetorical commitment to multi-ethnicity into achievable ends.

Starting in the spring of 1998, more than 10,000 Bosniaks (about half of the pre-war population) returned to Kozarac, a village just a few miles from Prijedor and a symbol of the wartime policy of ethnic cleansing. Some returns have occurred even in the town of Prijedor, a situation that international agencies considered impossible until not long ago. 'The lesson is clear: the removal of suspects indicted for war crimes, who are symbols of impunity and are among the most obstructionist, has a ripple effect that can fundamentally alter the disposition of an area towards DPA implementation' (ICG 1998b: 39). These developments have important implications for the role of the military in international intervention. At Dayton, the military refused to take over responsibility for enforcing the peace agreement, while oddly accepting the authority to do so. In the first post-settlement year, the Clinton administration had no desire to punish violators. The future and success of the mission was left to Admiral Leighton Smith, the commander of NATO forces in Bosnia, who did everything he could to prevent US intervention in the first place. After intervention was a fact, he interpreted IFOR's responsibilities as narrowly as possible, requiring IFOR to make arrests only when indicted war criminals were 'encountered' (Kerr 2004: 154–69). The example of Prijedor demonstrates that a more active military presence is important to ensure the implementation of the agreement and does not necessarily lead to a dangerous environment for international forces. Not a single soldier was killed in over ten years of military intervention. If this is the feared 'mission creep' (that is, the unwarranted process of expansion in the goals of the peace operation and in the responsibilities of interveners), it ought to have been welcomed. Instead, NATO troops continued to arrest on a case-by-case basis which so far has led to the apprehension of only a limited number of indicted war criminals.

International agencies responded to spontaneous return in the Prijedor region in two ways. First, they blamed the returnees for going back home. According to a former UNHCR official working in the Prijedor area, Bosniak

DPs and their leaders 'pressed ahead with an agenda of return without consideration of the safety of potential returnees' (Ito 2001b: 35). The sporadic violence that resulted from return was thus blamed on the returnees, and those who encouraged them to return 'too rapidly', instead of the perpetrators. As a local Bosniak leader pointed out, this argument was exactly the same one endorsed by Serb nationalists to justify the outbreak of violence against returnees.[12] Because of the unwillingness of NATO troops to provide security for the returnees, the victims of the attacks were once again blamed for their stubborn attempt to return to places from where they had been expelled. Second, international agencies also made an important change to their previous return strategy and created the Regional Return Task Force (RRTF). This coordinating body (which included all the major agencies involved in the return process, but still had no leverage to change NATO's reluctance to be more proactive) identified strategic axes of likely return movements *based on the interest of the DPs themselves.* Reversing the traditional top-down intervention approach, the RRTF's main innovation was the decision that international activities should follow the flow of DPs, instead of requiring DPs to follow the flow of international activities. This change was the critical policy innovation that would finally break Bosnia's population logjam.

Recipe for return

As a consequence of the improved security situation and the creation of the RRTF, minority returns improved considerably: 67,000 individuals returned during 2000 to their pre-war homes in areas where they would constitute an ethnic minority. More than 92,000 followed in 2001. The peak was reached in 2002, with 102,111 minority returnees. Since then, there has been a steady decline in the number of returns: 44,868 in 2003, 14,199 in 2004, 5,815 in 2005, and 4,596 in 2006, indicating that the process is slowly coming to a close (see Map 6.1) Since the signing of the DPA, more than a million refugees and DPs have returned to their pre-war homes. More than half a million returnees were individuals returning to areas under the control of another ethnic group, thus in part reversing the effects of ethnic cleansing.[13] At the current rate of return, another 150,000 returnees could be expected, increasing the total number to more than half of those who were displaced because they belonged to the 'wrong' ethnic group (Ivanisević 2004). The results achieved, combined with the fact that the number of returnees has decreased significantly since 2002, led the governments of Bosnia, Croatia, and Serbia and Montenegro to commit to solving the problem of remaining population displacement by the end of 2006, and to facilitate the return or local integration of refugees (UNHCR 2005). These population movements belie the scepticism about the possibility of return in the context of a society polarised by a brutal civil war, and raise two broader questions. First, what broke the minority return logjam and what does the process tell us about the possibility of restoring ethnic diversity in the context of profound divisions? Second, what is the impact of minority return on local communities and more broadly on the ethnic reintegration of the country? After addressing the first question, the remainder of this chapter will consider the issues of the impact and sustainability of minority return.

Improved implementation of property legislation, better coordination among international agencies, and the fact that the brutality of the war is slowly fading in the collective memory have all contributed to a breakthrough.[14] Worryingly, return occurred in a context in which less, not more, international assistance was available. UNHCR's budget shrunk from US$200 million in 1999 to $80 million in 2002. As a result, a mismatch between the willingness of the DPs to return home and the capacity of international agencies to assist them in doing so was created. The estimated need for housing units in support of return is 65,000 units. However, in 2004 available funds enabled the reconstruction of only 15–20 per cent of this estimate (UNHCR 2004: 10).

As the initial return to the villages outside the town of Prjiedor confirmed, return first occurred to destroyed rural communities with little strategic interest. Because these villages would still be inhabited by one ethnic group, local authorities were less opposed to allowing minorities to come back. Destroyed rural areas were politically much less sensitive than urban areas. Minority return could be tolerated to empty villages with little economic or strategic significance, or in small numbers to large urban centres, but outside those marginal situations it was consistently opposed (Cox 1999). In many of these cases return was spontaneous, occurring because DPs returned of their own initiative, often outside pre-established return-schemes and with little or no international help.

The key to making the return process an irreversible reality was securing individual property rights. During the war, all three communities tried to solidify their exclusionist territorial gains by promulgating property laws aimed at accommodating the large numbers of DPs belonging to their respective ethnic group. At the end of the war, the property regime made minority return practically impossible (Waters 1999). The DPA attempted to create the conditions necessary to reverse this state of affairs by upholding property rights. Annex 7 created the Commission on Real Property Claims of Refugees and Displaced Persons (CRPC), mandated with the task of certifying property rights and thus helping DPs to reclaim their homes. In an effort to take into account the significant number of Serbs who preferred to remain in the RS, the CRPC's mandate also allowed for financial compensation as an alternative to property restitution. The commission consisted of nine members, two representing each main national group, in addition to three international members appointed by the president of the European Court of Human Rights. By the time the CRPC mandate expired in 2003, the commission had received claims for nearly 320,000 properties and issued more than 312,000 decisions (CRPC 2004).

The enforcement of CRPC's decisions fell to Bosnian authorities, dominated by nationalist administrations opposed to property restitution (Philpott 2005). Furthermore, more than half of Bosnia's territory was socially owned land, much complicating the determination of property titles. In some cases, nationalist parties used socially owned land as strategic territory – a policy with a long history in the region. For centuries Austrian authorities settled Serbian peasants along the military frontier (*vojna krajina*) to protect their interests from the Ottomans.[15] In a similar vein, the creation of new settlements in Croat-controlled Herzegovina after the signing of the DPA appeared to be motivated by the desire to create frontier villages to guard the borders of Greater Croatia. The government in the RS similarly adopted a policy aimed to defeat the implementation of Annex 7 of the DPA (ESI 2002c).

Property repossession became part of international agencies' policy only in 1998, when the promulgation of new property laws in the Federation, and subsequently in the RS, created some legal certainty and cleared many obstacles for returnees. In 1999, the High Representative intervened to harmonise these laws in the two Entities. He imposed a package of property-related decrees to create the long-delayed legal framework to ease return and to reinforce 'the duty of the authorities at all levels ... to actively implement their [citizens'] rights to their homes and property' (OHR 1999). At last, a reasonably clear procedure was in place to make it more difficult for local housing offices to ignore requests for repossession and the need to evict illegal occupants who would not vacate the house of the returnees voluntarily. The presence of this framework, which applied in principle to all regardless of their ethnicity or status, was an important improvement towards establishing the rule of law based not on ethnic affiliation but on universal principles of equity.

With the legal framework in place, the creation of the Property Law Implementation Plan (PLIP) in 2000 gave the final necessary support to the return process. PLIP abandoned conditionality and positive discrimination in favour of the principle that the same pressures, demands, and expectations must be applied to all the officials and municipalities of Bosnia (Petritsch 2002a: 144–50; Philpott 2005: 9–10). Despite some resistance and delays, the process of enforcing the property laws soon became irreversible. Implementation initially focused on the cases of 'double' or 'multiple' occupancy. Multiple occupants were defined by their ability to meet their housing needs otherwise by dint of income or access to housing elsewhere. The enforcement of the new property laws focused on these cases.

While cases of 'multiple occupancy' were not too controversial (because those who were evicted had alternative accommodation), the cases of temporary occupants who could not meet their own housing needs and were therefore entitled to alternative accommodation were more politically and socially sensitive. UNHCR was concerned about the potential negative human costs of evicting individuals and families temporarily occupying

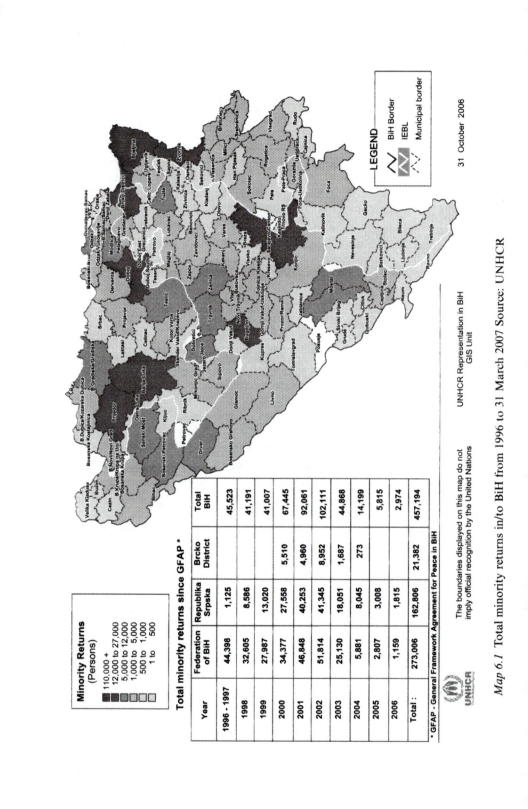

Minority Returns
(Persons)

- 110,000 +
- 12,000 to 27,000
- 5,000 to 12,000
- 1,000 to 5,000
- 500 to 1,000
- 1 to 500

Total minority returns since GFAP *

Year	Federation of BiH	Republika Srpska	Brcko District	Total BiH
1996 - 1997	44,398	1,125		45,523
1998	32,605	8,586		41,191
1999	27,987	13,020		41,007
2000	34,377	27,558	5,510	67,445
2001	46,848	40,253	4,960	92,061
2002	51,814	41,345	8,952	102,111
2003	25,130	18,051	1,687	44,868
2004	5,881	8,045	273	14,199
2005	2,807	3,008		5,815
2006	1,159	1,815		2,974
Total :	273,006	162,806	21,382	457,194

* GFAP - General Framework Agreement for Peace in BiH

LEGEND

- BiH Border
- IEBL
- Municipal border

31 October 2006

The boundaries displayed on this map do not imply official recognition by the United Nations

UNHCR Representation in BiH
GIS Unit

Map 6.1 Total minority returns in/to BiH from 1996 to 31 March 2007 Source: UNHCR

returnees' homes – but without a clear housing alternative. Paradoxically, the UNHCR position was anti-return, since postponing evictions could only buy time for local authorities wishing to obstruct the process. Because local authorities understood that international agencies would not push for the universal application of the property laws, they did not budget any resources in order to provide alternative accommodation for evicted families. Instead, local authorities gave temporary occupants an open-ended right to live in other people's claimed property. Compounding this problem was the housing authorities' discretion over the order of processing eviction cases, inviting both bribery and pressure not to act against politically protected families. As a UNHCR report noted, 'political interference, corruption, and often pure arbitrariness have dictated which claims are processed and when' (2002a: 4).

The solution was the introduction of 'chronological order' (Philpott 2005: 11–12). On 4 December 2001, amendments were imposed on the property laws, making the chronological processing of applications for property repossession an explicit legal obligation binding housing authorities. Property laws had to be implemented regardless of whether or not alternative accommodation was available for evicted families. This principle was once again tested in Prijedor before it became law in December 2001. In this municipality, there was no negative public reaction to the evictions. Four families without alternative accommodation moved in with friends and relatives. As the evictions were enforced according to the principle of chronological order, an increasing number of illegal occupants voluntarily turned over the properties they had occupied during the war or shortly after the signing of the peace agreement.[16] The policy's success in Prijedor was soon replicated in the rest of the country. Local authorities all over Bosnia had to confront the reality of evictions and the need to address the housing situation. Not only was the decision imposed by international agencies an important step in ending international micromanagement of domestic policy, but also it created domestic ownership of the policy, since local authorities had to take responsibility for the process and make resources available for it. In other words, international intervention does not necessarily create dependency and passivity but at times can improve the legitimacy and efficiency of domestic institutions.

Three lessons can be learned from the experience of Bosnian DPs. First, the key actors in facilitating return are the DPs themselves and their longing to go 'home'. It is only partly correct that many Bosnians of all ethnicities prefer to stay elsewhere than return to their homes (Chandler 1999: 105). Bosnian returnees voted with their feet, often preferring return to the other available options. Returning home has a meaning and depth that many cosmopolitans perhaps cannot fully comprehend.[17] Second, return became successful when it was no longer explicitly linked to minority issues and group rights in general, but to the respect of the rule of law and individual rights applying to everyone regardless of ethnic belonging. PLIP effectively decreased the politicisation of the property issue by treating repossession as a legal process of deciding and implementing individual return claims. This standardised and law-based approach gradually decreased the influence of partisan politics, and allowed DPs to go back to where they had been expelled from. Third, despite the international rhetoric of ownership and capacity building, the imposition of some key decisions, particularly those improving the legal framework, is necessary and justified as long as these are cast in individual human rights terms, impose the rule of law, and thus benefit everyone regardless of their ethnicity. The intervention that established legal certainty helped the DPs to assert their rights and forced local authorities to assume responsibility for the return process. In short, not all internationally imposed policies limit domestic governance.

Impact and sustainability

Is the return of minorities and the re-creation of some degree of ethnic inter-mixing a positive development furthering the peace process and promoting long-term stability? Or is minority return creating a fifth column or, as Susan Woodward has graphically argued, a 'Trojan Horse' with potentially devastating consequences should a new war break out? While the fear that ethnic remixing could be a recipe for future violence is legitimate and a matter of concern, the dynamics of the 1992–95 war provide prima facie evidence to reject the idea that the presence of a minority group surrounded by a majority group is a security threat for the majority. Again in the Prijedor region, for example, an area ethnically mixed prior to the war, the Bosniak minority was expelled and/or interned in concentration camps almost with no resistance. It is hard to imagine that their return could create a serious security concern for the current Serb majority population. This example should caution against the use of the Trojan Horse metaphor, which foresees an aggressive and hostile future role for individuals who were the victims, and not the perpetrators, of the recent conflict. As we shall see, the political impact of returnees on local communities suggests that at least some minority return is a positive development, particularly when compared to the alternative of internal displacement.

The impact of return

Through the Trojan Horse metaphor and the logic of the security dilemma (see Chapter 2), historical determinists suggest that a situation of ethnically mixed populations is potentially explosive. From their point of view, the more that hostile populations are intermixed, the more they feel insecure and ready to pre-empt surprise attacks by attacking first (Kaufmann 1999: 222–3). Accordingly, the only lasting solution to communal conflicts is supposedly the separation of the warring parties into defensible enclaves.

Instead of ethnic reintegration, international policy should focus on 'the long-term goal of ethnic reconciliation', even when such a goal requires the preservation of ethnic separation (Black 2001; Cox 1999). This argument is intertwined with the one advanced by autonomist critics of international intervention, who claim that the international agencies' insistence on defending the principle of ethnic diversity is both wrong and ultimately counter-productive (Chandler 1999). Marcus Cox (1999) concluded that, particularly in the early phase of the peace implementation process, any significant return would threaten the peace process itself.

These perspectives focus on security concerns and neglect the possibility that contacts between ethnic groups can foster mutual understanding and respect, rather than simply activating the security dilemma. The 'contact hypothesis' was first introduced in academic debates in the aftermath of World War II, and later proposed as a response to racial segregation in the United States. Advocates of this hypothesis differ on the question of whether inter-group or interpersonal contacts are more important, but they agree on the basic idea that frequent contact can reduce intolerance and improve inter-group relations. However, Bosnian population dynamics show that not all contacts are positive. Rather, contact can sour understanding if groups compete for resources. Demographic changes in the 1970s and 1980s increased competition for jobs at the level of the local municipalities (*opstina*). The increasing Bosniak population was able to access more jobs through ethnic quotas at the expense of a declining Serb population. Demographic indices of ethnic competition and population trends demonstrate the importance of resource competition as a source of conflict (Slack and Doyon 2001; Bougarel 1992).

Although both security concerns and resource competition seem to advise against post-war minority return, the relative success of this policy in post-Dayton Bosnia shows that, at least in come cases, inter-group contact can be an antidote against intolerance and extremism. True, several violent incidents have occurred since returns gained momentum. In two highly publicised incidents in May 2001, when mosques in Trebinje and Banja Luka were about to be rebuilt, an organised crowd of Serb protesters stopped the cornerstone ceremony by throwing rocks and attacking Bosniaks and some international officials in attendance. Nationalist parties threatened by the process of minority return often implicitly or openly supported and directed the violence. Occasionally violence has gone far beyond rioting. Six returnees have been killed since April 2000 in eastern RS (ICG 2002a). In 2002 in Prijedor, Zvornik, Doboj, Bratunac, Derventa and Modrica, unknown perpetrators planted bombs under returnees' cars or in their houses and yards (HCHR 2003b). In September 2002, during the celebration of the Yugoslav national team's victory at the World Basketball Championship in the United States, local Serbs vandalised houses and business premises of Bosniak returnees in Prijedor and Bijeljina. Explosives were planted and bombs thrown at several mosques. In most cases, the police failed to identify and arrest the perpetrators. On 24 December 2002, a young Bosniak killed a whole family of Croats in Kostajinica, near Konjic. Some violence against returnees, their properties and religious sites continues. In most cases, the perpetrators of these offences have never been found and tried (HCHR 2005).

What is most striking about these episodes is that violence has been generally limited. With tens of thousands of Bosnians estimated to be living in areas where they are a minority, the opportunities for violence could be endless. Moreover, one should keep in mind that Bosnia is a post-settlement society, not a post-conflict one. The expectation that never again will localised violence break out is quite unrealistic. Furthermore, from a security perspective, the alternative to return and to the establishment of some degree of ethnic intermixing is perhaps more dangerous than return itself. As argued earlier, displacement can be a breeding ground for extremism, even short of degeneration into the 'displaced warrior' phenomenon. DPs are frequently loyal supporters of local hard line nationalist leaders (Phuong 2000b), and nationalist rule is most unchallenged in mono-ethnic areas and municipalities (Pugh and Cobble 2001).

There remains the question of whether return has increased competition for resources and radicalised majorities and minorities alike. The case of Prijedor suggests that the increase in ethnic diversity can be a potential antidote to hard line politics. In this municipality the return of displaced Bosniaks and the election of Bosniak representatives to the municipal council had an important impact. At the 1997 elections, Bosniaks took 37 per cent of the seats on the municipal council. In 2000, the percentage of Bosniak seats decreased to 28 per cent (9 of 32 seats, reflecting a decrease in the number of Bosniaks voting with absentee ballots). Their vote, however, permitted the election of Nada Ševo, a member of the SNSD, one of the three relatively moderate parties that arose from the 1997 split of the SDS.[18] In addition to contributing towards electing a moderate Serb mayor, Bosniaks were able to obtain the appointment of one of their members as president of the municipal assembly.

This example suggests that the political participation of returnees (and potential returnees voting in absentia) can help marginalise hard liners and have an overall positive impact on accommodation and compromise. Contact between groups increased the need for a pragmatic approach among all political actors involved. The potentially negative effects of resource competition were avoided because returnees are often forced to rely on sources other than jobs (see next section). Many maintain welfare privileges from the 'other' Entity. Moreover, remittances from abroad help make ends meet. In Prijedor the returnee population almost doubles during the summer months, when many Bosniaks return from Western Europe to spend their holidays with family and friends, and bring with them much-needed hard currency.

Moreover, local politicians are often compelled to step up and provide solutions to diverse local demands. In 2002 the first Bosniak elementary school was opened in Prijedor – the first one in the RS. Municipal funds were allocated to implement projects in return areas – KM250,000 (approx. US$140,000) in 2001 and KM350,000 (approx. $195,000) in 2002. According to a UNHCR report on Prijedor, this new pragmatic stance 'comes as a result of both the pressure from the international community and the adoption of more moderate political platforms in order to gain the support of a larger returnee community' (2002b: 12). In May 2002, the United States acknowledged the many positive changes achieved and lifted the sanctions on Prijedor, previously imposed by the Lautenberg Amendment. Meanwhile, the municipality continued its transformation towards moderate, centrist politics. At the 2004 municipal elections Marko Pavić was elected new mayor, supported by all main parties with the exception of the nationalist SDS and SDA. Again, the presidency of the municipal assembly was obtained by a Bosniak, Azra Pasalić. The relationship between former enemies continued to improve. In April 2005, for example, the burial of the remains of 125 Bosniaks and Croats killed during the war was attended by local authorities of all ethnic groups, including the new Serb mayor.

The lessons of Prijedor apply to other municipalities as well. Instead of causing a backlash, in most instances return helped to diffuse tensions. Bosnian authorities have increasingly taken responsibility for the process. A return fund has been established at state level in order to finance return projects in selected municipalities. The overall positive impact of return convinced even some earlier sceptics. For example, Marcus Cox (1999) initially rejected return as a non-starter. In his later work (Cox and Garlick 2003: 79), he concluded that 'the Bosnian experience shows that one cannot wait until all of the tensions have been resolved before commencing return movements. In fact, it is the return movement itself which opens the way to peaceful coexistence.' Return improved the security situation and created conditions for social and political change.

Sustainability

Whether the patterns of return will be sustained is unclear. Often returnees are older people, beyond their reproductive age, who may or may not be joined by the younger generation. Furthermore, old and young alike are frequently frustrated by the lack of support they must endure after they take the difficult step of returning. International policy focused on achieving quantitative results, such as increasing the number of returnees, instead of qualitative ones, that is, improving the conditions for returnees to sustain themselves (Heimerl 2006; Ito 2001a: 121). As a result, 'many long-term minority returnees are disillusioned, trapped in poverty and feel abandoned by organisations who have ceased to have contact with them once they have signed off completed projects' (Hovey 2001: 21).

While the decision to return might not be always affected by economic considerations (Pickering 2003), the decision to stay needs to be based on the ability of returnees to sustain themselves. The official unemployment rate in Bosnia is at around 40 per cent, with peaks of 60–70 per cent in parts of eastern RS. The living conditions of returnees are particularly precarious. As Chapter 5 showed, the ethnicisation of the economy adds an additional hurdle. The unemployment rate is considerably worse for minority returnees, who are consistently discriminated against and find it almost impossible to find a job. It is estimated that about 80 per cent of returnees have no permanent employment. Discrimination remains one of the main obstacles to their sustainable return (AI 2006a). A UNHCR survey of minority returnees in the RS confirms that the grim reality of returnees' life. Out of the 194 persons interviewed, only one had found a job in the RS. This lucky person had been hired by an international organisation (Alfaro 2000: 29–30). The post-2002 constitutional changes, which were meant to counter the legacy of ethnic cleansing, support minority employment and encourage the long-term economic sustainability of returns, contributed only marginally to creating job opportunities. Women in particular suffer from the lack of labour laws protecting their full and equal access to employment. Because priority in recruitment is often given to demobilised soldiers, disabled war veterans, and families of deceased soldiers, it has been objectively difficult for women to access the job market (OSCE 1999b).

In some cases, returnees' chronic poverty has forced them to re-emigrate to areas where they can be more employable (Hovey 2001). The underrepresentation of minority officers in the police force, as well as limited educational opportunities, have also led some returnees to reconsider their choices. Many have decided to sell their apartment or house and exercise their right to 'voluntary relocation'. The July 2001 decision of the High Representative to end the two-year moratorium on the resale of property in the Federation has facilitated apartment sales in many areas. Because of the extremely difficult economic situation, eastern RS is particularly affected by this phenomenon. About 17,000 returnees from Bratunac and Janja (near Prijedor) are reported to be considering relocation again – also citing security reasons (HCHR 2003b: 10).

This situation was not inevitable. Donors could have adopted a set of 'Minority Employment Principles' in all contracts with government agencies and Bosnian enterprises (ICG 1998a). Similar principles have been adopted in the past. The MacBride Principles originated in the Irish American community to make US investment in Northern Ireland conditional on a balanced work force. Similarly, the Sullivan Principles were accepted in the 1980s by firms doing business with South Africa. Comparable initiatives for Bosnia could have amounted to a programme of affirmative action for minorities, but they were dismissed by international agencies as incompatible with market liberalisation. The creation of economic opportunities for returnees would have required a level of social and economic engineering that fits uncomfortably with the neo-liberal template focused on economic liberalisation (Donais 2005: 138–39).

Moreover, ensuring the sustainability of returns would also have required effective international coordination. While UNHCR can organise repatriation schemes, it does not possess either the human or material resources to ensure the sustainability of return. Accordingly, UNHCR defines return as 'successful' when the returnee spends one night in his or her house.[19] Because UNHCR is not a development agency, it cannot address the problems associated with post-settlement development and the reintegration of returnees in their former communities. This limitation has led the agency to seek collaboration with the World Bank and other international financial institutions. However, as argued in Chapter 5, economic aid has not paid particular attention to this aspect, and instead it has often reinforced the ethnicisation of the economy.

Confronted with their intrinsic limitations, international agencies have measured the success of the minority return policy in terms of quantitative instead of qualitative terms, overlooking the sustainability of returns (Ito 2001a: 119; Heimerl 2006). In one of the few statements of self-criticism, the Inter-Agency Working Group on Employment admitted that employment opportunities for returnees have not been given enough consideration: 'although the 24 May 2000 Peace Implementation Council highlighted the need to foster economic, educational and labour market opportunities for returnees, the actual implementation of these crucial objectives has not yet started' (cited in ICG 2002a: 15). According to UNHCR, 'much greater effort will have to be made successfully to anchor returnees in their original places of residence, if they are to regain productive livelihoods again' (2004: 9). At the same time, pro-active interventions in favour of minorities will not be enough. If the economy as a whole does not grow, the amount of available resources will shrink and competition between groups is likely to heighten, with one group trying to exclude the other(s).

Meanwhile, international agencies have moved to declare the issue resolved, thus moving one step closer to disengagement. The PIC on 30 January 2003 endorsed the transfer of responsibilities in the return sector to local authorities, handing over outstanding matters to the Bosnian Ministry for Human Rights and Refugees. The CRPC mandate expired at the end of 2003, despite the fact that many property claims were still unresolved. By the end of 2006, about 300,000 Bosnians remain internally displaced, while many of those who returned continued to struggle to achieve and maintain acceptable living standards.

Conclusion

The idea that ethnic diversity should be not only preserved, but also encouraged by helping individuals displaced by the war to return home, has been slow to emerge. International agencies have balanced their humanitarian work with other priorities and objectives. The forced repatriation of refugees from European states was not motivated by humanitarian reasons, but by the desire to relieve the Western welfare system from the presence of Bosnian refugees. Instead of contributing to peace and democratic consolidation, in the short term forced repatriation exacerbated existing tensions. Confronted with the risk that internally displaced persons could undermine the peace process, international agencies reluctantly and belatedly made minority return a priority. Eventually, a set of property laws, combined with the returnees' own initiatives, made return possible on a scale that very few had ever expected. Respect for property rights and the rule of law promoted inclusion, equality, and universal principles of justice.

Property repossession, followed in many cases by the return home, contributed to the consolidation of the peace process by preventing the mass of Bosnian DPs from turning into a destabilising factor. As the case of Prijedor suggests, return improved inter-ethnic relations and helped to moderate domestic political dynamics. Return home might also have created a precedent discouraging the future perpetration of ethnic cleansing in other divided societies. At the same time, serious problems remain with regard to the sustainability of return. Returnees continue to face considerable discrimination, particularly when searching for employment, and many have sold their properties and moved again. As the international presence in Bosnia winds down, the question remains whether the Bosnian state will be able effectively to address the demands of Bosnian citizens and those of the incipient process of integration into European institutions.

7　From NATO to the EU

While the terrorist attacks of 11 September 2001 have drastically altered and redefined states' priorities worldwide, in particular those of the United States, the transformation of international policy towards Bosnia has been a matter of degrees instead of a dramatic U-turn. The country has been downgraded to a position of marginal importance in the hierarchy of international concerns. Bosnia finds herself in a context broadly similar to the one which surrounded the dissolution of Yugoslavia in the early 1990s. The United States has a low strategic interest, limited to a narrow concern for the possible presence of al-Qaeda cells. European institutions are expected to provide security and stability for the foreseeable future by extending political, military and economic guarantees to the entire Southeast European region. While history does not always repeat itself, sometimes it rhymes. A similar scenario of marginal US interest and growing European involvement could not prevent bloodshed breaking out in Bosnia in 1992. Today the EU is much better equipped to play a constructive role, but the long-term outcome remains in balance.

This chapter addresses the future prospects for Bosnia. First, it examines how European institutions might support further peace consolidation and democratisation by replacing the 'push' of the OHR with the 'pull' of European integration. The country's progressive inclusion into European institutions might have a long-term moderating and stabilising effect. At the same time, however, it cannot address the immediate, short-term issues that stand in the way of European integration. Thus, the second part of the chapter outlines the elements of a possible 'post-settlement settlement', a reform aimed at increasing Bosnian responsibility in domestic governance, and improving the efficiency of the Bosnian state in order to augment its ability to implement EU regulations, guarantee the rule of law, and fight crime and corruption. The further strengthening of the state is necessary to move Bosnia from Dayton to Europe, that is, from post-war stabilisation to political, economic and social development. That said, the Bosnian conundrum cannot be solved by changing the constitution alone. A renewed commitment to supporting civil society is also needed to ground Bosnia's future on more solid foundations. As the previous two chapters have shown, important domestic resources exist at the level of society that should be mobilised further.

Future prospects I: European horizons

American military and political disengagement from Bosnia has been slow but constant. In early 2001, US defence secretary Donald Rumsfeld had declared the US military role in Bosnia as completed, suggesting that the remaining 3,800 US troops in the country should be brought home. The 11 September 2001 attack on the United States provided an additional reason to reconsider America's role and presence, since troops could be needed elsewhere in the fight against terrorism. In mid-2002 the American contribution to the Bosnian peace operation became intertwined with the creation of the International Criminal Court (ICC), scheduled to come into operation by July 2002. The US threatened to withdraw its troops from UN peacekeeping missions, starting with the Bosnian one, if not granted immunity from prosecution by the ICC. The announcement provoked worried reactions in Bosnia,[1] and strong objections in Europe, where both the European Union (EU) and NATO tried to find alternatives to the US presence. The episode revealed how low Bosnia figures among US foreign policy priorities.

From Dayton to Brussels

Declining American interest went hand-in-hand with the international agencies' progressive downsizing in view of the completion of their mission. In 2005, the PICSB had set the goal of transforming OHR into a less intrusive EU-led mission. Since March 2002 the High Representative has held a 'double-hatted position' representing both the PIC and acting as the EU's special representative with the mandate to steer the EU integration process. The limited American interest, combined with the continuing downsizing and likely withdrawal of (some) international agencies from Bosnia raise questions about future prospects.

The uncertainties related to handing over governing responsibilities to local authorities suggests that, if the peace operation in its current form is likely to terminate soon, international influence on local-policy making will be maintained in a different form. The new mantra of international intervention aims at integrating the Balkans into Europe 'both formally, in terms of shared structures and institutions, and informally, in terms of shared norms and ideals' (CFR 2003: 3–4). The goal of extending Kant's perpetual peace to the region is sought through the extension of European institutions and norms. The EU, the PIC, and international think tanks almost unanimously suggest that the Europeanisation of Southeastern Europe and its integration in European institutions is *the* long-term solution for the Bosnian conundrum. According to the International Commission on the Balkans (ICB) there is no realistic alternative to Europeanisation. Either Southeastern Europe develops the conditions to join the EU, or the EU will have to accept running protectorates in its backyard for decades to come (ICB 2005: 11). The ICB argues in favour of enlargement over empire, suggesting the EU should commit itself to integrate the Balkans by 2014 – on the centenary of the outbreak of World War I.

International authorities in Bosnia share the long-term view of the desirability of Europeanisation. For former High Representative Wolfgang Petritsch,

'Bosnia and Herzegovina's future is clear. It can be summed up in one word: Europe ... my job was not to work on an exit strategy for the International Community, but on an entry strategy for BiH: BiH's entry into Europe' (2002b). Petritsch's successor Paddy Ashdown similarly endorsed the idea that Bosnia's future should and will be anchored in Europe: 'one thing unites all the citizens of BiH, whatever their nationality: a yearning for the prosperity and security summed up by the word "Europe"' (2004). The last OHR Mission Implementation Plan under Ashdown's leadership confirmed that the overriding objective of the international presence in the country is 'to ensure that Bosnia and Herzegovina is a peaceful, viable state on course to European integration' (OHR 2005a). The transition from Dayton to Brussels was also the top priority of Christian Schwarz-Schilling, and remains so for Miroslav Lajčák. Opinion polls regularly confirm a high level of popular support for the European project.

For the EU and its member states there are important reasons to commit to Bosnia's long-term survival and her inclusion in European institutions. One such reason is strategic. After the 2004 enlargement to twenty-five members, only Southeastern Europe remains waiting on the doorstep. The accession of Bosnia and her neighbours can guarantee a stability and peace that will be ultimately beneficial for the entire continent. In addition, symbolic and normative considerations suggest that securing Bosnia's stability and prosperity is not a choice but a necessity. As the EU continues the process of expansion eastward, and as immigrants of all ethnic origins continue to choose the Old Continent as their final destination, Europe will increasingly face the problem of constructively addressing growing pluralisation and diversity. The 'New Europe' is premised upon political integration, national interdependence, and mutual accommodation, precisely the values and norms that xenophobic nationalism in Bosnia wants to undermine. While Southeastern Europe has often been perceived as a hopeless land of violence and fragmentation and kept at arms' length because of its perceived incompatibility with European values and norms, today this region has a symbolic importance because of the similarity of the problems and prospects it shares with the EU.

This newly found interest in Southeastern Europe is reflected in an increasing European focus on an agenda of enlargement instead of post-war stabilisation. Through the Stabilisation and Association Process (SAP), launched in May 1999, the EU has promised Bosnia and the other countries in Southeastern Europe that they are 'potential candidates' for membership. The SAP involves several steps, including the establishment of a Consultative Taskforce, the drafting of a feasibility study on a Stabilisation and Association Agreement (SAA) and the negotiation and ratification of the agreement – which in turn opens the way for an application for EU membership. At the EU-Balkan Thessaloniki summit of June 2003, the EU explicitly affirmed that the future of the region lies in integration with European institutions and that accession will be dependent upon fulfilling the same requirements applied to Central European states. Significantly, in late 2004 responsibility for Southeastern Europe (including, in addition to Bosnia, Macedonia, Serbia, Montenegro and Kosovo) was transferred to the new EU Enlargement Commissioner, Olli Rehn.

A concrete EU presence is already visible, although Bosnians do not always recognise it as a step forward from previous international engagement. Bosnia joined the Council of Europe (CoE) in April 2002, but the implementation of post-accession commitments remains problematic. In 2004, the CoE's Parliamentary Assembly pointed out how OHR powers in the country are hardly compatible with basic human rights and democratic principles (CoE, 2004). The failure to revise the electoral law and to adopt an education law also came under scrutiny (Solioz 2005: 121). More visible to ordinary Bosnians is the presence of an EU police and military force. The EU Police Mission (EUPM) began its operations in January 2003 with the task of supporting the establishment of a 'sustainable, professional and multi-ethnic police force operating in accordance with best European and international standards'. Moreover, the EU has taken increasing responsibility for military matters. The war and continuing instability in Iraq has accelerated US disengagement from Southeastern Europe, creating the need for greater European assertiveness. In October 2003, the American administration and the EU announced the forthcoming end of the SFOR presence and its replacement with a European force (EUFOR). Bosnians reacted with a mix of indifference and worry, wondering about the effectiveness of a military force operating without a strong American component (Hećimović 2003). In December 2004, EUFOR took over peacekeeping duties from SFOR. Its mission, which was dubbed operation Althea, included soldiers from thirty-three countries and was under the command of a British general. Despite the rhetoric about bridging Bosnia into Europe, Althea's mandate is still focused on providing deterrence and compliance with the DPA, instead of taking into account how conditions have changed since 1995. The fight against organised crime, for example, has been dropped from EUFOR's objectives, raising worries that the European military presence is premised upon obsolete thinking (Griffith and Jelacić 2004).

European hopes

European institutions have the potential to overcome some of the limitations evidenced by more than a decade of OHR administration, in particular by favouring a process of domestic reform without the blatant and problematic use of the Bonn powers. Recently, the lure of membership in European political and economic bodies has had an important reforming and moderating influence in Central and Eastern European states, which in a few years successfully reformed their political and economic institutions and were able to access the EU en masse in 2004. The experience of these states suggests the EU integration process is crucial in order to commit all major political forces, regardless of their political orientation, to the goal of EU membership (ESI 2005a). Current EU candidates, such as Croatia, Turkey and Macedonia, have already made dramatic progress in strengthening democratic institutions, guaranteeing the protection of human rights and ethnic minorities, and reforming the economy. Senior British diplomat Robert Cooper (2004) has invented the term 'voluntary empire' to describe the positive impact of the process of EU integration on both the political systems and societies of candidate states.

European institutions could provide three important functions to Bosnia. First, as Ashdown (2003) put it, the 'push' of the OHR should gradually be replaced by the 'pull' of the EU as a reform force. Bosnia must implement a wide range of structural changes to be considered for association and eventual membership in European institutions. Membership prospects can embolden reformers within government and society, and perhaps more importantly, they can provoke a change in nationalists' priorities even in politically sensitive matters such as military issues. For example, the replacement of three separate armies with the creation of a Bosnian common defence ministry under civilian control was one of the requirements to join the NATO-sponsored Partnership for Peace. This prospect raised much resistance, particularly in the RS where the ruling parties feared that a common defence structure could threaten the survival of their Entity. When RS president Dragan Čavić announced in spring 2003 that he would cooperate with SFOR to meet the conditions for Bosnia's access to the Partnership for Peace, he did so for tactical reasons. After two scandals, one of internal espionage and the other related to the selling of military equipment to Iraq, the RS president judged there was an urgent need to improve his Entity's legitimacy. But regardless of the immediate motivation for this decision, Čavić could justify it as a necessary step in the process towards European integration – a goal shared by Serbs as much as by the other groups. Similar considerations eventually convinced the RS leadership to arrest and deliver the first Serb indicted war criminal and deliver him to the ICTY in 2005.[2]

Second, European governance principles can contribute to improving policy-making and strengthening Bosnian institutions. The principle of 'subsidiarity', whereby decisions are taken at the lowest possible level and constant checks are made as to whether action at the national level is justified in light of the possibilities available at the cantonal or municipal level, has been adopted for European-level governance and could benefit Bosnia as well. The European Union itself is an important example of how sovereignty can be shared and pooled at the supranational level – an arrangement that helps improve domestic governance. In Bosnia the implementation of European governance and human rights standards and the country's inclusion into European institutions is likely to depoliticise some of the issues that Bosnians find difficult to compromise on and narrow the margins of disagreement among the parties. For example, the EU has demanded the introduction of a statewide customs administration and a value-added tax (VAT) as preconditions for signing an SAA. The introduction of VAT is an important state building measure, since it provides the state with an indispensable financial basis. The November 2004 parliamentary debate on tax matters revealed how Bosnian MPs have begun addressing such matters in terms of their economic and social impact, instead of arguing along predictable and hard to reconcile ethnic lines. The lines of political confrontation were drawn between government and opposition, not on the basis of ethnic belonging (Skrbić 2004). If this debate is an anticipation of what might occur in the future, then there is some reason for optimism about Bosnia's prospects. The inevitably difficult decisions required to comply with EU requirements are increasingly adopted and justified as a condition for joining Europe and enjoying the benefits of membership, not as a concession to former enemies.

Third, the EU can stimulate both respect for existing international borders and regional cooperation. For the best part of the post-Dayton period, it was the United States which applied pressure on Serbia and Croatia to respect Bosnia's political integrity. For example, in April 1998 the High Representative reported that illegal wartime structures had not been dissolved and that real power continued to reside outside official channels and institutions. He complained that Croatia's continuing support for their ethnic kin in Bosnia significantly weakened the Federation. The United States pressured Tudman to use his leverage to ensure Bosnian Croat compliance with the DPA. The United States' threat to block much-needed World Bank and IMF loans to Croatia proved convincing, and Tudman moderated his public statements. With America's systematic disengagement, the EU will need to apply similar pressure. For Serbia and Croatia, the prospect of integration in European institutions is more important than the partition of Bosnia between the two and the creation of greater Serbia and/ or greater Croatia. Significantly, since Croatia has applied for EU membership in early 2003, its nationalist HDZ-led government has gone to great lengths to reassure sceptical EU institutions that the country's reform will proceed apace. Finally, not only can the EU contribute to regional stability, but it can also create incentives for all states in the region to engage in democratic, transparent, and collaborative governance. European funds could require aspiring EU members to devise multi-year development plans collaboratively to address trans-border issues, such as the fight against organised crime, illegal trade and human trafficking.

In the long term, if integration in the EU will make borders less important, the redrawing of the regional political map will lose its appeal, particularly in view of the human, economic and social costs likely to be involved in the process. The answer to the problem of borders is not to redraw them, as historical determinists argue, but to make them increasingly irrelevant. 'Soft borders' can encourage regional and municipal cooperation across dividing lines. The experience of the Igman Initiative confirms that such cooperation can develop from the grass roots and thus be more locally flavoured and endorsed (see the fifth section of Chapter 5). As Bogdan Denitch (1996: 230) perceptively concludes, 'the softer the future borders of the states that emerge from the former Yugoslavia, the less it will matter on which side of the frontier one finds itself'. In January 2006 the EU proposed the creation of a regional free trade agreement among Bosnia, Serbia, Montenegro, Croatia, Albania and Macedonia (EU 2006a). In April of the same year these countries began negotiations on the agreement. If implemented, this proposal might further depoliticise border issues, while favouring legitimate travel and economic development.

European doubts

While membership within Europe's political, economic and security structures is expected to provide the long-term answer to the Bosnian conundrum, there are also reasons for concern. The spring 2005 rejection of the EU constitution by French and Dutch voters has poured cold water on the aspirations of would-be members. For many commentators and European policy-makers, the rejection of the constitution signified also the rejection of enlargement – complicating and probably postponing the prospect of EU accession for Southeastern European countries. Bosnian politicians have reacted by ignoring European demands. The day after the French referendum on the EU constitution, the RS parliament rejected once again a police reform package demanded by European institutions. Only after the EU demonstrated concretely its commitment to the region was it able to regain political leverage and stimulate the domestic endorsement of reform. The RS parliament accepted a very similar package of police reform in October 2005, agreeing to give control over police matters to state-level institutions, creating functional police regions (even crossing the IEBL when necessary) and removing political influence from operational matters. The RS decision came shortly after the EU decided to launch admission talks with Croatia and negotiations on an SAA with Serbia – leaving Bosnia the only country in the region without the prospect of membership (Moore 2005).

Despite the EU's renewed activism, the promise to extend Europe's stability and prosperity to the region remains quite insubstantial. After the rejection of its would-be constitution, the EU has cautiously confirmed its readiness to accept new states, but specified that future admissions will be granted on a country-by-country basis and not in groups. The fulfilment of specific criteria for admission will be monitored more closely, and the EU is likely to be less accommodating towards potential members. At the EU-Balkan meeting in Salzburg in March 2006, EU foreign ministers confirmed a tougher line on enlargement. They watered down previous commitments with reference to the EU's 'absorption capacity' and to an 'internal European debate on the future of enlargement' as potential barriers to accession (EU 2006a). In November 2006 the European Commission presented its 'enlargement strategy', including a 'special report on the EU's capacity to integrate new members'. This capacity is assessed on the basis of 'whether the EU can take in new members ... without jeopardizing the political and policy objectives established by the Treaties' (EU 2006b: 17).

Crucially, because the EU's 'absorption' or 'integration' capacity cannot be influenced by candidate states, meeting EU criteria might not be enough for accession. As a result, all Bosnian politicians, and Serb ones in particular, are increasingly tempted to renege on previous commitments: police reform has stalled again, disagreement over the distribution of revenue from VAT has arisen and constitutional amendments failed to reach the necessary two-thirds majority in parliament in April 2006 (see next section). By the end of 2006, six key reforms were holding up the conclusion of an SAA: full cooperation with the ICTY, implementation of police reform, adoption and implementation of a public broadcasting law, proper financing of state-level ministries, reform of the public administration, and the creation of an internal market across the entire country (EU 2006c). This context, dominated by EU soul-searching and Bosnian delaying tactics, is likely to lead to an increase in bilateral foreign policy, with countries such as Germany, Austria, Russia and Italy resurrecting their traditional and pernicious interest-based approach to the region.

Even if the EU was able to reassert a clear accession strategy, for Bosnia the prospect of inclusion in European institutions remains very distant. The completion of nineteen Road Map criteria between 2001 and 2003 led to an EU feasibility study in late 2003. The study identified sixteen areas needing reform to comply with the SAP and start negotiations on an SAA. The 'pull' of European integration led Bosnia's parties to agree on most reforms with no need for OHR to impose any laws or state building reforms required by the feasibility study (Recchia 2007: 25). Talks on an SAA formally opened in November 2005 and began in January 2006. Once an SAA is signed, a ten-year transition period will be needed before its implementation. The incorporation of over 100,000 pages of EU legislation will also require a long time. The EU, however, has not shown any interest in lowering the standards of admission,[3] thus raising fears that Bosnia will be kept in limbo. According to one calculation, if Bosnia proceeds to apply for EU membership immediately after the signing of an SAA, it will need four more years to be accepted as an official candidate and ten to be admitted to the EU (ESI 2005b). In the meantime, the economic and social gap between early candidates for EU admission (such as Croatia) and underdeveloped regions (such as Bosnia and Kosovo) will increase. The new European funding mechanism for the region, the Instrument of Pre-Accession (IPA), which came into effect on 1 January 2007, differentiates between candidate countries (Croatia and Macedonia) and potential candidate countries (in addition to Bosnia, Albania, Montenegro and Serbia). The paradox of the EU assistance programme is that the most advanced countries get the lion's share of EU assistance, leaving laggards like Bosnia further behind (ibid.).

However, the logic of demanding Bosnia's reform and development prior to extending the European carrot is far from compelling. European integration is a condition for continuing reform and development, instead of the other way round. In practice, reform, development and European integration should develop hand-in-hand to reinforce each other (Batt 2004; ESI 2005b). If not, the long-term time frame required by the accession process will continue to complicate the short-term local endorsement of reforms, since Bosnian leaders will be unable to muster support for their pro-European choices by delivering tangible results to their constituencies. A further risk is to unrealistically raise expectations among Bosnian citizens about the future benefits of membership, with little assurance of positive developments. The difficulty of delivering on promises explains Bosnians' widespread disillusionment with the EU. To cite the title of Danis Tanovic's remarkable 2002 film, Bosnia is in a 'no man's land', neither 'here' (in Europe, sharing and enjoying the benefits of membership), nor 'there' (in the Orient – symbolic more than geographical location of despotism and violence). Less stringent conditions for entering the SAP may be needed to sustain local interest, and provide Bosnia with resources to catch up and join Europe. In short, it is imperative that intermediate rewards for both Bosnian politicians and citizens be introduced, linking the adoption of difficult reforms (such as changing the Dayton constitution) to tangible, short-term benefits (Recchia 2007: 30).

Augmenting and improving EU engagement in Bosnia and more broadly in the broader Southeastern European region would be a positive but still incomplete step. As long as 'Europeanisation' is structured around the idea of the increasing involvement of the EU in Southeastern Europe with the intent of socialising this region into European norms, it reflects the same top-down approach to regional development based on external initiatives that characterised international intervention for the best part of the last decade. This approach makes Bosnia and the other countries in the region once again the recipient of strategies developed elsewhere, and not always endorsed by all. In 1999 Germany was particularly instrumental in launching the Stability Pact – heralded as the new Marshall Plan for the region. The pact's inefficiency in providing a framework and a sense of direction for international involvement led the EU to launch its SAP. As the rivalry between the two organisms suggests, institutional infighting might not diminish when international intervention becomes more squarely 'European'. Furthermore, to the extent that Bosnia's performance is measured only in terms of fulfilling the requirements for EU membership, there is a risk that reform will miss addressing the key domestic questions which are unique to this country, in particular the need to develop indigenous capacities for conflict management. Although long-term mechanisms are indispensable, and represent an important step forwards from the crisis-prone approach to intervention which characterised most of the post-Dayton period, these mechanisms are more likely to be effective if they are grounded in domestic political processes. Bosnians should be able to develop their own priorities, identify issues left unaddressed by the process of EU integration, and prepare strategies to address them.

In sum, the uncertainties surrounding European involvement and the limits inherent in the top-down Europeanisation process call for some caution. Until Bosnia is well on her way to Euro-Atlantic integration, European institutions can only have a disciplinary influence on Bosnian internal dynamics, not a reforming one. European discipline combines macro and micro dimensions of power. At the macro level, the economic and political power of the European giant can induce some degree of compliance with European demands, but will not generate a process of redefinition of the nature and purpose of the Bosnian state. At the micro level, constant European surveillance through a hierarchy of supervisors (international financial institutions, security organisations, and bilateral donors) might encourage self-discipline among unruly Bosnians. Like Jeremy Bentham's panopticon, surveillance practices are aimed at maximising restraint, developing reasoned (pro-EU) behaviour, and keeping in check unregulated (nationalist) emotions. Yet, surveillance is a weak strategy if it does not quickly evolve into a concrete offer of positive inducements. In short, the sooner Bosnian can be upgraded to EU candidate status, the sooner a deeper reform process is likely to take root.

Future prospects II: towards a 'post-settlement settlement'

In order for the country to enter Euro-Atlantic institutions, Bosnia's de facto international protectorate must be scrapped. The successful transition from international rule via OHR decrees to domestic ownership and integration into European institutions depends on the creation and/or strengthening of a range of state institutions effective in solving evolving policy issues and addressing societal demands. In light of the demands of the European integration process, Bosnia needs a 'post-settlement settlement' (Du Toit 2003) to overcome the institutional deficiencies of the DPA and strengthen the state, establish reliable civilian control of the military and create better conditions for domestic civil society, allowing it to have a more significant impact on political and social life.[4] The means to achieve these goals are to be found in dialogue and debate among all of the parties involved – international and domestic.

Institutional obstacles and the need for change

The main challenge post-Dayton Bosnia faces is overcoming the weak and divided nature of the state. Institutions have proved unable to foster economic development, build a legal and political framework in which civil society can consolidate itself and stop the proliferation of corruption, illegal trade and smuggling. In particular, consociationalism's propensity for inefficiency, bureaucratisation and patronage along ethnic lines has suited the interests of the political/economic elite that emerged from the war, and precluded the emergence and affirmation of civic-minded political and social forces. Furthermore, the ethnic character of Bosnian institutions subjugated the rights of Bosnian citizens to ethnic belonging. As the Constitutional Court has recognised in the constituent peoples case, ethnically defined Entities complicate the exercise of individual human rights, particularly opportunities for refugees and DPs permanently to return to areas where they constitute a minority. The 'thin' central state established at Dayton created a human rights vacuum that made law enforcement subject to the will of the Entities, the most likely abusers of the rights of returnees. As the Venice Commission (2005: para. 26) concluded, under these conditions Bosnia will not be able to progress towards European integration.

The problems related to the inefficient, discriminatory and unsustainable character of the state are widely recognised by Bosnians of all different ethnic backgrounds and political persuasions. Many Bosnians concede that the DPA was needed to end the war but will need reform to address changing conditions. The widespread perception that the DPA is a temporary arrangement contributes to perpetuating limited dedication to local institutions. The indigenous political process has been further discredited by years of nationalist corruption and international rule by decree. In this context, citizens have little or no expectations from politics and politicians. As the European Stability Initiative points out, this attitude creates a self-reinforcing dynamic: 'when citizens expect little from the political process, they make little effort to form into interest groups and place demands on politicians' (ESI 2004b: 7). As a result, the demand for domestically generated reforms is stifled, despite the apparent need for such reforms. When a debate about the shape and direction of the Bosnian state began as a result of the constituent peoples case, the impatience of international agencies blocked it. Despite their hyper-interventionist role, international agencies have demonstrated a strong status quo bias, preferring to preserve the current institutional and societal structures while promoting piecemeal reform.

There is little doubt that any future debate about reform will focus on how to strengthen the state and improve the efficiency and legitimacy of domestic institutions. The construction of a functional state is not an end in itself, but a means to enable the reconstruction of a broken and divided society (Bose 2002: 281). Furthermore, Bosnian institutions must possess the necessary legislative powers to create the conditions for an SAA, implement it, and ensure compliance with broader international obligations. The challenge Bosnia faces is to centralise enough power to make this possible, without marginalising or excluding any of its peoples and citizens. The Bosnian state can only be distinctively post-Westphalian in the sense that no single ethnic or national group should dominate it. A decade of post-Dayton experience suggests that such centralisation is not necessarily going to be opposed as long as it is premised on the inclusion of all relevant actors (and not as a tool for domination of the numerically stronger party – the Bosniaks) and is combined with self-government prerogatives of each group in areas where agreement is not at hand. Of course, there is no guarantee that Bosnian political elites will ever accept and commit to this goal. However, the eventual benefits of European integration and the possibility for substantial and meaningful careers in the central government might make Bosnian leaders more likely to become stakeholders in the preservation and development of the country. The slow growth from three to nine statewide ministries and the increase in the competence of the Bosnian state's agencies makes non-participation in these institutions a self-defeating strategy. The more the state develops its authority over an increasing number of policy areas, the more it will provide incentives to all groups to participate in joint institutions.

While overcoming the limits of the elite-based consociational framework should be the goal of institutional restructuring, it is important to keep a clear distinction between a desirable and a durable outcome. The preservation of the RS hardly qualifies as a desirable solution. As Bosniak politicians never fail to point out, the very existence of this Entity is based on massive human rights violations, in particular the expulsion of the non-Serb population during the war. Despite having achieved one of their main wartime goals through the creation of an ethnically pure Entity, Serb politicians have often defied international pressure to comply with various clauses of the peace agreement. Holbrooke has often remarked that had he known about the Serbs' lack of willingness to compromise, he would probably not have used his influence to stop the war when it was turning to the advantage of the Bosniak/Croat alliance. But the RS does exist and cannot be wished away. The Bosniaks' verbal attacks against the legitimacy of the Entity, often carried out with the sympathetic attitude of international agencies, have reinforced a siege mentality among Serbs that plays into the hands of nationalist parties and their extremist policies. Given that international agencies have not shown the slightest interest in taking any concrete initiative aimed at dissolving the RS, it is only self-defeating to question the legitimacy of that Entity. Instead, international agencies should refrain from verbal endorsement of anti-RS sentiments. In short, the preservation of the RS might not be a desirable outcome but it is the one likely to prevail, since any attempt to abolish it would probably be met with a vital interest veto from the Serb representatives.

Moreover, the Serbs remain generally in favour of seceding from Bosnia rather than accepting a centralised Bosnian state. Following Montenegro's successful referendum on independence from Serbia in May 2006, RS prime minister Milorad Dodik demanded the right to hold a similar referendum on secession. However, because 2006 was an election year, this demand owed as much to electoral posturing as to a realistic assessment of the possibility of gaining independence. Furthermore, despite the presence of strong secessionist feelings, many Serbs are willing to allow for some degree of state building as long as the survival of their Entity is not in jeopardy. Serbs' initial total rejection of statewide institutions has softened over time to a significantly higher degree of acceptance. While more than 50 per cent of Serbs still prefer either an independent RS or to secede from Bosnia and join Serbia, the number of those who support the Bosnian state has increased fourfold since 1996 (UNDP 2002b: 29). An increasing number of Serbs see the central institutions as not incompatible with their own self-governing structures. On the contrary, the presence of self-governing institutions makes them relatively more secure about their place in the country, and more open to the possibility that some governing functions could be transferred from the Entities to the central state.

The situation is different in the Federation, which was created in 1994 on the assumption that the Serbs would eventually join as an equal partner in a tri-communal state. The fact that the Serbs were granted their own semi-independent republic at Dayton left the Croats in an unequal and unbalanced position, providing the HDZ with the possibility of skilfully and regularly exploiting the real or supposed grievances of ordinary Croats. As long as the HDZ can play the ethnic card by raising the spectre of Croats' marginalisation, it will regularly outbid more moderate political parties, obtain the support of the electorate, and keep the peace building process unstable. However, even among Croats there are signs of important changes. Since the signing of the DPA, the number of Croats favouring 'a state of equal citizens and people' is larger than the number of those preferring the preservation of Croat parallel institutions (UNDP 2002b: 29). Croats' fear of becoming a powerless minority in a state dominated by Bosniaks and Serbs does not necessarily require the creation of a third Croat Entity, but can be softened with a reorganisation of the state. Moreover, since the post-Tudman government in Croatia has rescinded the main political and military links with their ethnic kin in Bosnia, Croats are more willing to accept a political future within the Bosnian state. In short, reform is needed and not necessarily opposed by either Serbs or Croats, the two groups suspicious of attempts at state centralisation. Four broad areas of reform can be identified, addressing institutional, electoral, military and civil society issues.

Improving domestic governance

As we shall see shortly, a package of constitutional reforms was discussed by the Bosnian parliament in April 2006, but narrowly failed to reach the two-thirds majority necessary for its adoption. Discussion on reform was triggered initially by the European Stability Initiative (ESI)'s proposal to eliminate the Federation. ESI envisioned that the current five layers of governance could be replaced by just three, turning the Bosnian state into a federal system with central, regional, and municipal governments (ESI 2004a). The new institutional setup would consist of the current ten cantons, in addition to the RS and the district of Brčko, which would acquire a standing equal to that of the other cantons. The elimination of the Federation could bring about several positive changes. Administratively, it would allow for the centralisation of all the prerogatives now invested in the Entity, and thus strengthen the central state. Politically, it would remove a continuing source of tension between Bosniaks and Croats, and probably undermine one of the reasons for Croats' radicalism. Financially, it would improve the state's budgetary status by reducing its enormous spending in sustaining public institutions and administrators – currently set at around 56 per cent of GDP, compared to the regional average of 40 per cent (ESI 2004b: 18). Finally, the elimination of the Federation would not involve the drawing of any new boundary and it would allow further development of what has been established in years of post-settlement institution building. Over time, the twelve cantons could also lose any ethnic label and become one layer of governance for all citizens regardless of their ethnic belonging. In other words, the creation of a federal system based on territorial instead of ethnic principles could reduce the salience of ethnicity and become a useful conflict management tool.

Other proposals have been advanced. In March 2005, the Venice Commission of the Council of Europe issued an important opinion about the constitutional structure of the Bosnian state, arguing that constitutional reform is indispensable (Venice Commission 2005). The commission pointed out the incompatibility of the Bonn powers with the rule of law, suggested that such powers should be gradually abandoned and emphasised the need for reform to strengthen the state and make it more efficient. According to the commission, the long-term aim of constitutional reform is to move from a state based on peoples to a state based on citizens. To achieve this goal, a number of changes are deemed crucial: the transfer of responsibilities from the Entities to the central state, the streamlining of decision-making procedures, especially with regard to the vital interest veto, and the reform of the composition and election of the presidency and the House of Peoples.

Following the Venice Commission's opinion, a debate about constitutional reform among Bosnia's political actors formally began. Throughout 2005, a constitutional working group met eight times – the last two occasions being in November in Brussels and then in Washington DC (Hitchner 2006). International organisations and civil servants were instrumental in facilitating the meetings. Retired US diplomat and former Deputy High Representative Donald Hayes was at the forefront of the reform effort, also facilitated by the US Institute of Peace and the American NGO the Dayton Peace Accord Project. Holbrooke and other negotiators for the DPA expressed support for the talks as an opportunity to correct the limits of the document which emerged from Dayton. In November, on the eve of Dayton's tenth anniversary, the working group endorsed a constitutional plan aimed at strengthening the central government and national parliament at the expense of the Entities – which would nonetheless retain their place in the constitution. The new Bosnian state would consist of a unicameral parliament in which the exercise of veto rights would be limited. A largely ceremonial president would be elected directly, and decision-making powers would be centralised in a single cabinet headed by a prime minister. To meet the demands of European integration, two more ministries would be created: a ministry of agriculture and a ministry of technology, science and environmental protection. Stronger human rights mechanisms to strengthen individual human rights vis-à-vis group rights would also be established. After public and parliamentary debate, the reform package was expected to be voted by parliament in March 2006 – a date dictated by the need to implement the changes prior to the October elections and put in place a new government with strengthened powers for the next four years.

The amendments presented to parliament for adoption closely reflected the agreement reached in Washington. The amendments envisioned the reform of five main parts of the constitution:

- on human rights and fundamental freedoms;
- on the responsibilities of and relations between the Entities and state institutions;
- on the Parliamentary Assembly;
- on the Presidency;
- on the Council of Ministers.

The amendments aimed to reduce significantly the power of the Entities vis-à-vis the government via the adoption of the three main changes: the Entity-based national election for the presidency would be scrapped, the Entities would not be able to recover powers ceded to the state without the consent of the government, and the government would be allowed to negotiate, adopt and implement all measures necessary to comply with commitments to the EU (CWG 2006). The three-member presidency would be replaced by a single president and two vice presidents elected by parliament.

In a new opinion, the Venice Commission hailed the changes, welcoming the granting of increased powers to the state level, the strengthening of the Council of Ministers and the House of Representatives and the reduced role of the collective presidency and the House of Peoples. At the same time, the commission pointed out that the changes envisioned are still of a piecemeal nature and do not arise from a systematic reflection on the needs of the country. In particular, the new human rights text was found insufficient. The broad and ambitious catalogue of rights was judged as too vague and 'not really destined to be applied by courts to concrete cases' (Venice Commission 2006: para. 82). Accordingly, the commission advised against its adoption.

It is an irony of Bosnian political development that, when the reform package failed to produce a two-thirds majority in parliament in April 2006 (twenty-six deputies voted in favour and sixteen against), the new human rights text was one of the few reforms eventually adopted. Bosnian politicians often see human rights as peripheral and inconsequential because, contrary to political and administrative office, human rights do not offer room for patronage. Accordingly, this is one of the few areas where political parties were able to reach an agreement. Substantively, the reform fiasco high-lighted the deep divisions still affecting the country (CEIS 2006). The 'no' votes were mostly cast by the deputies from HDZ 1990, a breakaway party which split from the HDZ earlier the same month, and which argued in favour of the creation of a third Croat Entity. Serb politicians, including RS prime minister Milorad Dodik, offered support for Croat calls for a third Entity, calculating that it would cement the RS position in the current institutional framework. The other negative votes came from the Party for Bosnia (SBiH) of Haris Silajdžić, who reasoned that rejecting the reforms as imposed by international agencies to consolidate the existence of the RS would help him in the upcoming elections. Accordingly, he condemned the amendments as cosmetic because of the failure to abolish the two Entities system (Skrbić and Vogel 2006).

The failure of constitutional reform exposed two limits of the international approach. First, because international officials feared a backlash from nationalist voters, the early stages of the negotiations were veiled in secrecy, a circumstance which did not create a sense of ownership among the general public. The fact that an agreement on the principles of reform was reached under American pressure during an event in Washington marking the tenth anniversary of the DPA did not help Bosnians feel they were in the driver's seat of reform. Second, throughout the post-Dayton period international agencies have often let the Bosniak leadership take control of the state building agenda. Serbs and Croats willingly limited their engagement in central institutions – preferring instead to run their ethnic enclaves. As a result, state building remained primarily a Bosniak project, and was viewed with suspicion by the other communities.

Whether this or a similar reform package will win parliamentary support in the future remains unclear. Perhaps only the influence of the EU, through a set of economic incentives, can help recalcitrant politicians to adopt much-needed reforms. Ultimately, the main lesson arising from the failed reform attempt is that Bosnia's stateness problem cannot be addressed simply by changing the constitution – desirable as this goal might be. Bosnians lack a common sense of belonging, and political divisions often reflect this social reality. A process of constitutional reform will be successful only to the extent that it goes hand-in-hand with social development and the strengthening of a less conflictual sense of identity and belonging among Bosnian citizens.

Reforming the election law

As noted, the composition and methods of the presidential and House of Peoples elections have been the subject of extensive criticism because of their discriminatory nature. The Venice Commission suggested replacing the current three-member presidency with a single president with limited executive powers, elected indirectly by the Parliamentary Assembly with a wide majority. A rotation rule ensuring that the president may not belong to the same constituent people as his or her predecessor could build support for this solution (Venice Commission 2005).

The 2006 constitutional packaged included an electoral reform along the lines proposed by the Venice Commission, but was rejected along with the other constitutional measures. Unlikely as it might be because of nationalist opposition, the future adoption of an integrationist formula for the election of the presidency would be a positive state building measure. Cross-voting favours moderate candidates who possess appeal beyond their own ethnic communities (Reilly 2001). The 2006 election experience suggests that cross-voting can have important moderating effects. Željko Komšić, an ethnic Croat and an SDP member, was elected to the tri-partite presidency as a representative of the Croat people. Komšić fought in the 1992–95 war for the BiH army rather than the Croatian Defence Council. His opponents (largely HDZ supporters) accused him of being the choice of Bosniaks, not Croats, since he failed to win a majority of votes in any of the cantons with a Croat majority. This outcome was possible because in the Federation both Bosniak and Croat candidates appeared on one ballot, giving voters the right to choose between the two regardless of their ethnicity.

It is undeniable that Komšić won the vote of Bosniaks who did not wish to choose Silajdžić. After he blocked constitutional reform, Silajdžić was seen by many as an opportunistic politician willing to trade Bosnia's future to ensure his own political success. In other words, Komšić was chosen by Bosnian citizens in the Federation voting not as ethnic Croats or Bosniaks, but as voters choosing among political alternatives. On the same ground, these voters preferred Komšić to more politically extreme candidates, most notably the one put forward by the HDZ. As discussed in Chapter 3, consociationalists condemn this kind of ethnic cross-voting because it supposedly undermines the legitimacy of leaders and their capacity to govern on behalf of their group. Instead, consociationalists believe that voters should pick their own ethnic leader without external influence (Bose 2002: 239). This view, also held by HDZ members and supporters who complained about Komšić's victory, rests on weak grounds. To begin with, the controversy would not have even arisen had voters chosen the HDZ candidate over Komšić. This raises the question of whether only hard line nationalists can represent their own ethnic group or whether political moderates such as Komšić are legitimate choices. Clearly, the logic of representation would be turned upside down if only hard liners were legitimate options.

More serious is a second type of criticism of cross-voting, that is, the fact that numerically smaller groups cannot exercise the same degree of influence in the choice of political representatives of other groups. For example, the creation of a nationwide electoral base for the election of the three-member presidency (a key adjustment in the direction of an effective integrationist approach) can be criticised on the grounds that it would give an unfair advantage to the Bosniaks, allowing them to have a disproportionate influence in the selection of the two non-Bosniak members of the presidency. However, even this objection is not entirely convincing. Bosniaks are the relative majority in the country and therefore it would not be an unrepresentative outcome if their votes weighed comparatively more in determining political outcomes. On the contrary, one could argue that a collective presidency elected by all Bosnian citizens would be even more legitimate because it would be more representative. That said, in order to minimise nationalist opposition to this formula, cross-voting could even be adjusted to have the same effect on each community regardless of its relative size – as argued by Loizides and Keskiner (2004) in their analysis of the potential moderating effects of cross-voting in Cyprus.

Making war obsolete

Throughout the post-DPA period a major source of tension and disagreement among the parties has been the presence and role of the armed forces. The DPA permitted the Entities to preserve their own armies. An initial post-Dayton military build-up of the Bosniak army created a situation of equilibrium among the parties that was successful in preventing the outbreak of a new war. The fact that such a military build-up occurred while the presence of NATO troops discouraged the return to violence makes it impossible to assess whether stability was achieved by a domestic military balance of power or by the foreign military deterrent. Nevertheless, the progressive downsizing of military personnel since the signing of the DPA has reduced the armies' size but has not reduced their fighting ability. This poses risks to long-term stability, which is likely to be secured only when the very capacity to wage war is no longer available.

The problems raised by the presence of three ethnic armies have turned Bosnia into a 'security welfare state'[5] dependent on foreign troops for its own survival. The Dayton framework has not encouraged the Bosnian government and the governments of the Entities to invest in creating the military and policing capacity necessary to make the country stand on its own. This is not only because they want foreign powers to bear the costs of such investment, but also because the more local parties develop self-governing institutions and structures, the closer the day international patrons will declare the mission successful and leave. But the three main groups all have an interest in keeping foreign forces stationed in the country. Since the signing of the DPA, NATO's patrolling of the IEBL has provided an invaluable security service to the RS – a practically indefensible Entity. In fact, the closure of the Posavina corridor around Brčko would break off the two halves of the Entity and make them extremely vulnerable. Because elements of the Bosniak leadership have intermittently toyed with the idea of a possible military solution to the Bosnian conundrum, some of the worries that exist in the RS seem justified. Thus, the departure of foreign troops would create a potential security gap.

At the same time, while Bosniaks might be in the position to inflict short-term revenge upon former enemies, their long-term survival is intertwined with international political and military guarantees concerning the preservation of Bosnia as an independent and unitary state (although internally divided). Croats have less explicit advantages from the international presence. It is perhaps not surprising that the biggest challenge to the DPA came from them in 2001. Their demand for a third Entity or re-cantonisation of the country signalled their discontent and the possibility of additional protests. But even Croats can find in the international military presence a long-term reassurance that Serb expansionism will be prevented. In short, the presence of three armies is a continuing source of instability and a reason for perpetuating the international presence.

Only an imaginative solution to this problem will guarantee long-term security. As we have seen, the EU has demanded the creation of a joint command for the three Bosnian armies. While this development might be an improvement on the previous situation, it might not be enough. Two Entity armies under a joint command do not erase the ethnic character of the different units but dangerously perpetuate them. Other alternatives could be explored. Bogdan Denitch (1996: 168) suggested that Bosnia and the surrounding region should become a military-free zone. A different and perhaps more achievable proposal is gradually to incorporate both the Federation and the RS armies into NATO, and have this organisation guarantee the long-term stability of the country. This solution would create an arrangement similar to the one established in the aftermath of World War II in West Germany, where the German military was fully integrated into NATO.

In the transition period to Bosnia's entry into NATO, a short-term solution is to adopt for military matters what has been successful for political/institutional ones: foreign nationals could be appointed as members of the central military command to create a 'joint sovereignty' arrangement of a kind successful in a number of other Bosnian institutions. Of course, the presence of foreign nationals is no guarantee of long-term stability, but would provide greater transparency and civilian control over the armed forces. In the long term, the reduction of military spending is indispensable to free up resources for economic and social development. Despite post-settlement military downsizing, Bosnia remains the country with the highest military spending in the world in relation to its GDP. Defence spending still absorbs a high share of Entity budgets – approximately 6 per cent of GDP – compared with an EU average of 1.5 per cent.

Furthermore, Bosnia needs to reduce the availability and possible circulation of weapons. It is estimated that twelve weapons sites and twenty-eight ammunition depots hold more than 300,000 small and light weapons and tens of millions of rounds of ammunition (SEESAC 2004). The reduction of

Bosnia's armed forces to 10,000 men has raised questions about how to secure the safety of storage sites and how to dispose of excess weapons. Conflicting international interests complicate the search for a solution. Most EU member states and international agencies want the weapons destroyed, fearing that such weapons might end up, via the grey market, in other conflict areas. By contrast, the United States supports a policy of selling weapons to those countries enjoying a close relationship with the Pentagon. Since 2002, weapons and ammunition have been exported not only to the US but also to the United Kingdom and Israel. The Pentagon also arranged the secret shipment of tens of thousands of weapons from Bosnia to Iraq. The weapons were supposed to arm the fledging Iraqi military, but no tracking mechanism was put in place to ensure they would not fall into the wrong hands (AI 2006b). More importantly, from the point of view of Bosnian security, export schemes of this kind undermine projects aimed at destroying weapons, since Bosnian authorities at all levels are reluctant to surrender weapons that might draw in money.

Sustaining civil society

State building measures involving constitutional changes, electoral reform and military restructuring could also benefit Bosnian civil society as a whole. Because civil society organisations have no material power (such as control over the use of force and the state's repressive apparatus), their influence in the political process relies on alternative mechanisms. As human rights groups worldwide know very well, their impact on the political process largely depends on the presence of a functioning and accountable state and on the rule of law. Not only does the absence of a functioning state complicate the enforcement of individual human rights, but it also diminishes the effectiveness of domestic human rights groups pursuing a broad public policy agenda. The strengthening of the state creates an indispensable domestic interlocutor for these groups. It is not civil society that creates the foundation of a strong and legitimate state, but it is the presence of representative and responsive state institutions that permits civil society to develop (Belloni 2008).

State building is only one part of the civil society building strategy. Bosnian civil society organisations need also to become progressively less dependent on foreign resources for their funding. Civil society organisations are unlikely to be an expression of grass roots democracy and inter-ethnic reconciliation when they are more accountable to their international donors than their local constituencies. By providing local civil society groups with the money and resources to address needs in their own communities, international agencies might end up, albeit unwittingly, controlling local groups' agendas. An alternative approach should seek to stimulate the agenda, not to create it or control it. The positive experience with the Bulldozer Initiative (see Chapter 5), among others, shows the soundness of this approach.

While there is no clear-cut solution to organisations' dependency on their donors, it is at least possible to imagine alternatives that would improve the workings of Bosnian organisations. One simple but far-reaching initiative would be to make funding available for projects with a time frame longer than the current six months to one year period. Funding cycles should be at least three years long, with periodic progress assessments. Over time, the solution to the problem of organisations' dependency on foreign resources is to generate domestic financial support, a very difficult task given the current low level of economic development. In the short term, the creation of a Bosnian Civil Society Foundation with enough resources to fund at least some high profile and potentially controversial initiatives would also be an important positive development. The creation of such a foundation was proposed shortly after the end of the war (Smillie 1996: 15–21), but never materialised into an effective engine for civil society development. Instead, due to Bosnia's legal jungle, the foundation had to register in the Netherlands.

The most important reform should address the very approach international agencies adopt in their civil society support programmes. As Chapters 5 and 6 argued, international agencies often treat Bosnian society as a blank slate, ignoring the existence of local capacities. The prevailing approach to civil society development downplays the existence of local resources and knowledge. International engagement reinforces the view that local communities have needs which can be met through international funding channelled via domestic NGOs. Domestic community leaders learn that the best way to attract international funding is to disparage their own community, downplay the existing resources, and emphasise their problems. There are needs to be addressed, and only outside experts and funding can provide the necessary help. Citizens become customers, consumers of services and clients. The costs of this strategy should be clear. As a result of pressures from above, local civil society groups transform themselves from potential agents of domestic advocacy and political and social change into service providers for communities in need. Instead of developing existing human and social resources, civil society groups are given incentives to downplay the existence of these resources and rely on external support.

An effective civil society development strategy requires shifting international policy from a needs-based strategy to an asset- or strength-based approach (Belloni 2008). Even in the unfavourable conditions of division and mistrust, deepened by the experience of war, Bosnia does possess a network of community groups and individuals committed to peaceful change. International support should develop local strengths and assets, rather than continuously identify real or perceived gaps and needs – usually to be met with a dose of international money and expertise. International engagement should support local civil society in what Gramsci (1971) called a 'war of position' – the slow building of the political and social foundations of a new state with wider opportunities for participation and social inclusion beyond the narrow boundaries of ethnic politics. A new focus on a bottom-up, civil society contributions to peace building and democratisation might also be a solution to the dilemma confronting international agencies. Since 2000 the High Representative has faced the dual problem of promoting Bosnian ownership without handing over the country to nationalist parties, and imposing laws and removing obstructing officials without discouraging Bosnian ownership. The development of civil society through the expansion of opportunities for participation and debate is the long-term answer to both neo-imperial international rule and to virulent and xenophobic nationalism.

Conclusion

Since the events of 11 September 2001, not only has the international military and civilian presence in Bosnia been progressively downsized, but intervention has increasingly shifted its focus from an emphasis on stabilisation within the framework of the DPA to a process of integration with European institutions. 'Europeanisation' is the new mantra shared by international and domestic actors alike. The 'pull' of Europe is expected gradually to replace the 'push' of the OHR in the completion of the internationally driven state building process. In the long run, integration into Euro-Atlantic institutions might help to depoliticise some of the issues Bosnians find difficult to compromise on. Furthermore, Bosnia's inclusion in European institutions will help demystify the importance of exclusive control over territory and support economic and social development. However, as it stands, the prospects for integration remain distant and quite insubstantial. Bosnia is left in a limbo between the expectation of long-term prosperity and development and the short-term reality of fragmentation and division. As argued in this chapter, continuing reform requires European institutions to provide short-term incentives to Bosnian politicians and citizens.

A 'post-settlement settlement' aimed at strengthening state institutions is indispensable to enhance the prospects for Europeanisation. Such a settlement should address not only institutional issues, but also social ones, in particular the need to develop existing resources within civil society. Bosnia's main political parties, pressured by their American and European sponsors, began a debate about institutional reform but failed to agree on a list of specific changes. The differences between the parties revealed persisting mistrust and a zero-sum conception of the political process. More than a decade after the signing of the DPA, there remain doubts about the long-term impact of international intervention.

8 Conclusion

The long-term future of Bosnia remains in the balance. Instead of enjoying democratic stability and prosperity, Bosnia continues to experience a low-intensity peace. Nationalist rhetoric still predominates. The economy is weak, corruption is extensive, and collusion between political power and illegal interests is widespread. Civil society struggles to establish itself as an arena for social and political change. Minority returnees are often intimidated and excluded from the economic and social life of their communities. Many have sold their properties to relocate again in areas controlled by their own ethnic groups. Despite its growth in size and competencies, the state still lacks many of the capabilities of functioning and effective institutions, and ministries remain chronically understaffed.

One of this book's main arguments is that this situation was not entirely inevitable. Rather, the choices and strategies of international agencies contributed to complicating the process of post-war state building. To begin with, third parties have been less than clear about their objectives in intervening in Bosnia with a massive military and civil presence. Realist concerns for stability merged uneasily with efforts to guarantee human rights protection and even reverse wartime ethnic cleansing. Second, despite the robust and assertive foreign presence, intervention had a bias towards maintaining the status quo. By focusing on stability, international agencies did not pay enough attention to the need for change. Third, pressured to achieve short-term, visible results, these agencies adopted a top-down approach to social engineering that framed Bosnian civil society as a blank slate on which to build a 'new' peaceful and democratic society.

At the same time, the temptation to reject the international presence as ultimately counter-productive should be resisted. The second major argument of this book is that international intervention had an undeniably positive impact and that there are encouraging lessons that can be drawn from the Bosnian experience and applied to other cases. First, 'shared sovereignty' institutions have proved to be a useful and efficient middle ground between the neo-colonial, hyper-interventionist approach and naive calls for local autonomy. Furthermore, local resources exist which provide opportunities for democratisation and peace building to be grounded on more solid foundations. In particular, the protection of individual human rights has provided Bosnian citizens with an avenue to begin reshaping the Bosnian polity from below. In the next few years, as the process of transition from international trusteeship to local governance continues, greater citizen involvement could contribute to peace consolidation. For example, by improving the flow of information about the transition process and by allowing for citizen input on at least major policy decisions, the legitimacy and sustainability of institution building can improve.

This concluding chapter briefly expands on both these two arguments. First, it reviews the limits of the international strategy, suggesting that these limits are not insurmountable. Second, it takes stock of the positive lessons, arguing in particular that the move from the OHR trusteeship to EU peace building could represent an overall viable response to the shortcomings of intervention. The long-term policy of the Europeanisation of Bosnia and the surrounding region is an important step forwards from short-term, ad hoc conflict management strategies.

The limits of international intervention

Multiple objectives

Third parties have different reasons and incentives for providing resources and support to the Bosnian peace process. Large-scale international intervention has been justified in terms of asserting human rights norms, which are diametrically opposed to ethnic cleansing. Bosnia has been the 'battleground' in a struggle between domestic practices of exclusion, ethnic segregation and sectarianism, and the international promotion of diversity, pluralism, and coexistence. At the same time, however, the international commitment to ethnic pluralism and human rights has been far from absolute. The goal of third parties to curtail ethnic cleansing was thwarted by competing objectives. In the name of stability, international agencies have compromised on the right to return. Particularly in the first few post-Dayton years, the primary international agenda was to repatriate refugees from Western countries in order to end the burden posed on the host states' welfare systems – not to return refugees home. Premature forced repatriation increased ethnic divisions instead of alleviating them. Furthermore, international agencies have been at least as interested in re-structuring and consolidating themselves as they have been in defending and deepening the Bosnian peace. For many agencies, the Bosnian mission has become the defining operation of the post-Cold War period, allowing them to find a new role in international peace and security and thus preparing the ground for future missions. NATO's timid role in apprehending indicted war criminals reflected this stance, while allowing for the organisation's first out-of-area mission. In the post-9/11 environment, the United States' interest in fighting terrorism worldwide has once again added a supplementary external layer to an already complex set of priorities. The case of the 'Algerian six' illustrates how the 'war against terror' fits uneasily with peace building goals and how it can even frustrate attempts to consolidate Bosnian institutions.

The main consequence of this complex set of international priorities is uncertainty over which norms, rules and principles international agencies have promoted in Bosnia. Third parties failed to insist on the implementation of norms and practices consistent with their commitment to promoting multi-ethnicity, mutual accommodation and democratic and inclusive politics. International agencies' approach to intervention oscillated between accepting and legitimising the ethnic separation that emerged from the war and promoting human rights protection, minority return, civil society development and regional cooperation. As a result, they have been less than clear about what constitutes compliant behaviour and fulfilment of the obligations the DPA imposes on all parties. The ambiguous and changing criteria for obtaining international support allowed Bosnian politicians to make cosmetic changes, continue their violation of the commitments subscribed to at Dayton and delay the deepening of the peace process. The international support for Dodik shows that it is possible to be extremely ambivalent on the right to return and still be part of the 'in-group', benefiting from international economic and political support. Even the weak performance of the moderate Alliance for Change in 2000–2 can be explained by international agencies' willingness to turn a blind eye to patronage-style politics in the attempt to bolster politicians and coalitions nominally in favour of Western democracy and multi-ethnic politics. While Bosnian politicians have the lion's share of responsibility for this situation, international agencies have been at best negligent and at worst complicit in the process.

The early post-Dayton phase set the basic constraints for later intervention. International agencies were willing to tolerate almost any nationalist obstruction that would not provoke a new full-scale war. International intervention failed to put pressure on Bosnian elites to embrace liberal values and institutions and instead accepted and endorsed ethnic separation and the rule of nationalist parties. After this initial policy failed to provide tangible results, international intervention switched to an agenda more clearly centred on the protection and promotion of human rights. SFOR became increasingly active in arresting indicted war criminals, minority return was elevated to one of the central goals of intervention and local civil society came to be seen as a promising avenue to promote an alternative world-view to that of ethnic segregation.

This change of policy provided some positive results, allowing for a dramatic improvement in the political and social stabilisation of the country. At the same time, international agencies continued to accept ethnicity as the primary organising principle of political life, guaranteed the survival of a discriminatory constitutional system, hindered the emergence of alternative political projects, and often subordinated human rights protection to the goal of preventing backlash against international interveners. In short, years of international intervention demonstrate that the view of international agencies as 'missionaries of our time' (Barnett and Finnemore 2004: 33), that is, agents for the transmission of human rights and governance norms from the international to the domestic domain, is only in part accurate. International agencies are not simply staunch defenders of human rights, but are also organisations with their own institutional interests, priorities and objectives resulting from the self-interest of their member states. Because this self-interest is not necessarily in tune with the needs of a country recovering from war, the overall coherence and effectiveness of international intervention will always be difficult to ensure.

To some extent, these shortcomings of international engagement in weak and failing states are inescapable. However, third parties' different interests do need not require the sacrifice of liberal human rights norms. The DPA committed international agencies to an agenda which includes human rights, the prosecution of war criminals, the return of refugees, and economic and social reconstruction. This agenda is in tune with the identity of those Western states most engaged in Southeastern Europe and thus the insistence on its implementation is not an unrealistic strategy. Moreover, it is a strategy that so far has yielded the most far-reaching positive results.

Hyper-interventionism and the status quo

The second lesson about international intervention concerns the contradictory strategy of assertively promoting reform while guaranteeing the continued existence of the DPA. Despite all of its flaws, the international role has contributed to improve the life of most Bosnians. At the same time, however, and despite the number of initiatives undertaken and decisions imposed, the major flaw with international engagement is its orientation to the status quo. International agencies have interpreted the DPA as an end in itself, instead of a means to creating a society and institutions that are more inclusive, democratic and open. The DPA is 'like the Bible', as one American official put it, and 'it should be read as it was written' (Cohen 2002: 139). This attitude has dampened domestic aspirations to further democratisation. The Serb Civic Council's initiative on the constituent peoples had to be carried out initially against the will of international agencies, who preferred stability to the supposed risks involved in making substantial changes to the DPA. International agencies made the issue central to peace building only after local actors raised it and the Constitutional Court ruled in favour of eliminating the discriminatory aspects of the Bosnian constitutional structure. The paradox in the international attitude explains the frustration of some Bosnian intellectuals, who have often found international commitment to the DPA difficult to explain (Pajić 2002: 128).

Instead of focusing on overcoming the structural limitations of local institutions, international agencies have largely concentrated on individuals, firing those who restrict the democratisation process while attempting to promote those who rhetorically support it. Aggressive use of the Bonn powers led to the dismissal of more than 200 politicians and officials accused of obstructing the implementation of the DPA and proved to be a useful short-term strategy for promoting political, economic and social reform. However, it could not ameliorate the conditions where sectarianism thrives, nor could it help moderate political and social forces to emerge. As Florian Bieber has aptly argued, the assumption that existing institutional structures don't need reform but rather the encouragement of moderate political forces, 'created a curious situation where multi-ethnic parties and candidates promoting a more inclusive conception of political processes are discouraged by the structure of the political institutions, but promoted by those who designed and defended them' (2002: 215).

This focus on stability merged uneasily with the international agencies' attempt to overcompensate for the failings of domestic institutions by imposing legislation and sacking domestic officials. Instead of favouring inter-ethnic cooperation, international hyper-interventionism has backfired. This approach allows politicians to free ride on international initiatives. They can make decisions that are popular with their own constituencies, aware that those decisions will be overturned. Ethnic leaders can raise unrealistic expectations among their constituencies to gain popular support, knowing that international agencies will intervene when these promises are in violation of the DPA or when they can bankrupt local institutions. Because the political costs of compromise will be assumed by international agencies, ethnic elites and entrepreneurs can maintain an intransigent attitude and then blame international agencies for their own failure to make good on their electoral promises (Cox 2001: 14). Thus, domestic inter-ethnic cooperation becomes less urgent and less likely. Because the possibility of imposition is always present, 'politicians have had little incentive to compromise, preferring to keep open the option of opposing a High Representative's imposition' (ESI 2002a: 10). As a result, local nationalists can maintain their uncompromising stance, aware that the international agencies will relent and find a way out. In short, international hyper-activism hinders the development of the domestic political process and makes Bosnians' mutual intransigence less costly (Belloni 2003).

Not only does the international agencies' hyper-interventionism relieve local parties of the need to negotiate and compromise, but it also hinders citizens' participation and prevents the mobilisation of domestic civic constituencies. The more responsibilites international agencies assume in local governance, the more they release local parties from their responsibilities in the conduct of local public affairs, creating a deep crisis of political representation whereby various Bosnian governments are unresponsive to their electorates. The redirection of political accountability towards international agencies further diminishes citizens' impact on the political process. The external imposition of policies sidesteps domestic elected officials and contributes to citizens' disenchantment with and alienation from politics. Public mistrust of democratic institutions and the gap dividing elites from the public have become a troubling political liability. The steady decrease in voter turnout at successive post-war elections confirms that citizens are increasingly abdicating their role as political and social agents, complicating local involvement in and endorsement of reforms.

The main policy implication is not that international agencies should become constitutional Jacobins to change the status quo. Clearly the mandate of the High Representative is to implement the DPA and not to change it. Moreover, as the history of post-World War II Yugoslavia demonstrates, the adoption of four different constitutions did not solve political problems but merely shifted the focus away from those problems temporarily until the emergence of a new crisis exposed them. Rather, international agencies should favour a process of domestic reform. The exact shape reform will take needs to be negotiated among the local parties, with the input and support of European institutions and perhaps international analysts. However, the broad contours for change are clear. Bosnia needs to strengthen its institutions to favour efficient decision-making and the emergence and consolidation of a pluralistic and inclusive political space. Chapter 7 outlined how a 'post-settlement settlement' might move Bosnia in this direction, making local institutions more legitimate and effective, and increasing civil society's involvement in political and social life. The presence of 'shared sovereignty' entities and the appointment of foreign nationals in local institutions can contribute to improving these institutions' efficiency and legitimacy – in particular by enhancing norms of fairness and due process.

Short-termism and projectism

The third lesson from international intervention derives from the short-term timeframe that international agencies apply to their programmes and projects (Jarstad 2004). All international agencies are under tremendous institutional pressure to minimise risks of failure and maximise visible gains. Often international agencies, including leading ones such as the OHR and the OSCE, must be able to demonstrate immediate progress. The High Representative reports to the UN Security Council and the PIC every six months. The ad hoc nature of this organisation, not having a history of successful missions prior to the one in Bosnia, intensifies the pressure to show that intervention 'is working'. Similarly, the OSCE head of mission regularly reports to the OSCE parliamentary assembly in Vienna. Since the organisation was created in 1993 (before that date it was a 'conference' with no permanent staff and offices), the mission to Bosnia-Herzegovina has defined its very existence and identity, using about half of the organisation's funds. Most international personnel are seconded to the OHR and the OSCE for a period of only six months or one year, with considerable turnover and consequent loss of institutional memory. Furthermore, despite the long-term nature of the Bosnian operation, frequent staff turnover prevents language training, with negative consequences particularly in the realm of policing.

Short-termism, or 'imperialism in a hurry' (Ignatieff 2003: 22), exposes the contradictions at the heart of international intervention in weak and failing states such as Bosnia. A formally sovereign and democratic state cannot be ruled by international administrators indefinitely – at least in our post-colonial age. Short-term deadlines, often linked to the holding of national elections, help to justify the exercise of international authority and make such authority more acceptable to both the local people and the electorate of those states contributing military and civilian personnel to peace operations. At the same time, the need for 'instant gratification', and a short implementation timeframe explains 'projectism', the tendency to treat democratisation and peace building as a set of discrete interventions incorporated into a project with a relatively clear beginning, implementation and evaluation, usually with a six-month time span, or at best a year. 'Projectism' leads to at least three important distortions. First, it makes international intervention a top-down enterprise. Because of the brevity of projects, international agencies have little scope to develop significant local partnerships and include local actors in a process of joint planning, implementation, and assessment. Instead, they make important decisions about the priorities and allocation of international assistance in the initial phases of a project, when international understanding of local conditions is limited. Seen in this light, the idea of developing 'local ownership' of the peace process sounds at best naive. The pressure to show immediate and concrete results militates against capacity building and domestic ownership (Sampson 2002).

Second, in order to achieve immediate results, international agencies are geared towards attempting to manipulate short-term outcomes, instead of creating the long-term conditions for peace to take hold indigenously. Not only can this short-term focus backfire (as with the international manipulation of election rules), but it is unsustainable. The performance of the Alliance for Change between 2000 and 2002 demonstrates that, in the absence of structural changes, even multi-ethnic and civic parties might be driven to adopt the same patronage style of government that characterises the behaviour of nationalist parties. Third, the greater the international role and need for short-term results, the more international agencies fear that recognising problems may be perceived as an admission of failure. Yet, as the United States' ambassador to Bosnia has unambiguously stated, 'failure is not an option' (Gienger and Loza 2003). The more subtle side of this tendency to 'show results' is the problematic inclination to blame local actors for delays, obstacles and drawbacks in the process. While success has a thousand fathers, failure is an orphan. Lack of progress is frequently blamed on the 'Balkan mentality', the supposedly combined effects of socialism and war, instead of dubious international choices. When Bosnians choose not to follow the paternal advice and priorities of international agencies, their behaviour is seen as puzzling and explained away as the result of the lack of democratic traditions in the region or the influence of post-war trauma.

These distortions caution against a widely held view on how to improve the efficiency of peace operations in Bosnia and elsewhere – the idea that the privatisation of foreign aid and the sub-contracting of various components of peace operations to private companies is needed to improve the effectiveness of international intervention (Chayes *et al.* 1997). Businesses are even less inclined than international organisations to spend the time and resources necessary to incorporate local actors into planning and decision-making. Furthermore, sub-contracting can lead to a worsening of standards. For example, a UN internal report charged the UN police mission in Bosnia with misconduct, sexual impropriety and corruption. In the case of the US contingent, the job of selecting and training police officers was given to a Texas-based private corporation, but the record of the American policemen was no better than that of the other contingents (AFP 2001).

Instead of privatising peace missions, the reasons for sub-optimal results need to be carefully evaluated. To some extent, short-termism is an inevitable characteristic of peace operations. No country would contribute peacekeepers, civilian personnel and financial resources knowing at the outset that such a contribution would be needed for a generation or more. But the Bosnian case demonstrates that the current approach is myopic and, as a result, less effective, more costly and more time-consuming. An early, accurate and realistic evaluation of what is necessary for a successful intervention is a much more viable strategy, particularly if such an evaluation includes a discussion about burden sharing among intervening states and organisations. If the costs of intervention can be shared among many actors, governments will find it a much more tolerable task and will be able better to justify to their constituencies the use of national resources for peace operations abroad. A realistic evaluation could also provide clarity of purpose and a better focus on the needs of the country undergoing the post-settlement transition, instead of the needs of those countries facilitating it.

To summarise, the analysis of more than a decade of post-settlement international intervention demonstrates that competing international objectives, the contradiction between hyper-interventionism and status-quo orientation, and short-termism and projectism, limited the positive impact of international intervention and left many questions open about Bosnia's future prospects. As Principal Deputy High Representative Donald Hays (2004) concluded in one of the rare hints of self-criticism to come from international officials,

> if we had known then what we know now, the international community might well have taken the time immediately after the signing of the Dayton Peace Agreement to develop *a comprehensive, multi-year plan*, with a robust administrative and political structure in order to *implement* that plan and with the full and coherent support of the international agencies and countries involved.
>
> (Hays 2004, emphasis in the original)

Taking stock of positive lessons

Despite its limits, international intervention in Bosnia has allowed much progress to be achieved that would not have been possible otherwise. The one single lesson that Bosnia teaches to international interveners is the necessity of focusing on strengthening political institutions, the rule of law and, more broadly, the legitimacy of domestic decision-making bodies. When necessary, 'shared sovereignty' arrangements might be needed to allow for the transparent and efficient work of local institutions. Shared-sovereignty institutions are a voluntary agreement between national political authorities and an external actor to govern difficult issues (Krasner 2004). This type of agreement is more acceptable if it is negotiated with multi-lateral actors, instead of a single powerful state – thus minimising the fear of post-colonial control. In Bosnia, for example, mixed international and domestic management boards could help curb corruption and nepotism in local industries. Similar arrangements could be devised for sensitive security areas such as the army, the police and tax collection.

Bosnia's post-Dayton experience shows that a particular kind of 'shared sovereignty' can be especially effective in ensuring efficient policy-making. The appointment of foreign nationals to local institutions has been an effective alternative to international rule by decree, preserving domestic sovereignty and strengthening domestic governance. Against expectations to the contrary, the Constitutional Court established itself as a key Bosnian institution thanks to the presence of three international judges. The Constitutional Court's decision on the constituent peoples, which removed discriminatory clauses from both the RS and Federation constitutions, contributed to addressing Bosnia's stateness problem by increasing domestic institutions' legitimacy and stability. While Serb and Croat judges voted against the constituent peoples ruling, and several politicians protested at this decision, the court's legitimacy was not in question. The presence of foreign judges on the court allowed it to overcome a stalemate along ethnic lines, and further legitimised this important domestic judicial organ.[1] Similarly, the central bank, directed for the first five years by an Australian national, was very effective in providing financial stability to the recovering post-war economy. Notably, of about 170 staff, only three are foreign nationals. Even the Bosnian Electoral Commission benefited from a similar structure. When the OSCE handed over its electoral responsibilities to Bosnian authorities in 2001, three international members of the seven-member electoral commission helped to make the 2002 elections a technical success. The CRPC, a third of whom were international members appointed by the European Court of Human Rights, proved crucial in certifying property claims and in creating the conditions for post-war property restitution and refugee return. The success of these institutions was due to their being 'de-linked' from nationalist politics (Caplan 2005: 92) and has later justified the creation of other domestic bodies (the Communication

Regulation Agency and the Human Rights Commission) with the presence of foreign nationals in key positions.

Most of these institutions do not have veto provisions, but decisions are taken by simple majority. The absence of the vital interest veto both streamlined decision-making and improved the efficiency and legitimacy of these institutions. In her analysis of post-war governance, Nina Caspersen (2004b: 585) concluded that 'integrative institutions worked more smoothly than consociational institutions ... and their establishment was remarkably problem-free'. This finding is even more important as some of the integrative institutions (such as the Constitutional Court) are central pillars of the state instead of lacking, as Caspersen suggests, the 'symbolic importance of the consociational institutions'. During the debate over constitutional reform, Bosniak president Tihić proposed that decisions in the Council of Ministers be made by majority vote rather than consensus, while Serb and Croat parties argued that consensus was common practice in most countries. Serbs and Croats oppose majoritarianism, fearing that it could lead to their being outvoted by the Bosniak relative majority.

These fears are legitimate and go to the heart of the disagreement between the three main groups. However, strengthening the efficiency of state institutions does not need to conflict with the preservation of guarantees for group rights and does not need to lead to subordination and exclusion. The participation of Croats in central institutions, where they currently enjoy one third of the power with much less than a third of the country's population, suggests that state building cannot simply be equated with the Bosniaks' drive for domination. The preservation of the RS as the largest canton in a restructured federal state is another obvious rebuttal to these fears. But all cantons can in effect become the counterpoint of a central and efficient state. The development of an effective state requires Bosnia to move beyond perfect proportionality (as currently enshrined in the consociational system) and ensure a workable mix of representation and governability.

European institutions have an obvious and important role in such a renewed state building strategy. The prospect for integration into European security, political, economic and legal institutions can overcome the pitfalls of post-Dayton international intervention, namely, the incoherent, stability-oriented and short-term international approach. Instead, Bosnia's gradual involvement in European institutions can provide a long-term political alternative based on domestic endorsement of reform aimed at addressing Bosnia's stateness problem. The experience of European integration shows that the long-term benefits of joining European institutions can give national politicians positive incentives to undertake a process of restructuring and development, even at the risk of alienating their domestic constituencies. The Italian government, for example, was able to adopt painful (but indispensable) economic reforms in the 1990s, citing the need to meet the parameters for joining the common European currency – at the same time saving the Italian state from possible economic and financial default.

Similarly, Bosnian politicians could endorse political, economic and social change in view of enjoying the European carrot. Eventually, membership in the EU will add a new layer of governance, helping to transform the role of the state in mediating between alternative and sometimes conflicting positions. EU member states delegate some sovereign prerogatives to European institutions, thus removing potentially problematic issues from local decision-making. The EU Council of Ministers, by taking decisions in most areas on the basis of majority rule, allows for policy-making even in the absence of local agreement. Moreover, and perhaps most importantly, the EU is also instrumental in softening identities by adding a new layer to existing local identities, thus potentially helping to reduce ethno-national exclusiveness. As a whole, the EU motto of 'unity in diversity' is particularly fitting for a state like Bosnia torn between competing allegiances.

The second positive lesson to be learned from Bosnia lies in the existence of positive bottom-up resources which can be mobilised for more effective peace building. In particular, the protection of individual human rights is an important avenue for improving the quality of individual and collective life. Human rights permit individuals to have more freedom in choosing their version of the good life, and even to opt out of their ethnic group, as my interlocutor in Bihać pressed me to understand (see Chapter 1). Furthermore, rights-bearing citizens can (re)shape political and social relations, mediate communal divisions and create a new polity 'from below'. In its most extreme form – such as the attempt to undo ethnic cleansing through minority return – the consequences of human rights protection can be far-reaching. As Christine Bell argues, 'human rights institutions aim not merely to police the division between law and politics found in the polity, as in the classic liberal-democratic state, but also to create the polity by mediating communal divisions' (Bell 2000: 199).

The return home of many Bosnians to areas under the control of an ethnic group other than the one to which the returnee belongs confirms that the principled protection of individual rights can have an important impact on the recreation of ethnic diversity. More importantly, Bosnia provides some evidence that the increased contact between members of different groups can help alleviate conflict and even marginalise extreme nationalist parties. Ethnic heterogeneity has moderating effects among the electorate (Pugh and Cobble 2001). Croats living in central Bosnia – where they are intermixed with (primarily) Bosniaks – are much more likely to support moderate parties than Croats in ethnically homogeneous hard line Herzegovina. Similarly, as Chapter 6 showed, minority return has an overall positive impact on strengthening the peace process and promoting inclusive and moderate political processes. The surprising return of Bosniaks to the municipality of Prijedor contributed to defusing tensions between the two Entities. Moreover, it allowed the marginalisation of those nationalist parties and politicians more implicated in the war, while promoting centrist and pragmatic views on multi-ethnic co-existence. By contrast, segregation in ethnic enclaves is more likely to be associated with hard and uncompromising ethnic identities. In sum, the contact between individuals of different ethnic groups diminishes the salience of extreme political views and the overall likelihood of violence – an outcome also confirmed by Ashutosh Varshney (2002) in his study of Muslim-Hindu relations in India.

Beyond Bosnia

A promising development is the establishment in late 2005 of a United Nations Peacebuilding Commission. The commission is a direct response to the limits evidenced by a decade and a half of international missions in war-torn regions. While Bosnia escaped a relapse into war, half of all countries emerging from conflict revert to violence within five years. But even cases with low levels of violence remain politically, economically and socially unstable. Changing international priorities, lack of comprehensive strategies, and short-term and top-down planning continue to plague international intervention. By focusing on five key areas, the commission has the potential to address the shortcomings of intervention. The commission's tasks of improving coordination among all relevant actors, advising on integrated strategies for peace building and sustainable development, developing best practices, ensuring predictable funding and extending the period of attention of the international community is likely to increase the chances that international intervention will be more effective.

At the same time, doubts about the impact of the Peacebuilding Commission remain. In particular, the terms of cooperation among the various stakeholders remain unclear. The commission includes members from the Security Council, from the Economic and Social Council, additional members elected by the General Assembly to ensure regional representation and the top providers of financial resources and of military and civilian personnel. Other actors can be involved in country-specific operations to enhance the legitimacy and effectiveness of the operation – including national and transnational authorities, regional actors and organisations, troop contributors and major donors of the country in question. The role of national authorities of those countries under consideration remains uncertain, in particular the extent to which their views should shape the commission's agenda and strategy. Moreover, no particular role is foreseen for humanitarian organisations, local and international civil society groups, and academic/regional experts.

Bosnia's Peace Implementation Council (PIC) provides lessons and warnings for the Peacebuilding Commission and its future role. Despite the presence of the PIC, no cohesive approach to intervention has been adopted in Bosnia. PIC declarations resulted from a largely behind-the-scenes process of negotiation between American and European diplomats. Often these declarations failed to move the democratisation and peace building process forward or even to identify key areas for international involvement. Only in

2000 did the PIC recognise the need to focus on state building as a means to foster democratic consolidation and a gradual process of international exit. Bosnia can teach the Peacebuilding Commission that addressing the problems of weak and failing states requires a structure of global governance where leading states accept that effective intervention needs time, money and manpower, as well as the political will to engage constructively with the major security concern of the twenty-first century.

Notes

1 Introduction

1 This is revealed by an ongoing study conducted at the Department of Peace and Conflict Research and the Uppsala Programme for Holocaust and Genocide Research, Uppsala University. Thanks to Roland Kostić for this data.
2 With regard to Bosnia, see in particular Armakolas 2001; Bougarel *et al.* 2007; Lovrenović 2001.

2 Bosnia and international intervention

1 Useful works on Yugoslavia are: Allcock 2000; Banac 1984; Lampe 1996; Ramet 1992.
2 Steven Kull and Clay Ramsay (2003) argue that the Clinton administration did not have an accurate perception of the public's attitude. The American public was positively inclined about the US involvement in Bosnia, as long as such involvement was multi-lateral and its costs fairly shared between the US and its allies.
3 Holbrooke singled out the British delegation at Dayton, and in particular Pauline Neville-Jones, for arguing that, as Holbrooke stated it, 'the legacy of Northern Ireland precluded her government from allowing police officers to make arrests on foreign soil' (1998: 251). Neville-Jones replied that 'no one wanted IFOR soldiers to get involved' in executing police functions (1996–97: 52). See also (Chollet 2005: 149).
4 Only in 1999 did the OSCE change the 'Area of Responsibility' of each field office, to increase the possibility for cross-ethnic contacts, exchanges, and cooperation.
5 Schwarz-Schilling drastically reversed the trend towards an ever-increasing use of the Bonn powers: Westendorp used these powers 76 times, Petritsch 250 times and Ashdown 447 times. Although Ashdown used the Bonn powers more than any other High Representative, his interventions declined over time (OHR 2007).
6 The labelling of these three approaches is my own, and incorporates previous research. Such research has investigated various aspects of international intervention, in particular the strengths and limits of international trusteeship (see e.g. Caplan 2005; Zaum 2007) and its two main alternatives: managed partition (see e.g. Kaufmann 1999; Licklider and Bloom 2007) and local self-government (see e.g. Chandler 1999; Knaus and Martin 2003). The Bosnian case figures prominently as a key test for each approach.
7 Similar views are not uncommon among intellectuals from various post-Yugoslav states (Denitch 1996: 210).
8 Since early 2005, the High Representative has issued decisions removing the restrictions in a number of individual cases.

9 Throughout the Cold War period, the only boundary changes not related to the end of colonialism were the creation of Bangladesh, the annexation of the Golan Heights and the absorption of South Vietnam.

10 For critiques of Balkanism, see Todorova 1997; Bijelić 2005; Bjelić and Savić 2002.

11 As Banac (1984) argues with reference to the Serbs' attempts at domination after World War I.

3 Democracy from scratch

1 For example, about a quarter of all parliamentary sessions between 1996 and 2000 were spent in internal wrangling about the agenda (ICG 1999: 53, footnote 99).

2 See Holbrooke's memoirs (1998) and those of Daniel Serwer (1999) who was the main American negotiator for the Federation at Dayton.

3 The refusal of hard-line Nikola Poplašen to nominate Milorad Dodik for the post of prime minister provoked a reaction from OHR which cost him the presidency of the RS in March 1999.

4 At Dayton the parties could not agree on the fate of this strategically located town between the eastern and western part of the RS. An arbitration decision in March 1999 has made Brčko a district ruled jointly by the RS and the Federation and under the authority of the common institutions of Bosnia.

5 As Lijphart (1977) acknowledges, the worst-case scenario cannot be excluded – as in the collapse in 1975 of the consociational National Pact in Lebanon leading to a bloody civil war.

6 In 2003, a probe into the HDZ Hercegovačka Banka implicated Jelavić and other top Bosnian Croat leaders for illegal use of funds and corruption. Jelavić was arrested in January 2004.

7 Author's interview, Sarajevo, July 2002.

8 Prce was arrested in January 2004 in relation to the irregularities surrounding the management of the Hercegovačka Banka. In October he was sentenced to five years in prison.

9 Author's personal communication with Szebor Dizdarević, December 2003.

10 Author's interview, Sarajevo, July 2001.

11 'Text of the Agreement on Constitutional Changes in BiH', Sarajevo, 27 March 2002 (ONASA). For a discussion, see ICG 2002b.

12 Author's interview with Jacob Finci, Chair of the Federation Commission, Sarajevo, July 2002. Finci suggested that the unstated desire of Petritsch to 'leave an important legacy behind at the end of his mandate as High Representative also played an important role'.

13 According to a 2001 poll, 83.3 per cent of Croats support the constitutionality of peoples across the country, in addition to 62 per cent of Serbs (UNDP 2001b: 13).

14 'Zahtje: za Bosnu I Hercegovinu – Trecu Republiku' (press release). Thanks to Florian Bieber for providing me with a copy of this document. See also Finci (2004) for a proposal to create regions based on criteria other than the ethnic principle.

15 Author's interview, Prijedor, July 2004.

4 Elections and electoral engineering

1 The SDA focus on cementing its control over the Federation was perhaps most evident in the failure of Bosniak voters to cross the IEBL and vote in the RS. Despite expectations to the contrary, only one Bosniak former resident of

Srebrenica appeared to cast his vote. However, the responsibility should not be attributed entirely to the SDA's political agenda. As an electoral supervisor at the time, I was present at meetings with local Serb authorities in the area of Srebrenica where the prospect of Bosniaks returning to vote was welcomed as an opportunity to 'finish the job of the war'. Needless to say, this type of atmosphere did not encourage Bosniaks to return in person to cast their ballots.

2 At first sight, this finding seems to advise against the post-war return home of refugees and displaced persons to areas where they constitute an ethnic minority, because such a return might increase support for nationalists and raise ethnic tensions. However, as argued in Chapter 6, return actually often contributed to decrease ethnic tensions and marginalise nationalist parties. Support for nationalist parties might be due more to the level of pre-war violence than to the level of ethnic inter-mixing, and such support has nonetheless decreased over time.

3 The Bosnian Constitution makes no ruling on the length of mandates at all levels. Consequently, until the adoption of the final election law, the Election Commission (chaired by the OSCE head of mission) had the discretion to decide the frequency of elections.

4 For an opposite view see Bose (2002: 228) who suggests that 'it is really difficult to find fault with this measure'.

5 American and British ambassadors operated independently from other international agencies. The exclusion of the High Representative further deteriorated the already troubled relationship between Petritsch and the American and British embassy. Author's confidential interview with OHR official, Sarajevo, July 2002.

6 Author's interview with Dieter Woltman, OSCE deputy head of mission, Sarajevo, July 2002.

7 *Mathieu Mohin and Clerfayt v. Belgium*, case no. 9/1985/95/143, of 2 February 1987. More recently, the ECHR confirmed its intention to leave to states a wide margin of discretion in the area of election law in *Melnychenko v. Ukraine* of 19 October 2004. See the court's website at www.hchr.coe.int/echr

8 Author's interview with Dieter Woltmann, OSCE deputy head of mission, Sarajevo, July 2001.

9 The OSCE's director of elections raised doubts about the enforceability of this provision well before the elections. Author's interview with Domenico Taccinardi, Sarajevo, July 2002.

5 The limits and virtues of civil society

1 The late Paul Szasz, one of the American lawyers who drafted the DPA, made this point during a conference in Washington DC in March 1999.

2 There is nothing unintended about this. As the World Bank proudly states, 'the Bank was successful in hiring well-qualified local staff ... by offering compensation well above that paid to civil servants' (WBOED 2004: 8).

3 Author's interview with Joe Ingram, World Bank director of the mission to BiH, Sarajevo, July 2002.

4 The governor was Peter Nicholl, who served from 1997 to 2003. Having received Bosnian citizenship he was re-appointed again in May 2003.

5 Thanks to Chip Gagnon for drawing my attention to the importance of this point.

6 By way of disclosure, I should report that I served as the OSCE member to the consulting body working on this project throughout 1998.

7 Author's interview with Muhamed Džemidžić, board of directors, Helsinki Committee for Human Rights, Sarajevo, July 2003.

8 Author's interview with Madeleine Rees, UN High Commissioner for Human Rights in BiH, Sarajevo, July 2004.

9 Author's interview with Muhamed Džemidžić, board of directors, Helsinki Committee for Human Rights, Sarajevo, July 2003.

10 The weakness of the Stability Pact can be attributed to two reasons. First, the initial exclusion of Yugoslavia, due to Milošević's indictment for war crimes, severely damaged the idea of promoting a regional approach. Second, the Stability Pact's focus on working with legitimate governments could only have a limited impact on domestic civil society. Author's interview with Erhard Busek, the Stability Pact's coordinator, Cambridge, October 2003.

11 This meeting was preceded by other smaller but important steps. In February 2002, the Yugoslav president publicly expressed support for a visa-free border regime between Bosnia, Croatia, and Yugoslavia (RSNA 2002).

12 For example, the OSCE (2002a) launched a Civic Dialogue Alternative project, explicitly 'based on the experience of the Igman Initiative'.

13 As one of the promoters of the initiative has explained, the ICTY's position is unwarranted. There is no inherent conflict between the work of the tribunal and the work of a truth commission: while a trial focuses on the specific crimes of the perpetrators, a truth commission focuses on the experience of the victims. Author's interview with Jacob Finci, Sarajevo, July 2003. See also Finci (2001).

6 The antinomies of refugee return

1 Thus, those authors who argue that the right to return home sets the Bosnian peace mission apart from similar international interventions overlook these broader developments (Rosand 1998; Phuong 2000a).

2 The expression 'minority return' refers to return to an area where one's own national group is not demographically predominant. In the Bosnian context this expression can be deceiving because a minority is not a constituent nation, regardless of size in a given area. Consequently, Bosniaks, Croats and Serbs are not minorities because they are constituent peoples of the state of Bosnia and Herzegovina.

3 Author's interview with Michele Simone, UNHCR Protection Officer, Banja Luka, July 2002.

4 It should be noted that the DPA was not signed by the Bosnian Serbs and the Bosnian Croats who were represented at Dayton by the FRY and Croatia respectively. Occasionally this issue is raised by the opponents of the agreement to either question the authority of the OHR or the binding nature of specific aspects of the DPA, such as refugee return. However, successive Bosnian governments never openly rejected the DPA, and it would be hollow to pick and choose among its clauses (on the issues raised by the legitimacy of international administrations and local consent, see Zaum 2007). Above all, the fact that the agreement was signed by the presidents of the two neighbouring countries testifies to the international character of the 1992–95 war in Bosnia.

5 Author's confidential interview with OSCE Human Rights Officer, Sarajevo, July 2003.

6 While Germany attracted much criticism of its behaviour, repatriation was not a German anomaly. Instead, it resulted from and contributed to the process of European integration in the direction of so-called 'Fortress Europe' – the building of a European architecture impermeable to the waves of refugees escaping war and persecution, and the simultaneous weakening of legal norms of refugee protection. Germany should not be singled out for having hosted the majority of these refugees during the Bosnian war and therefore for having conducted the majority of repatriations at the time when both the EU and its member states were beginning to become more impermeable to migration flows. On the containment of war-ridden zones, see Duffield 2001.

7 See, for example, the open letter that Physicians for Human Rights wrote to the interior ministers of Germany's sixteen federal states on 4 June 1999. Copy on file with author.

8 For conflicting interpretations see: Andersen 1996; Bagshaw 1997; Hathaway 1997.

9 Senator Frank Lautenberg sponsored the War Crimes Prosecution Facilitation Act of 1997 (S804, 23 May 1997) instructing the US executive director to the international financial institutions to vote against any aid or grants to countries, entities or cantons providing sanctuary to indicted war criminals. It was incorporated into the Foreign Operations Appropriations Act for 1998, Section 573 of HR 2159, and became law on 12 November 1997.

10 This newly found activism was facilitated by the fact that the prosecutor, Louise Arbour, started to issue sealed – that is, secret – indictments (Kerr 2004: 159). This strategy allowed NATO the advantage of surprise and thus the ability to minimise possible casualties. Arbour focused on more important cases, dropping the indictment of low-level persons, and thus raising the profile and effectiveness of the tribunal.

11 This is what the municipality staff communicated to international officials asking to meet him. Author's interview with Massimo Moratti, OSCE Human Rights Officer, Sarajevo, July 2002. Stakić was later arrested in early 2001 in Belgrade and sent to The Hague to stand trial at the ICTY. In September 2003 he was convicted of crimes against humanity, crimes against the laws and customs of war, and murder, and sentenced to life imprisonment.

12 Author's interview with Muharem Murselović, President of the Municipal Council, Prijedor, July 2004.

13 Statistics on minority returns, regularly updated, can be found at www.unhcr.ba/return/index.htm; the total number of minority returns is deceiving, since many returnees do not signal their presence to the authorities, while others return only to sell their property and move again. I shall come back to the issue of sustainability of returns later in the chapter.

14 Author's interview with Wernon Blatter, Chief of Mission of UNHCR in BiH, Sarajevo, July 2001.

15 These Serb communities no longer live here. In August 1995 Croatia launched Operation Storm, which took control of the region and created approximately 150,000 Serb refugees.

16 Author's interview with Jose Luis Martinez Llopis, OSCE Head of Office, Prijedor, July 2002.

17 As Katherine Verdery (1999) has shown in her fascinating study of the 'political role of dead bodies', Bosnians have extremely strong ties to the earth, as well as the houses and the graves of their ancestors.

18 The other two are the Serb People's Alliance (SNS) and the Party of Democratic Progress (PDP). See Caspersen 2004a.

19 Author's interview with Wernon Blatter, Chief of Mission of UNHCR in BiH, Sarajevo, July 2001.

7 From NATO to the EU

1 See for example Ashdown (2002b), who fails to identify the source of the crisis (the US administration), preferring to blame the UN – an easy but ultimately useless exercise. On the importance of the US military presence in Bosnia, see Evans 2001.

2 Many more war-crime indictees remain at large, including Radovan Karadžić and Ratko Mladić. Limited collaboration on this issue continues to be the crucial stumbling block to Bosnia's admission to the Partnership for Peace and further Euro-Atlantic integration (OHR 2005c).

3 Author's interview with Stefan Simosas, Political Adviser, Delegation of the European Commission to BiH, Sarajevo, July 2005.
4 I trust the reader will agree that the analytic attempt to identify necessary reforms is not in contradiction with the view, shared by this study, that Bosnians themselves must be the engine of those reforms.
5 The expression is from Zalmay Khalilzad, president Bush's special envoy to Afghanistan. The general implications of this concept are discussed in Fearon and Laitin 2004.

8 Conclusion

1 The question of whether decisions of the Constitutional Court should be valid only if one judge from each constituent people supports them was brought to the attention of the Venice Commission in 2005. The commission argued that requiring a positive vote from each group (effectively a veto right) is 'alien to the very nature of judicial decision making' (Venice Commission 2005: para. 4).

Bibliography

AEO (Association of Election Officials of BiH) (2001) 'Technical Series No. 1/2001', Online. Available at: www.aeobih.com.ba/tech_series1p7.htm (accessed 3 July 2002)

AFP (Agence France-Presse) (1999) 'Capitalism as Tool of Cleansing?!', 6 August.

—— (2001) 'UN Mission in Bosnia Commits Abuses, Gets Off Lightly', 29 May.

—— (2003) 'Bosnia Violated Rights of Terror Suspects Handed to US: Court,' 5 April.

AI (Amnesty International) (1998) 'Bosnia-Herzegovina. All the Way Home: Safe "Minority Returns" as a Just Remedy for a Secure Future', 1 February (EUR 63/02/1998).

—— (2002) 'Bosnia-Herzegovina: Human Rights Chambers Decision in the Algerian Case Must be Implemented by Bosnia', 11 October (EUR 63/017/2002).

—— (2003a) 'Bosnia-Herzegovina: Abolition of Human Rights Chamber Leaves Citizens Unprotected', 11 June (EUR 63/015/2003).

—— (2003b) 'Unlawful Detention of Six Men from Bosnia-Herzegovina in Guantanamo Bay,' 30 May (EUR 63/013/2003).

—— (2006a) 'Bosnia and Herzegovina. Behind Closed Gates: Ethnic Discrimination in Employment', 26 January (EUR 63/001/2006).

—— (2006b) 'Dead on Time: Arms Transportation, Brokering and the Threat to Human Rights', 12 May (ACT 30/008/2006).

Alfaro, M. (2000) *Return Monitoring Study: Minority Returnees to Republika Srpska, Bosnia and Herzegovina*, Sarajevo: UNHCR.

Alić, A. (2002) 'Dissecting Nationalist Success', *Transitions Online*, 1 November. Online. Available at: www.tol.cz (accessed 2 November 2002)

—— (2003a) 'Bosnia: Compensating for Guantanamo', *Transitions Online*, 22 December. Online. Available at: www.tol.cz (accessed 4 January 2004).

—— (2003b) 'Bosnia: Serbia and Montenegro Apologize', *Balkan Report*, 17 November.

—— (2003c) 'Living in a Paradox', *Transitions Online*, 17 September. Online. Available at: www.tol.cz (accessed 18 September 2003).

Allcock, J. B. (2000) *Explaining Yugoslvia*, London: Hurst.

—— (2004) 'Come Back, Dayton: All Is Forgiven!', in C. Solioz and T. Vogel (eds) *Dayton and Beyond: Perspectives on the Future of Bosnia and Herzegovina*. Baden-Baden, Germany: Nomos.

Andersen, E. (1996) 'The Role of Asylum States in Promoting Safe and Peaceful Repatriation Under the Dayton Agreements', *European Journal of International Law*, 7: 193–206.

Anderson, B. (1991) *Imagined Communities: Reflections on the Origin and Spread of Nationalism*. London: Verso.

Andjelić, N. (2003) *Bosnia-Herzegovina: The End of A Legacy*, Portland OR: Frank Cass.

Andreas, P. (2004) 'The Clandestine Political Economy of War and Peace in Bosnia', *International Studies Quarterly*, 48: 29–51.

Armakolas, I. (2001) 'A Field Trip to Bosnia: The Dilemmas of the First-Time Researcher', in M. Smyth and G. Robinson (eds) *Researching Violently Divided Societies: Ethical and Methodological Issues*, Tokyo and London: United Nations University and Pluto Press.

Ashdown, P. (2002a) *Inaugural Speech, State Parliament of Bosnia and Herzegovina*, Sarajevo, 27 May.

—— (2002b) 'What I Learned in Bosnia', *New York Times*, 28 October.

—— (2003) 'Peace Stabilisation: The Lessons from Bosnia and Herzegovina', lecture at the London School of Economics, London, 8 December.

—— (2004) 'From Dayton to Brussels', *Reporter*, 12 May.

Ayoob, M. (2004) 'Third World Perspectives on Humanitarian Intervention and International Administration', *Global Governance*, 10: 99–118.

Bagshaw, S. (1997) 'Benchmarks or Deutschmarks? Determining the Criteria for the Repatriation of Refugees to Bosnia-Herzegovina', *International Journal of Refugee Law* 9: 566–92.

Banac, I. (1984) *The National Question in Yugoslavia: Origins, History and Politics*, Ithaca NY and London: Cornell University Press.

Barnett, M. and Finnemore, M. (2004) *Rules for the World: International Organizations in Global Politics*, London and Ithaca NY: Cornell University Press.

Batt, J. (ed.) (2004) *The Western Balkans: Moving On*, Paris: Institute for Security Studies, Chaillot Paper no. 70, October.

BCR (Balkan Crisis Report) (2002). 'Bosnia: Key Vote on Constitutional Change', no. 328, 4 April.

Bell, C. (2000) *Human Rights and Peace Agreements*, Oxford: Oxford University Press.

Belloni, R. (2003) 'A Dubious Democracy by Fiat', *Transitions Online*, 22 August. Online. Available at: www.tol.cz (accessed 22 August 2003).

—— (2004) 'Bosnia: The Limits of Neocolonial Rule', Silver City NM and Washington DC: *Foreign Policy in Focus*, 5 August.

—— (2007) 'Rethinking "Nation-building": The Contradictions of the Wilsonian Approach at Democracy Promotion', *Whitehead Journal of Diplomacy and International Relations*, 7: 97–109.

—— (2008) 'Civil Society in War-to-Democracy Transitions', in A. Jarstad and T. D. Sisk (eds) *From War to Democracy*. Cambridge: Cambridge University Press, forthcoming.

Belloni, R. and Deane, S. (2005) 'From Belfast to Bosnia: Piecemeal Peacemaking and the Role of Institutional Learning', *Civil Wars*, 7: 219–43.

Bieber, F. (2001) 'Croat Self-Government in Bosnia: A Challenge for Dayton?', ECMI, Brief #5.

—— (2002) 'Governing Post-war Bosnia-Herzegovina', in K. Gál (ed.) *Minority Governance Concepts in Europe on the Threshold of the Twenty-first Century*, Budapest: LGI.

—— (2006a) *Post-War Bosnia: Ethnicity, Inequality and Public Sector Governance*, Houndsmills UK: Palgrave and Sarajevo: United Nations Research Institute for Social Development.

—— (2006b) 'Bosnia-Herzegovina: Slow Progress towards a Functional State', *Southeast European and Black Sea Studies*, 6: 43–64.

BiH (Bosnia and Herzegovina) (2004) *BiH Medium Term Development Strategy: Poverty Reduction Strategy Paper, 2004–2007*, Sarajevo, March.

BiH Media Round-up, daily news reviews provided by the Office of the High Representative. Online. Available at: www.ohr.int

Bildt, C. (1998) *Peace Journey: The Struggle for Peace in Bosnia*, London: Weidenfeld and Nicolson.

Bisogno, M. and Chong, A. (2002) 'Poverty and Inequality in Bosnia and Herzegovina After the Civil War', *World Development*, 30: 61–75.

Bijelić, B. (2005) 'Balkans, Stereotypes, Violence and Responsibility', in F. Bieber and C. Wieland (eds) *Facing the Past, Facing the Future: Confronting Ethnicity and Conflict in Bosnia and Former Yugoslavia*, Ravenna, Italy: Longo.

Bjelić, D. I. and Savić, O. (eds) (2002) *Balkan as Metaphor: Between Globalization and Fragmentation*, Cambridge MA: MIT Press.

Black, R. (2001) 'Return and Reconstruction in Bosnia-Herzegovina', *SAIS-Review*. 21: 177–99.

Black, R., Koser, K. and Walsh, M. (1998) *Conditions for the Return of Displaced Persons from the European Union*, Luxembourg: European Commission.

Bogović, N. (2002) 'Novi Sad, Osijek, Tuzla: une tradition de bonnes relations'. *Courrier des Balkans*, 19 January.

Bojičić-Dželilovic, V., Caušević, M. and Tomaš, R. (2004) *Bosnia and Herzegovina – Understanding Reform*, Vienna : Global Development Network Southeast Europe.

Bojičić-Dželilovic, V. and Kaldor, M. 1999. 'The Abnormal Economy of Bosnia-Herzegovina', in C. Schierup (ed.) *Scramble for the Balkans: Nationalism, Globalism and the Political Economy of Reconstruction*, New York: St Martin's Press.

Bose, S. (2002) *Bosnia after Dayton: Nationalist Partition and International Intervention*, Oxford: Oxford University Press.

—— (2006) 'The Bosnian State a Decade After Dayton', in D. Chandler (ed.) *Peace Without Politics? Ten Years of International State-Building in Bosnia*, London and New York: Routledge.

Bougarel, X. (1992) 'Bosnia-Herzegovine: anatomie d'un poudrière', *Herodote*, 67: 84–147.

—— (1996). *Bosnie: Anatomie d'un conflit*, Paris: La Découverte.

—— (2003) 'Islam and Politics in the Post-communist Balkans, 1990–2000', in D. Keridis, E. Elias-Bursac and N. Yatromanolakis (eds) *New Approaches to Balkan Studies*, Dulles VA: Brassey's.

Bougarel, X., Helms, E. and Duijzings, G. (eds) (2007) *The New Bosnian Mosaic: Identities, Memories and Moral Claims in a Post-war Society*, Aldershot UK: Ashgate.

Boyd, C. G. (1998) 'Making Bosnia Work', *Foreign Affairs*, 77: 42–55.

Bricker, M. K. (2005) 'Bosnian NGOs: The Quest for Sustainability', *Transition Online*, 9 June.

Burg, S. L. (1997) 'Bosnia and Herzegovina: A Case of Failed Democratization', in K. Dawisha and B. Parrot (eds) *Politics, Power, and the Struggle for Democracy in South-east Europe*, Cambridge: Cambridge University Press.

Burg, S. L. and Shoup, P. S. (1999) *The War in Bosnia-Herzegovina: Ethnic Conflict and International Intervention*, Armonk NY: M. E. Sharpe.

Campbell, D. (1998) *National Deconstruction: Violence, Identity and Justice in Bosnia*, Minneapolis MN: University of Minnesota Press.

Campbell, I. (2002) 'Each People in the Entire BiH has Constitutional Basis to Protect its Own Interests', Sarajevo: OHR, 4 April.

Caplan, R. (2005) *International Governance of War-torn Territories: Rule and Reconstruction*, Oxford: Oxford University Press.

Caspersen, N. (2004a) 'Intra-Ethnic Challenges to Nationalist Parties: SDS and Serb Opposition Before, During, and After the War', paper presented to the 7th international seminar on Democracy and Human Rights in Multi-Ethnic Societies, Konjić, Bosnia, July.

—— (2004b) 'Good Fences Make Good Neighbours? A Comparison of Conflict Regulation Strategies in Post-war Bosnia', *Journal of Peace Research*, 41: 569–88.

CEIS (Center for European Integration Strategies) (2006) *Overcoming the War in the Heads: Renewing Bosnia's Constitutional Debate*, Sarajevo/Geneva/Vienna, Policy Brief no. 5.

CFR (Council on Foreign Relations) (2003) *Balkans 2003*, New York: CFR.

Chandler, D. (1999) *Bosnia: Faking Democracy After Dayton*, London: Pluto.

—— (2004) 'Imposing the "Rule of Law": The Lessons of BiH for Peacebuilding in Iraq', *International Peacekeeping*, 11: 312–33.

Chayes, A., Chayes, A. and Raach, G. (1997) 'Beyond Reform: Restructuring for More Effective Conflict Intervention', *Global Governance*, 3: 117–45.

Chesterman, S., Ignatieff, M. and Thakur, R. (eds) (2005) *Making States Work: State Failure and the Crisis of Governance*, Tokyo: United Nations University Press.

Chollet, D. (2005) *The Road to the Dayton Accords: A Study in American Statecraft*, New York: Palgrave.

Circle 99 (1997) 'In Support of the Declaration of the Serb Civic Council', *99: Review of Free Thought*, 7–8: 81.

CoE (Council of Europe) (2004) 'Strengthening the Democratic Institutions in Bosnia and Herzegovina', Resolution 1384, 23 June.

Cohen, L. J. (2002) 'Fabricating Federalism in "Dayton Bosnia": Political Development and Future Options', in A. Heinemann-Gruder (ed.) *Federalism Doomed? European Federalism Between Integration and Separation*, New York and Oxford: Berghan.

CWG (Constitutional Working Group) (2006) *Amendments to the Constitution of Bosnia and Herzegovina*, Medford: The Dayton Peace Accords Project. Online. Available at: www.daytonproject.org (accessed 2 August 2006).

Cooper, R. (2004) *The Breaking of Nations: Order and Chaos in the Twenty-first Century*, London: Atlantic.

Cousens, E. M. and Cater, C. K. (2001) *Toward Peace in Bosnia: Implementing the Dayton Accords*, Boulder CO and London: Lynne Rienner.

Cox, M. (1999) 'The Dayton Agreement in Bosnia and Herzegovina: A Study of Implementation Strategies', *The British Yearbook of International Law 1999*, Oxford: Clarendon Press.

—— (2001) *State Building and Post-war Reconstruction: Lessons from Bosnia*, Geneva: Center for Applied Studies in International Negotiation (CASIN).

Cox, M. and Garlick, M. (2003) 'Musical Chairs: Property Repossession and Return Strategies in Bosnia and Herzegovina', in S. Leckie (ed.) *Returning Home: Housing and Property Restitution Rights of Refugees and Displaced Persons*, Ardsley NY: Transnational Publishers.

CRPC (Commission on Real Property Claims) (2004) *End of Mandate Report (1996–2003)*, Sarajevo: CRPC.

CRPC and UNHCR (1997) *Return, Relocation, and Property Rights: A Discussion Paper*, Sarajevo: CRCP and UNHCR, December.

Ćurak, N. (1998) 'Electing to Change', *Transitions*, 5: 28–33.

Cvijanović, Z. (2000) 'The Prophet: Ten Misconceptions about Milorad Dodik', *Dani*, 25 August.

Dani (2000) 'Deset tesa za Bosnu i Hercegovine,' Sarajevo: *Dani*, 28 January.

Deacon, B. and Stubbs, P. (1998) 'International Actors and Social Policy Development in Bosnia-Herzegovina', *Journal of European Social Policy*, 8: 99–115.

Deets, S. (2006) 'Public Policy in the Passive-Aggressive State: Health Care Reform in Bosnia-Hercegovina', *Europe-Asia Studies*, 58: 57–80.

Denitch, B. (1996) *Ethnic Nationalism: The Tragic Death of Yugoslavia*, Minneapolis: University of Minnesota Press.

Dobbins, J. F. (2003–4) 'America's Role in Nation-building: From Germany to Iraq', *Survival*, 45: 87–110.

Donais, T. (2005) *The Political Economy of Peacebuilding in Post-Dayton Bosnia*, London and New York: Routledge.

Donia, R. J. and Fine, J. V. A. (1994) *Bosnia and Herzegovina: A Tradition Betrayed*, New York: Columbia University Press.

Downes, A. B. (2007) 'The Problem with Negotiated Settlements to Ethnic Civil Wars', in M. Bloom and R. Licklider (eds) *Living Together After Ethnic Cleansing: Exploring the Chaim Kaufmann Argument*, New York: Routledge.

Du Toit, P. (2003) 'Why Post-settlement Settlements?', *Journal of Democracy*, 14: 104–18.

Duffield, M. (2001) *Global Governance and the New Wars: The Merging of Development and Security*, London and New York: Zed.

Elazar, D. (1985) 'Constitution-making: The Preeminently Political Act', in K. G. Baniting and R. Simeon (eds) *The Politics of Constitutional Change in Industrial Nations: Redesigning the State*, London: Macmillan.

ESI (European Stability Initiative) (2000) *Turning Point: The Brussels PIC Declaration and a State-Building Agenda for Bosnia and Herzegovina*, Berlin, Brussels and Istanbul: ESI, June.

—— (2002a) *A Real Life Story of Private Sector Growth in Bosnia*, Berlin, Brussels and Istanbul: ESI, February.

—— (2002b) *Imposing Constitutional Reform? The Case for Ownership*, Berlin, Brussels and Istanbul: ESI, March.

—— (2002c) *From Dayton to Europe: Land, Development and the Future of Democratic Planning*, Berlin, Brussels and Istanbul: ESI, December.

—— (2004a) *Making Federalism Work – A Radical Proposal for Practical Reform*, Berlin, Brussels and Istanbul: ESI, January.

—— (2004b) *Governance and Democracy in Bosnia and Herzegovina: Post-industrial Society and the Authoritarian Temptation*, Berlin, Brussels and Istanbul: ESI, June.

—— (2005a) *The Helsinki Moment: European Member-state Building in the Balkans*, Berlin, Brussels and Istanbul: ESI, February.

—— (2005b) *Breaking Out of the Balkan Ghetto: Why IPA Should Be Changed*, Berlin, Brussels and Istanbul: ESI, June.

—— (2007) *Legal Dynamite: How a Bosnian Court May Bring Closer the End of the Bosnian Protectorate*, Berlin, Brussels and Istanbul: ESI, March.

Evans, G. (2001) 'Sorry, the Boys Should Darn Well Stay in Bosnia', *International Herald Tribune*, 25 May.

EU (European Union) (2006a) *The Western Balkans on the Road to the EU: Consolidating Stability and Raising Prosperity*, Brussels: European Commission, 27 January.

—— (2006b) *Enlargement Strategy and Main Challenges 2006 – 2007: Including Annexed Special Report on the EU's Capacity to Integrate New Members*, Brussels: European Commission, 8 November.

—— (2006c) *Commission Staff Working Document: Bosnia and Herzegovina 2006 Progess Report*, Brussels: European Commission, 8 November.

EUWB (European Union/Western Balkans) (2006) *Joint Press Statement*, Salzburg, Austria, 11 March.

Evans-Kent, B. and Bleiker, R. (2003) 'Peace Beyond the State? NGOs in Bosnia and Herzegovina', *International Peacekeeping*, 10: 103–19.

Everly, R. (2006) 'Complex Public Power Regulation in Bosnia and Herzegovina after the Dayton Peace Agreement', *Ethnopolitics*, 5: 33–48.

Fagan, A. (2006) 'Civil Society in Bosnia Ten Years After Dayton', in D. Chandler (ed.) *Peace Without Politics? Ten Years of International State-Building in Bosnia*, London and New York: Routledge.

Fanon, F. (1991) *Black Skin, White Masks*, New York: Grove Press.

Fearon, J. D. and Laitin, D. (2004) 'Neotrusteeship and the Problem of Weak States', *International Security*, 28: 5–43.

Finci, J. (2001) 'Truth and Reconciliation Commission in B-H', in conference proceedings: Bosnia and Herzegovina in Europe, Sarajevo, 21–23 March.

—— (2004) 'The Federal Republic of Bosnia and Herzegovina', in C. Solioz and T. Vogel (eds) *Dayton and Beyond: Perspectives on the Future of Bosnia and Herzegovina*, Baden-Baden, Germany: Nomos.

Fischel de Andrade, J. and Delaney, N. (2001) 'Minority Return to South-Eastern Bosnia and Herzegovina: A Review of the Return Season,' *Journal of Refugee Studies*, 14: 315–30.

Freedom House (2001) 'Bosnia-Herzegovina', in *Nations in Transit 2001*, Washington DC: Freedom House.

Friedman, T. L. (2001) 'Not Happening', *New York Times*, 26 January.

Fox, W. and Wallich, C. (1997) *Fiscal Federalism in Bosnia-Hercegovina: The Dayton Challenge*, Washington DC: World Bank.

Fukuyama, F. (2004) *State Building: Governance and World Order in the Twenty-first Century*, London: Profile Books.

Gagnon, V. P. (2002) 'International NGOs in Bosnia-Herzegovina: Attempting to Build Civil Society', in S. E. Mendelson and J. K. Glenn (eds) *The Power and Limits of NGOs: A Critical Look at Building Democracy in Eastern Europe and Eurasia*, New York: Columbia University Press.

Gall, C. (2000) 'Three Main Nationalist Parties Showing Strength in Bosnia Vote', *New York Times*, 14 November.

Gienger, V. and Loza, T. (2003) 'Failure is not an Option', *Transitions Online*, 7 March. Online. Available at: www.tol.cz (accessed 8 March 2003).

Glenny, M. (1999) *The Balkans: Nationalism, War and the Great Powers. 1804–1999*, London: Viking.

Glover, J. (2002) 'King Paddy', *Guardian*, 11 October.

Gramsci, A. (1971) *Selections from the Prison Notebooks*, trans. Q. Hoare and G. Nowell-Smith, New York: International Publishers.

Grandits, H. (2007) 'The Power of "Armchair Politicians": Ethnic Loyalty and Political Factionalism among Herzegovinian Croats', in X. Bougarel, E. Helms and G. Duijzings (eds) *The New Bosnian Mosaic: Identities, Memories and Moral Claims in a Post-war Society*, Aldershot, UK: Ashgate.

Griffith, H. and Jelacić, N. (2004) 'Will Europe Take on Bosnia's Mafia?' *Balkan Crisis Report*, no. 531, 2 December.

Hadžiahmetović, A. (2006) 'The Economy of Bosnia-Herzegovina – Ten Years On', *Bosnia Report*, December/March, new series: 49–50. Online. Available at: www.bosnia.org.uk (accessed 8 February 2007).

Hathaway, J. C. (1997) 'The Meaning of Repatriation', *International Journal of Refugee Law*, 9: 551–58.

Hayden, R. M. (1999) *Blueprints for a House Divided: The Constitutional Logic of the Yugoslav Conflicts*, Ann Arbor MI: University of Michigan Press.

—— (2005) '"Democracy" without a Demos? The Bosnian Constitutional Experiment and the Intentional Construction of Nonfunctioning States', *East European Politics and Societies*, 19: 226–59.

Hays, D. (2004) 'Lessons We Re-learned in the Balkan Conflicts', keynote address at the Conference, Boston College, Boston MA, October.

HCHR (Helsinki Committee on Human Rights) (2003a) *Human Rights in Bosnia-Herzegovina*, Sarajevo: HCHR.

—— (2003b) *Report on the State of Human Rights in Bosnia and Herzegovina*. Sarajevo: HCHR, December.

—— (2005) *Report on the Status of Human Rights in Bosnia and Herzegovina*, Sarajevo: HCHR, January.

Hećimović, E. (2003) 'Amerikanci Prepustaju BIH Evropi,' *Dani*, 6 October.

—— (2006) 'Abu Hamzina javna tajna,' *Dani*, 3 November.

Hećimović, E. and Selimbegović, V. (2002) 'Deportacija uprkos zakonima,' *Dani*, 25 January.

Hedges, C. (1999) 'Leaders in Bosnia Are Said to Steal Up to $US 1 billion', *New York Times*, 17 August.

Hedl, D. (2001) 'Croatia Proposes Cantonisation', *Balkan Crisis Report*, no. 226, 14 March.

Heimerl, D. (2006) 'The Return of Refugees and Internally Displaced Persons: From Coercion to Sustainability?' in D. Chandler (ed.) *Peace Without Politics? Ten Years of International State-building in Bosnia*, London and New York: Routledge.

Hertić, Z., Sapčanin, S. and Woodward, S. L. (2001) 'Bosnia and Herzegovina', in S. Forman and S. Patrick (eds) *Good Intentions: Pledges of Aid for Post-conflict Recovery*, Boulder CO: Lynne Rienner.

Herzberg, B. (2004) *Investment Climate Reform: Going the Last Mile. The Bulldozer Initiative in Bosnia and Herzegovina*, Washington DC and Sarajevo: World Bank.

Hitchner, R. B. (2006) 'From Dayton to Brussels: The Story Behind the Constitutional Reform Process in Bosnia and Herzegovina', *The Fletcher Forum of World Affairs*, 30: 125–35.

Hockstader, L. (1997) 'Scattered Signs of Progress in Bosnia', *Washington Post*, 16 September.

Holbrooke, R. (1998) *To End a War*, New York: Random House.

Horowitz, D. (2000) *Ethnic Groups in Conflict*, 2nd edn, Berkeley CA: University of California Press.

Hovey, G. (2000) 'The Rehabilitation of Homes and Return of Minorities to Republika Srpska, Bosnia and Herzegovina', *Forced Migration Review*, 4: 8–11.

—— (2001) 'Discontent with Assistance to the Bosnian Return Process', *Forced Migration Review*, 11: 21–22.

HRCC (Human Rights Coordination Center) (1998) *LEA/LINK Draft Law on Association and Foundations*, Sarajevo: HRCC, June.

ICB (International Commission on the Balkans) (2005) *The Balkans in Europe's Future*, Sofia: Centre for Liberal Strategies, April.

ICG (International Crisis Group) (1996a) *Elections in Bosnia and Herzegovina, Part 1*, Sarajevo, 22 September. Online. Available at: www.crisisweb.org (all ICG reports available at this website).

—— (1996b) *The Dayton Peace Accord: A Six Month Review*, Sarajevo, 13 June.

—— (1997) *House Burnings: Obstruction to the Right to Return to Drvar*, Sarajevo, 9 June.

—— (1998a) *Minority Employment Principles*, Sarajevo, 1 December.

—— (1998b) *The Konjic Conundrum: Why Minorities Have Failed to Return to Model Open City*, Sarajevo, 19 July.

—— (1998c) *Minority Return or Mass Relocation?* Sarajevo, 14 May. Online.

—— (1998d) *Changing the Logic of Bosnian Politics*, Sarajevo, 10 March. Online.

—— (1999) *Is Dayton Failing? Bosnia Four Years After the Peace Agreement*, Sarajevo, 28 October.

—— (2001a) *Bosnia's Precarious Economy: Still Not Open for Business*, Sarajevo, 7 August.

—— (2001b) *Turning Strife to Advantage: A Blueprint to Integrate the Croats in Bosnia and Herzegovina*, Sarajevo, 15 March.

—— (2002a) *The Continuing Challenge of Minority Return in Bosnia and Herzegovina*, Sarajevo, 13 December.

—— (2002b) *Implementing Equality: The Constituent People Decision in Bosnia-Herzegovina*, Sarajevo, 16 April.

—— (2003a) *Building Bridges in Mostar*, Sarajevo, 20 November.

—— (2003b) *Bosnia's Nationalist Governments: Paddy Ashdown and the Paradoxes of State Building*, Sarajevo, 22 July.

—— (2007) *Ensuring Bosnia's Future: A New International Engagement Strategy*, Sarajevo, 15 February.

IEOM (International Election Observation Mission) (2002) *General Elections – Bosnia and Herzegovina 2002*, Sarajevo: IEOM, 6 October.

Ignatieff, M. (2003) *Empire Lite: Nation-building in Bosnia, Kosovo and Afghanistan*, London: Penguin.

Ingram, J. K. (2001) 'BiH Competitiveness Report: A Milestone in the Development Process', speech delivered at the Academy of Science and Arts of Bosnia-Herzegovina, 18 May, Sarajevo (typescript).

Ito, A. (2001a) 'Politicisation of Minority Return in Bosnia and Herzegovina – The First Five Years Examined', *International Journal of Refugee Law*, 13: 98–122.

—— (2001b) 'Return to Prijedor: Politics and UNHCR', *Forced Migration Review*, 10: 35–7.

Ivanić, M. (2005) 'The International Community and Bosnia-Herzegovina', *Cambridge Review of International Affairs*, 18: 275–82.

Ivanisević, B. (2004) *Legacy of War: Minority Returns in the Balkans*, New York: Human Rights Watch, January.

Izetbegović, A. (2003) *Inescapable Questions: Autobiographical Notes*, Leicester UK: The Islamic Foundation.

Jackson-Preece, J. (2005) *Minority Rights: Between Diversity and Community*, Cambridge: Polity.

Jarstad, A. (2004) *International Assistance to Democratisation and Reconciliation in Bosnia and Herzegovina*, Uppsala, Sweden: Report no. 4 of the project 'Democratisation and Reconciliation in Post-intrastate Conflict Situations', Department of Peace and Conflict Research, Uppsala University.

Jelacić, N. and Ahmetasević, N. (2003) 'Bosnia: Strikes Reflect Economic Woes,' *Balkan Crisis Report*, no. 462, 3 October.

—— (2006) 'Truth Commission Divides Bosnia', *Balkan Insight*, 31 March.

Kaldor, M. (1999) *New and Old Wars: Organized Violence in a Global Era*, Stanford CA: Stanford University Press.

Katana, G. (1999) 'NGOs in Republika Srpska: Bashful Support of the Regime', *AIM Banja Luka*, 20 September.

—— (2003) 'Bosnian Serbs Select President', *Balkan Crisis Report*, no. 424, 17 April.

—— (2005) 'New Bosnian Serb Government Underwhelms', *Balkan Crisis Report*, no. 536, 14 January.

—— (2006) 'Bosnian Serbs to Challenge Symbols Ruling', *Balkan Insight*, 10 May.

Kaufmann, C. D. (1999) 'When All Else Fails: Evaluating Population Transfers and Partition as Solutions to Ethnic Conflict', in B. F. Walter and J. Snyder (eds) *Civil Wars, Insecurity and Intervention*, New York: Columbia University Press.

Keane, R. (2001) *Reconstituting Sovereignty: Post-Dayton Bosnia Uncovered*, Aldershot UK: Ashgate.

Kerr, R. (2004) *The International Criminal Tribunal for the Former Yugoslavia: An Exercise in Law, Politics, and Diplomacy*, Oxford: Oxford University Press.

Knaus, G. and Martin, F. (2003) 'Travails of the European Raj', *Journal of Democracy*, 14: 60–74.

Kostakos, G. (1998) 'Division of Labor Among International Organizations: The Bosnian Experience', *Global Governance*, 4: 461–84.

Krasner, S. D. (2004) 'Sharing Sovereignty: New Institutions for Collapsed and Failing States,' *International Security*, 29: 85–120.

Kull, S. and Ramsay, C. (2003) 'U.S. Public Opinion on Intervention in Bosnia', in R. Sobel and E. Shiraev (eds) *International Public Opinion and the Bosnia Crisis*, Lanham MD: Lexington.

Lampe, J. R. (1996) *Yugoslavia as History: Twice There was a Country*, Cambridge: Cambridge University Press.

Licklider, R. (1995) 'The Consequences of Negotiated Settlements in Civil Wars, 1945–1993', *American Political Science Review*, 89: 681–90.

Licklider, R. and Bloom, M. (eds) (2007) *Living Together After Ethnic Killing: Exploring the Chaim Kaufmann Argument*, New York: Routledge.

Lijphart, A. (1977) *Democracy in Plural Societies: A Comparative Exploration*, New Haven CT: Yale University Press.

—— (1999) *Patterns of Democracy: Government Forms and Performance in Thirty-six Countries*, New Haven CT: Yale University Press.

—— (2003) 'Consociationalism and Bosnia', email (30 October).

Lindvall, D. (2003) 'The Resurrection of Bosnia on the Dayton Respirator', in S. Kuhnle and D. Sokolović (eds) *The Balkans: Searching for Solutions*, Bergen, Norway: Stein Rokkan Center for Social Studies.

Linz, J. J. and Stepan, A. (1996) *Problems of Democratic Transition and Consolidation: Southern Europe, South America, and Post-Communist Europe*, Baltimore MD and London: Johns Hopkins University Press.

Lippman, P. (1999) *The Advocacy Project: OTR Bosnia*, 12 May. Online. Available at: www.advocacynet.autoupdate (accessed 12 November 2002).

Lischer-Kenyon, S. (2003) 'Collateral Damage: Humanitarian Assistance as Cause of Conflict,' *International Security*, 28: 79–109.

Lithander, A. (ed.) (2001) *Engendering the Peace Process: A Gender Approach to Dayton and Beyond*, Stockholm: Kvinna till Kvinna Foundation.

Lovrenović, Ivan (2001) *Bosnia: A Cultural History*, London: Saqi Books.

Lyon, J. M. B. (2000) 'Will Bosnia Survive Dayton?', *Current History*, March: 110–16.

Loizides, N. and Keskiner E. (2004) 'The Aftermath of the Annan Plan Referendums: Cross-voting Moderation for Cyprus?', *Southeast European Politics*, 5: 158–71.

Loza, T. (2004) 'Unlocking the Future', in C. Solioz and T. Vogel (eds) *Dayton and Beyond: Perspectives on the Future of Bosnia and Herzegovina*, Baden-Baden, Germany: Nomos.

Luttwak, E. N. (1999) 'Give War a Chance', *Foreign Affairs*, 78: 36–44.

Malcolm, N. (1996) *A Short History of Bosnia*, New York: Columbia University Press.

Mann, M. (2004) *The Dark Side of Democracy: Explaining Ethnic Cleansing*, Cambridge: Cambridge University Press.

Manning, C. and Antić, M. (2003) 'Democracy in Search of a State? Elections in Bosnia-Herzegovina, 1996–2002', *Journal of Democracy*, 14: 45–59.

Mansfield, A. M. (2003) 'Ethnic but Equal: The Quest for a New Democratic Order in Bosnia and Herzegovina', *Columbia Law Review*, 103: 2052–93.

Moore, P. (2005) 'Bosnian Serbs Accept Poice Reform', RFE/RL Newsline, 6 October.

MRGI (Minority Rights Group International) (2003) *The Decision of the Constitutional Court of Bosnia and Herzegovina on the Constituent Status of Peoples and the Process of Return*, London, June.

MSI (Management System International) (2000) *United States Agency for International Development/Bosnia and Herzegovina: Civic Participation and Organizing Assessment*, Sarajevo: MSI, 30 March.

Mueller, J. (2000) 'The Banality of "Ethnic War"', *International Security*, 25: 42–70.

Nazi, F. and Rutzen, D. (2003) 'Iraq Reconstruction – Heeding Balkan Lessons,' *Balkan Crisis Report*, no. 427, 2 May.

NDI (National Democratic Institute for International Affairs) (2002) 'A Survey of Voter Attitudes in B and H: Summary Report', 28 February.

Neville-Jones, P. (1996–97) 'Dayton, IFOR, and Alliance Relations in Bosnia,' *Survival* 38: 45–65.

Nowak, M. (2001) 'Human Rights and Refugee Return', in G. de Vergottini and R. H. Evans (eds) *Strategies for the Future of Bosnia-Herzegovina and Croatia*, Turin, Italy: Giappichelli.

—— (2004) 'Has Dayton Failed?', in C. Solioz and T. Vogel (eds) *Dayton and Beyond: Perspectives on the Future of Bosnia and Herzegovina*, Baden-Baden, Germany: Nomos.

OHR (Office of the High Representative) (1999) *A Comprehensive Strategy for a Just and Efficient Returns Process in Bosnia and Herzegovina*, Sarajevo: OHR, 27 October.

—— (2001a) *Communique of The Steering Board of the Peace Implementation Council*, Sarajevo: OHR, 21 June.

—— (2001b) *Decision Establishing Interim Procedures to Protect Vital Interests of Constituent Peoples and Others, Including Freedom from Discrimination*, Sarajevo: OHR, 11 January.

—— (2003) *Brcko Supervisor Launches Public Debate on District Election Law*, Sarajevo: OHR, 6 June.

—— (2005a) *Mission Implementation Plan*. Sarajevo: OHR, March.

—— (2005b) *Communique by the PIC Steering Board*, Sarajevo: OHR, 24 June.

—— (2005c) *Communique by the PIC Steering Board*, Sarajevo: OHR, 15 December.

—— (2007) *High Representative's Decisions by Topic*, Sarajevo: OHR. Online. Available at: http://ohr.int/decisions/archive.asp (accessed 10 April 2007)

Omanović, S. (2005) *Accepting Responsibility: Moving Beyond Political and Economic Dependence in Post-conflict Bosnia and Herzegovina*, Washington DC: Center For International Private Enterprise, 9 February.

Orentilicher, D. (1998) 'Separation Anxiety: International Responses to Ethno-separatist Claims', *Yale Journal of International Law*, 23: 1–78.

OSCE (Organization for Security and Cooperation in Europe) (1998) *Information and Strategy on the Neglected Areas*, Sarajevo: OSCE, 20 June.

—— (1999a) *Democratization Department Semi-annual Report: January–June 1998*, Sarajevo: OSCE, January.

—— (1999b) *Employment Discrimination in Bosnia and Herzegovina*, Sarajevo: OSCE, June.

—— (2000a) 'PEC Adopts Rules on Federation House of Peoples and Federation President, Vice President', Sarajevo: OSCE, 19 October.

—— (2000b) 'PEC Adopts New Rules for General Elections', Sarajevo: OSCE, 31 May.

—— (2000c) 'Domi Reaffirms Draft Election Law's Preferential Voting System', Sarajevo: OSCE, 5 January.

—— (2002a) 'Fostering Regional Dialogues Through Media', Pristina: OSCE, 29 November.

—— (2002b) 'Fact Sheet on the 2002 BiH Elections', Sarajevo: OSCE, July.

—— (2002c) 'Implementation of the Constitutional Amendments to Entity Constitutions on the Constituent Peoples Decision of the Constitutional Court,' Sarajevo: OSCE, May.

Oslobođenje (2003) 'Deklaraciju o Nužnosti Izmjena Ustava Bosna I Hercegovine I o Ustrojstvu "Federalne Republike Bosne I Hercegovine"',12 July.

Owen, D. (1995) *Balkan Odyssey*, New York: Harcourt Brace.

Pajić, Z. (2002) 'The Role of Institutions in Peace Building: (Rule of Law in Bosnia and Herzegovina)', in F. Butler (ed.) *Human Rights Protection: Methods and Effectiveness*. London: Kluwer Law.

Papić, Ž. (1999) 'Etnička privatizacija: neogranicene mogucosti', *Dani*, 6 August.

—— (2001) 'The General Situation in B-H and International Support Policies', in Ž. Papić (ed.) *International Support Policies to SEE Countries – Lessons (Not) Learned in Bosnia-Herzegovina*, Sarajevo: Mueller.

—— (2006) 'Eleven Theses on the Future of Bosnia-Herzegovina', *Bosnia Report*, December/ March, new series 49/50. Online. Available at: www.bosnia.org.uk (accessed 20 February 2007).

Paris, R. (2004) *At War's End: Building Peace After Civil Conflict*, Cambridge: Cambridge University Press.

Partos, G. (1999) 'Return in Slow Motion', *Transitions*, 6: 42–5.

Pecanin, S. (2002) 'Protectorate Makes More Sense', *Dani*, 25 October.

Pejanović, M. (2002) *Through Bosnian Eyes: The Political Memoirs of a Bosnian Serb*, Sarajevo: TDK.

Perić, B. (2000) 'Post-Electoral Analyses: Why Did Dodik Fail?', AIM Banja Luka, 17 November, available at: www.aimpress.ch/dyn/trae/archive/data/200011/01122-002-trae-sar.htm

Petritsch, W. (2002a) *Bosna i Hercegovina od Daytona do Evrope*, Sarajevo: Svjetlost.

—— (2002b) 'BiH's Future is Europe', *Oslobojenje*, 20 May.

—— (2002c) 'Press Conference of the High Representative on the Completion of the Constitutional Reform Process in Bosnia and Herzegovina's Entities', Sarajevo, 19 April (transcript).

Pfaff, W. (2002) 'Time to Concede Defeat in Bosnia', *International Herald Tribune*, 10 October.

Philpott, C. (2005) 'Though the Dog is Dead, the Pig Must be Killed: Finishing with Property Restitution to Bosnia-Herzegovina's IDPs and Refugees', *Journal of Refugee Studies*, 18: 1–24.

Phuong, C. (2000a) 'Freely to Return: Reversing Ethnic Cleansing in Bosnia and Herzegovina', *Journal of Refugee Studies*, 13: 165–83.

—— (2000b) 'At the Heart of the Return Process: Solving Property Issues in Bosnia-Herzegovina', *Forced Migration Review* (April): 5–7.

PIC (Peace Implementation Council) (1997a) *Bosnia and Herzegovina 1998: Self-Sustaining Structures*, Bonn, Germany: PIC, 9–10 December.

—— (1997b). *Political Declaration from the Ministerial Meeting of the Steering Board*, Sintra: PIC, 30 May.

—— (1998) *Declaration of the Peace Implementation Council*, Madrid: PIC, 16 December.

—— (2000) *Declaration of the Peace Implementation Council*, Brussels: PIC, 22 May.

—— (2007) *Communiqué by the PIC Steering Board*, Brussels: PIC, 27 February.

Pickering, P. M. (2003) 'The Choices that Minorities Make: Strategies of Negotiation with the Majority in Post-war Bosnia-Herzegovina', in D. Keridis (ed.) *New Approaches to Balkan Studies*, San Francisco: Brassey's.

—— (2006) 'Generating Social Capital for Bridging Ethnic Divisions in the Balkans: Case Studies of Two Bosniak Cities', *Ethnic and Racial Studies*, 29: 79–103.

Popper, K. R. (1961) *The Poverty of Historicism*, London: Routledge and Kegan Paul.

Prce, M. (2001) 'Revising Dayton Using European Solutions', *Fletcher Forum of World Affairs*, 25: 143–51.

Pugh, M. (2006) 'Transformation in the Political Economy of Bosnia Since Dayton', in D. Chandler (ed.) *Peace Without Politics? Ten Years of International State-building in Bosnia*, London and New York: Routledge.

Pugh, M. and Cobble, M. (2001) 'Non-nationalist Voting in Bosnia Municipal Elections: Implications for Democracy and Peacebuilding', *Journal of Peace Research*, 38: 27–47.

Pupavac, V. (2006) 'Empowering Women? An Assessment of International Gender Policies in Bosnia', in D. Chandler (ed.) *Peace Without Politics? Ten Years of International State-building in Bosnia*, London: Routledge.

Raguz, V. M. (2001) 'A New Era Calls for New Thinking About Dayton', *Financial Times*, 1–2 June.

Ramet, S. P. (1992) *Nationalism and Federalism in Yugoslavia, 1962–1991*, Bloomington IN: Indiana University Press.

Rao, R. (2004) 'The Empire Writes Back (to Michael Ignatieff)', *Millennium: Journal of International Studies*, 33: 145–66.

Recchia, S. (2007) *Beyond International Trusteeship: EU Peacebuilding in Bosnia and Herzegovina*, Paris: Institute for Security Studies, Occassional Paper no. 66, February.

Rees, M. (2002) 'Protection in Conflict and Peacebuilding: Some Lessons from Bosnia-Herzegovina', *Humanitarian Practice Network*. Online. Avalaible at: www.odihpn.org/report.asp?ID = 2517 (accessed 15 September 2002).

Reilly, B. (2001) *Democracy in Deeply Divided Societies: Electoral Engineering for Conflict Management*, Cambridge: Cambridge University Press.

—— (2002) 'Post-conflict Elections: Constraints and Dangers', *International Peacekeeping*, 9: 118–39.

Reuters (1997) 'Swiss Stick to Plan to Repatriate Bosnian Refugees', 9 June.

Richmond, O. P. (2002) *Maintaining Order, Making Peace*, Houndmills UK: Palgrave.

Roeder, P. G. and Rotchild, D. (eds) (2005) *Sustainable Peace: Democracy and Power-dividing Institutions After Civil Wars*, Ithaca NY: Cornell University Press.

Rosand, E. (1998) 'The Right to Return Under International Law Following Mass Dislocation: The Bosnia Precedent?', *Michigan Journal of International Law*, 19: 1091–1139.

Rose, G. (1998) 'The Exit Strategy Delusion', *Foreign Affairs*, 77: 56–67.

Ross, H. M. (2001) 'Evaluation in Conflict Resolution Training and Practice,' in R. M. Schoenhaus (ed.) *Conflict Management Training: Advancing Best Practices*, Washington DC: Peaceworks 36, January.

Rotberg, R. I. (2004) 'The Failure and Collapse of Nation-states: Breakdown, Prevention and Repair', in R. I. Rotberg (ed.) *When States Fail: Causes and Consequences*, Princeton NJ: Princeton University Press.

RRTF (Regional Return Task Force) (1998) *1999 RRTF Action Plan*, Sarajevo: RRTF, 13 December.

RSNA (Serbian Press Agency) (2002) 'Yugoslav President Supports NGO Initiative for Visa-Free Border Regime', 22 February.

Rusinow, D. (1995) 'The Avoidable Catastrophe', in S. P. Ramet and L. Adamovich (eds) *Beyond Yugoslavia: Politics, Economics, and Culture in a Shattered Community*, Boulder CO: Westview.

Šabić, S. S. (2005) 'Post-war State Building: Germany in 1945 and Bosnia-Herzegovina in 1995', in F. Bieber and C. Wieland (eds) *Facing the Past, Facing the Future: Confronting Ethnicity and Conflict in Bosnia and Former Yugoslavia*, Ravenna, Italy: Longo.

Sali-Terzić, S. (2001) 'Civil Society', in Z. Papić (ed.) *International Support Policies to SEE Countries – Lessons (Not) Learned in Bosnia-Herzegovina*, Sarajevo: Mueller.

Sampson, S. (2002) *Weak States, Uncivil Societies and Thousands of NGOs: Western Democracy Exported as Benevolent Colonialism in the Balkans*, Lund, Sweden, June, draft.

Sartori, G. (1997) *Comparative Constitutional Engineering: An Inquiry into Structures, Incentives, and Outcomes*, Houndsmills, UK: Macmillan.

SCC (Serb Civic Council) (1997) 'Declaration of the Serb Civic Council of Bosnia-Herzegovina on the Human Right to Political and National Equality', *Bosnia*

Report, June/August, 19. Online. Available at: www.bosniareport.org (accessed 10 February 2002).

—— (1998) *Extract from the Platform of Activities and Development of the Serb Civic Council Civic Movement of Equality*, Sarajevo: SCC.

Schwarz-Schilling, C. (2006) 'Bosnia's Way Forward', *IP Global Issues*, spring: 84–86.

SEESAC (South Eastern Europe Clearing House for the Control of Small Arms and Light Weapons) (2004) *Bosnia and Herzegovina: Small Arms and Light Weapons Ammunition Demilitarization Feasibility Study*, Belgrade: SEESAC.

Selimbegović, V. (2001) 'Intervju Dana: Robert Barry "Nije to ta diskriminacija"', *Dani*, 20 April.

Sell, L. (2000) 'The Serbs' Flight From Sarajevo: Dayton's First Failure', *East European Politics and Societies*, 14: 179–202.

Serwer, D. (1999) 'A Bosnian Federation Memoir', in C. Crocker, F. O. Hampson and P. Hall (eds) *Herding Cats: Multiparty Mediation in a Complex World*, Washington DC: United States Institute of Peace Press.

Shoup, P. (1997) 'The Elections in Bosnia and Herzegovina: The End of an Illusion', *Problems of Post-Communism*, 44: 3–15.

Silajdžić, H. (2000) 'Why Dayton Must be Change', *Bosnia Report*, March/June. Online. Available at: www.bosniareport.org (accessed 10 February 2002).

Silber, L. and Little, A. (1996) *Yugoslavia: Death of a Nation*, London: Penguin.

Simić, D. (2002) 'The Algerian Case: Between Politics and Principles', *AIM*, 2 February.

Simpson, D. (2003) 'A Nation Unbuilt: Where Did All That Money in Bosnia Go?', *New York Times*, 16 February.

Sinanović, E. (2003) 'Building Democracy Top-down: The Role of International Factors in Promoting Civil Society and Democracy in Bosnia and Herzegovina', in C. Solioz and S. Dizdarevic (eds) *Ownership Process in Bosnia and Herzegovina*. Baden-Baden, Germany: Nomos.

Sinanović, N. (2000) 'The Question of Cantonization', *Bosnia Report*, March/June, new series 15/16. Online. Available at: www.bosniareport.org (accessed 20 February 2002).

Singer, P. W. (2000) 'Bosnia 2000: Phoenix or Flames?' *World Policy Journal*, 27: 31–37.

Skrbić, M. (2004) 'Bosnia: the VAT spat', *Transitions Online*, 15 November. Online. Available at: www.tol.cz (accessed 17 November 2004).

—— (2005) 'Bosnia: A Meaty Indictment', *Transitions Online*, 7 March. Online. Available at: www.tol.cz (accessed 7 March 2005).

Skrbić, M. and Vogel, T. K. (2006) 'Constitutional Reform Falters', *Transitions Online*, 27 April. Online. Available at: www.tol.cz (accessed 28 April 2006).

Slack, A. J. and Doyon, R. R. (2001) 'Population Dynamics and the Susceptibility of Ethnic Conflict', *Journal of Peace Research*, 38: 139–61.

Slatina, J. (1999) 'Empty Declaration,' *Institute of War and Peace Reporting*, 27 August.

Slatina, S. (2002) 'Hands Off Pledge over Bosnia,' *Balkan Crisis Report*, 351, 18 July.

Smillie, I. (1996) *Service Delivery or Civil Society? Non-governmental Organizations in Bosnia and Herzegovina*, Sarajevo: Care Canada.

Smillie, I. and Todorović, G. (2001) 'Reconstructing Bosnia, Constructing Civil Society: Disjuncture and Convergence', in I. Smillie (ed.) *Patronage or Partnership: Local Capacity Building in Humanitarian Crisis*, Bloomfield CT: Kumarian Press.

Smith, J. (2000) 'West is Trying to Rebuild Bosnia; Five Years After War's End, Efforts Have Largely Failed', *Washington Post*, 25 November.

Smyth, M. and Robinson, G. (2001) (eds) *Researching Violently Divided Societies: Ethical and Methodological Issues*, Tokyo: United Nations University Press and London: Pluto.

Sokolović, D. (2001) 'Social Reconstruction and Moral Restoration', in D. Sokolović and F. Bieber (eds) *Reconstructing Multiethnic Societies: The Case of Bosnia-Herzegovina*, Aldershot, UK: Ashgate.

Solioz, C. (2005) *Turning-Points in Post-war Bosnia: Ownership Process and European Integration*, Baden-Baden, Germany: Nomos.

Sonn, M. (2003) 'Ownership in Institution Building', in C. Solioz and S. Dizdarević (eds) *Ownership Process in Bosnia and Herzegovina*, Baden-Baden, Germany: Nomos.

SPAI (Stability Pact Anti-Corruption Initiative) (2002) *Empowering Civil Society in the Fight Against Corruption in South East Europe: Bosnia and Herzegovina Civil Society Assessment Report*, Sarajevo: SPAI (SPAI/SG/MON/CS(02)BiH).

Stark, D. and Bruszt, L. (1998) *Postsocialist Pathways : Transforming Politics and Property in East Central Europe*, Cambridge: Cambridge University Press.

Stedman, S. J. (2002) 'Policy Implications', in S. J. Stedman, D. Rotchild and E. Cousens (eds) *Ending Civil Wars: The Implementation of Peace Agreements*, Boulder CO: Lynne Rienner.

Sterland, B. (2003) *Serving the Community: An Assessment of Civil Society in Rural BiH*, Sarajevo: Daedalos Association for Peace Education Work.

Stiglmayer, A. (2002) 'Constitutional Reform in BiH: RS Is Becoming Multi-Ethnic', *Jutarnje Novine*, 15 April.

Stokes, G. (2003) 'Solving the Wars of Yugoslav Secession', in N. M. Mainark and H. Case (eds) *Yugoslavia and Its Historians: Understanding the Balkan Wars of the 1990s*, Stanford CA: Stanford University Press.

Stroschein, S. (2003) 'What Belgium Can Teach Bosnia: The Uses of Autonomy in "Divided House" States,' *Journal on Ethnopolitics and Minority Issues in Europe*, 3. Online. Available at: www.de/jemie7download/Focus3–2003_stroschein.pdf (accessed 2 June 2006)

—— (2005). 'Examining Ethnic Violence and Partition in Bosnia-Herzegovina,' *Ethnopolitics*, 4: 1–16.

Stubbs, P. (1999) *Displaced Promises: Forced Migration, Refugees and Return in Croatia and Bosnia-Herzegovina*, Uppsala, Sweden: Life and Peace Institute.

—— (2000) 'Partnership or Colonisation? The Relationship between International Agencies and Local Non-governmental Organisations in Bosnia-Herzegovina', in B. Deacon (ed.) *Civil Society, NGOs, and Global Governance*, Sheffield UK: GASPP Occasional Paper no. 7/2000.

Todorova, M. (1997) *Imagining the Balkans*, Oxford: Oxford University Press.

Tokić, S. (2003) 'Present and Future in Bosnia and Herzegovina', in C. Solioz and S. Dizdarević (eds) *Ownership Process in Bosnia and Herzegovina*, Baden-Baden, Germany: Nomos.

TI (Transparency International) (2006) *Annual Report*, Berlin: Transparency International.

Traynor, I. (2007) 'German Bosnia Chief "Fired" After Just a Year', *Guardian*, 24 January.

TWST (To Work and Succeed Together) (2002) *A Strategy for the Development of a Viable Non-government Sector in BiH*, Sarajevo: TWST.

Tzifakis, N. and Tsardanidis, C. (2006) 'Economic Reconstruction of Bosnia and Herzegovina: The Lost Decade', *Ethnopolitics*, 5: 67–84.

Udovički, J. (1997) 'Conclusion', in J. Udovički and J. Ridgeway (eds) *Burn this House: The Making and Unmaking of Yugoslavia*, Durham NC and London: Duke University Press.

UNDF (United Nations Development Fund for Women) (2004) *Gender Profile of the Conflict in Bosnia and Herzegovina*, New York: UNDF.

UNDP (United Nations Development Programme) (1999) *Human Development Report. Bosnia-Herzegovina 1998*, Sarajevo: UNDP.

—— (2000) *Human Development Report. Bosnia-Herzegovina 2000: Youth*, Sarajevo: UNDP.

—— (2001a) *Early Warning System: Annual Report*, Sarajevo: UNDP.

—— (2001b) *Early Warning System, April-June 2001*, Sarajevo: UNDP.

—— (2002a) *Human Development Report 2002: Bosnia and Herzegovina*, Sarajevo: UNDP.

—— (2002b) *Early Warning System: Annual Report*, Sarajevo: UNDP.

—— (2002c) *Early Warning System: Bosnia and Herzegovina 2002 – Election Special*, Sarajevo: UNDP.

UNHCR (United Nations High Commissioner for Refugees) (1997) *The State of the World's Refugees: A Humanitarian Agenda*, Oxford: Oxford University Press.

—— (2000) *Daunting Prospects – Minority Women: Obstacles to their Return and Reintegration*, Sarajevo: UNHCR.

—— (2001) *Collective Centres Reports*, Sarajevo: UNHCR.

—— (2002a) *A New Strategic Direction: Proposed Ways Ahead for Property Law Implementation in a Time of Decreasing IC Resources*, Sarajevo: UNHCR.

—— (2002b) *Prijedor: Municipality Background Report*, Banja Luka: UNHCR.

—— (2003) *UNHCR's Concerns with the Designation of Bosnia and Herzegovina as a Safe County of Origin*, Sarajevo: UNHCR.

—— (2004) *Closing the Circle: From Emergency Humanitarian Relief to Sustainable Development in South Eastern Europe*, Geneva: UNHCR.

—— (2005) *Balkan Governments Seek to Close Refugee Chapter in Region*, Sarajevo: UNHCR.

Ustavni sud BiH (2000) Case no. U-98/5 III, 1 July (all cases available at www.ccbh.ba/en/decisions).

—— (2004a) Case no. U-2/04, 28 May.

—— (2004b) Case no. U-2/04, 25 June.

—— (2004c) Case no. U-44/01, 22 September.

—— (2005) Case no. U-8/04, 25 June.

—— (2006) Case no. U-4/04, 31 March.

Varshney, A. (2002) *Ethnic Conflict and Civic Life: Hindus and Muslims in India*, New Haven CT: Yale University Press.

Venice Commission (2001) 'Opinion on the Electoral Law of Bosnia and Herzegovina', Strasbourg: Venice Commission, 24 October.

—— (2005) 'Opinion on the Constitutional Situation in Bosnia and Herzegovina and the Powers of the High Representative', Venice: Venice Commission, 12 March.

—— (2006) 'Preliminary Opinion on the Draft Amendments to the Constitution of Bosnia and Herzegovina', Venice: Venice Commission, 7 April.

Verdery, K. (1999) *The Political Lives of Dead Bodies: Reburial and Post-socialist Change*, New York: Columbia University Press.

Walter, B. F. (1999) 'Designing Transitions from Civil War', in B. F. Walter and J. Snyder (eds) *Civil Wars, Insecurity, and Intervention*, New York: Columbia University Press.

Waters, T. W. (1999) 'The Naked Land: The Dayton Accord, Property Disputes, and Bosnia's Real Constitution', *Harvard International Law Journal*, 40: 517–93.

—— (2004) 'Contemplating Failure and Creating Alternatives in the Balkans: Bosnia's Peoples, Democracy, and the Shape of Self-Determination', *Yale International Law Journal*, 29: 423–75.

WBOED (World Bank Operations Evaluation Department) (2004) *Bosnia and Herzegovina: Post-conflict Reconstruction and the Transition to a Market Economy*, Washington DC: World Bank.

Wedel, J. (1998) *Collision and Collusion: The Strange Case of Western Aid to Eastern Europe 1989–1998*, New York: St Martin's Press.

Wesselingh, I. and Valeurin, A. (2003) *Bosnia: La mémoire à vif: Prijedor, laboratoire de la purification ethnique*, Paris: Buchet/Chastel.

Wheeler, M. (2003) 'Exit or Integration: The International Agenda in Bosnia and Hercegovina Over the Next Three Years', in D. Sokolovic (ed.) *Democracy Papers*, Konjić: Institute for Strengthening Democracy.

Wippman, D. (1998) 'Practical and Legal Constraints on International Power-sharing', in D. Wippman (ed.) *International Law and Ethnic Conflict*, Ithaca NY and London: Cornell University Press.

Wood, N. (2004) 'Bosnia Seeks Return of 6 Detainees Held by US in Bomb Plot', *New York Times*, 22 October.

Woodward, S. L. (1995) *Balkan Tragedy: Chaos and Dissolution After the Cold War*, Washington DC: Brookings Institution Press.

—— (1999) 'How Not to End a Civil War', in J. Snyder and B. Walter (eds) *Civil War, Insecurity, and Intervention*, New York: Columbia University Press.

World Bank (1997) *Bosnia and Herzegovina: From Recovery to Sustainable Growth*, Washington DC: World Bank.

—— (2002) *Local Level Institutions and Social Capital Study*, vol. 1, June, Washington DC: World Bank.

—— (2003) *Breaking the Conflict Trap: Civil War and Development Policy*, Washington DC: World Bank and Oxford: Oxford University Press.

Zaum, D. (2007) *The Sovereignty Paradox: The Norms and Politics of International Statebuilding*, Oxford: Oxford University Press.

Index

Acton, Lord J. 2
aid 33, 52, 96–97, 100–102, 105, 109, 149, 180; conditionality 135; NGOs dependency on 110–12; to the RS 86; in wartime 107.
Alagić, M. 134
'Algerians' case' 115–17, 174
Alliance for Change 2, 85–86, 99, 175, 179
Al-Qaeda 115, 151
Aluminij Mostar 105
Amnesty International (AI) 68, 116, 134
Ashdown, P. 25, 31, 32, 39, 93, 123, 124, 153, 155, 186n5
Association of Multi-Ethnic Cities of Southeastern Europe 120
autonomists 3–4, 28, 37–38, 67; author's criticism of 38–40, 67–68

Banja Luka: Ferhadija mosque in 117, 145; refugee returns to 135–36
Barry, R. 84, 89
'Barry Rule' 84–86
Belgium 17; consociationalism in 44, 46; electoral system in 89
Belkacem, B. 115
Bell, C. 183
Bentham, J. 160
Bieber, F. 177
BiH Women Initiative 118–19
Bihać 8
Bildt, C. 22, 23, 44, 133
Bose, S. 40, 83
Bosnian Civil Society Foundation 171
Boyd, C. 101
Bratunac 148
Brčko: status in BiH 49, 163–64, 187n; election law 94

Brecht, B. 86
Budiša, D. 56
Bukejlović, P. 93
Bulldozer Initiative 106, 170

Campbell, I. 67
Caspersen, N. 182
Čavić, D. 93, 155
Chandler, D. 38, 67
Circle 99 59
Clarke, H. 94
Clausewitz, C. 78
Clinton, B. 96, 138, 186n2
CoE (Council of Europe) 87, 114; BiH accession to 154; and critique of Bonn powers 31 see also Venice Commission
conclusions 173–85; and the limits of international intervention 174–80; and positive lessons 181–84
consociationalism 3, 43, 44, 167; and 1996–98 elections 74–78; and electoral rules 76; problems with 50–54, 72, 160–61; in Yugoslavia 19
constituent peoples' case 11, 44, 58–70, 161, 181; constitutional changes 65–66; constitutional commissions 63–65; impact of 62, 66–70
constitutional court 32, 51, 88, 161, 176, 182, 191n1; constituent peoples' case 11, 44, 49, 58–70, 87, 181; as shared-sovereignty institution 62; vital interest clause 70–71
'contact hypothesis' 145, 146, 183–84
Cooper, R. 155
corruption 25, 26, 30, 93–94, 99, 106, 108, 109, 143, 151, 160, 173, 180, 181; misuse of aid 101–2.
Cotti, F. 132

Council of the Congress of Bosniak
  Intellectuals 59
Čović, D. 51, 92
Cox, M. 145, 147
crime, organised 25, 51, 94, 99, 125,
  151, 154, 156,
Croat National Council 55
Croatia 18–19, 119, 139, 157;
  democratisation in 35–36; and
  Herzeg-Bosna 48; and Herzegovina
  104; refugees from BiH 126; support
  for Bosnian Croats 34, 156, 163
CRPC (Commission on Real Property
  Claims) 129, 140–41, 149, 181
Czech Republic: privatisation in 103

Dayton Project 121
Denitch, B. 157, 169
Dodik, M. 138, 162, 175; and 2000
  elections 83, 84; and 2002 elections
  92; and 2006 elections 55, 77; and
  constitutional reform 166; and
  minority return 102, 136
Donais, T. 108
DPA (Dayton Peace Agreement) 1, 42,
  73, 176; and consociationalism 44,
  50, 69; contradictory aspects of 17,
  38; the Entities 47–50, 98, 168; ethnic
  discrimination in 53; HDZ challenge
  54; implementation 138;
  international aspects 20–23; local
  views 43, 189n4; negotiations leading
  to 16; proposals to change 54–58;
  reform 163–66; and right to return
  123, 127–33; and statewide
  institutions 45–47, 103; and voting
  rights 75
Drvar 80, 132
Džemidžić, M. 116

ECHR (European Court of Human
  Rights) 62, 140, 181; views on
  electoral rules 89
Elazar, D. 65
election law 87–91
electoral engineering 78–87
electoral reforms 166–68
electoral results: of 1996–98 77–78; of
  2002 92; of 2006 77
electoral system 1996–98 76
ESI (European Stability Initiative) 65,
  69, 161, 163
ethnic cleansing 125; and DPA 127; in
  post-DPA period 23

EU (European Union) 151, 153, 155,
  169, 183; absorption capacity 158;
  BiH accession prospects 154–60;
  'Europeanisation' 33, 152, 159–60;
  police mission of 154; refugees in
  126; and SAA 153, 155, 157, 158,
  161; and SAP 153, 158, 159.
EUFOR (European Force) 154
European Convention on Human
  Rights 32, 74, 88, 116
EUSR (European Union Special
  Representative) 25, 152

Fanon, F. 30
Fearon, J. 30
Federation: 2006 presidential elections
  in 167–68; constituent peoples in 53;
  constituent peoples' case 60, 63–66,
  69–70; constitutional structure of 46–
  48, 59; economic viability 98;
  elections of House of Peoples 84–87;
  HDZ protest 56, 85; NGO legislation
  113–15; poverty 106; property laws
  141, 148; Serb return 132
Ferhadija mosque 117
FDI (Foreign Direct Investment) 105,
  106
Filipović, K. 86
foteljaši 81
Friedman, T. 35, 36
Fukuyama, F. 37

Geneva Convention on Refugees 132
Germany 66, 101; post-war
  reconstruction of 28; Bosnian
  refugees in 126, 131, 189n6
Glenny, M. 35
Gramsci, A. 77, 171

Halilović, S. 86
Han Pijesak 32
Hayden, R. 34, 46, 62
Hays, D. 121, 164, 180
HDZ (Croat Democratic Union) 54,
  56, 75, 76, 163; and Aluminij Mostar
  105; attitude towards refugee return
  128; and constitutional commissions
  63–64; in Croatia 156; in Drvar 132;
  and Herceg-Bosna 48; protest against
  'Barry Rule' 84–85
HDZ 1990 (New Croatian Democratic
  Union 1990) 77, 166
Helsinki Committee for Human Rights
  116, 117

Herceg-Bosna 48, 85
Herzegovina 104, 128, 141, 183
historical determinists 2–3; 28, 33–34,
  67; author's criticism of 34–37
Holbrooke, R. 20, 42, 84, 137, 162, 164
Horowitz, D. 78
Human Rights Chamber 116, 117
Hungary: privatisation in 103

ICC (International Criminal Court)
  152
ICG (International Crisis Group) 79,
  85
ICTY (International Criminal Tribunal
  for the Former Yugoslavia) 24, 137,
  189n13; views about Truth and
  Reconciliation Commission 120
IEBL (Inter Entity Boundary Line) 16,
  23, 157, 168
IFOR (Implementation Force) 128,
  138; mandate 21 *see also* NATO
Igman Initiative 119–20, 156
Ignatieff, M. 29
Inter-Agency Working Group on
  Employment 149
Inter-Church Council of the
  Netherlands 120
International Centre for Not-for-Profit
  Law 114
International Commission on the
  Balkans 152
International Federation of Human
  Rights 120
IPTF (International Police Task Force)
  128, 132
Istočni Stari Grad 80
Ivanić, M. 64, 77, 86, 92
Izetbegović, A. 59, 75

Janja 148
Japan: post-war reconstruction 28
Jelavić, A. 54
Jelisić, G. 137

Kaldor, M. 125
Kalesija 118, 122
Kalinić, D. 64
Karadžić, R. 31, 32, 75, 93
Kaufmann, C. 33, 36, 40
Keskiner, E. 168
Komšić I. 55
Komšić, Ž. 167
Kosovo 66, 125
Kostajinica 146

Kozarac 138
Križanović, J. 54
Kukić, S. 117

Lagumdžia, Z. 64, 86
Laitin, D. 30
Lajčák, M. 25, 153
Lautemberg Amendment 137, 147,
  190n9
LEA/LINK (Law Education Advocacy
  and Networking) 113–15
Lijphart, A. 44, 49
Linz, J. 17
Loizides, N. 168
Loza, T. 39

Malcolm, N. 20
Mann, M. 27
Marović, S. 120
Matić, B. 86, 87
Mazowiecki, T. 69
Mill, J. S. 2
Miller, T. 62
Milošević, S. 35
MMCs (Multi-member constituencies)
  82
Modrica 145
Morawiec Mansfield, A. 49, 62
Mostar 101
Mrakovica-Sarajevo agreement 63–64,
  65
(MZ) *mjesna zajednica* 118

national anthem 4
NATO (North Atlantic Treaty
  Organization) 15, 21, 23, 75, 125,
  138, 168, 169, 174; return policy 133,
  136, 139 *see also* IFOR and SFOR
NDI (National Democratic Institute)
  99
neglected areas strategy 111–12
New Croatian Initiative 77
'new wars' 125
NGOs (Non-governmental
  Organisations) 11, 97, 109, 118, 119,
  122; legal framework for 112–15;
  problems with international support
  110–12, 122, 170–72
Nowak, M. 54

OHR (Office of the High
  Representative) 21–22, 24, 32, 45,
  117, 153, 156, 178; accountability of
  38–39; aid coordination 100;

ambivalence towards refugee return 133; attempt to foster local ownership 52, 62, 109, 172; and Bonn powers 24, 25, 31, 58, 64–65, 78, 93, 115, 164, 176–78; EU mandate of 152; imposition of constitutional amendments 64–66; imposition of property laws 141, 148; establishment of constitutional commissions 63–64; role in democratisation 57–58
open cities 135
OSCE (Organisation for Security and Cooperation in Europe) 22, 24, 91, 120, 132, 178, 181; assessment of constitutional reforms 67; electoral rules 80–87; misuse of Belgian example 80, 89–90
Oštra Luka 80
Owen, D. 34

Pack, D. 31
Pajić, Z. 54
Paravać, B. 93
Paris, R. 26, 29,
Partnership for Peace Programme 93, 155
Pasalić, A. 147
Pavić, M. 147
PDP (Party of Democratic Progress) 2, 77, 86
Peacebuilding Commission 8, 184
Petritsch 24, 85, 152–53, 186n5; constituent peoples' case 62–65
PIC (Peace Implementation Council) 22, 23, 24, 25, 109, 137, 149, 152, 178, 184–85; and electoral engineering 79; Steering Board 22, 152
Plavišić, B. 83, 138
PLIP (Property Law Implementation Plan) 141, 143–44
Poplašen, N. 83
Popper, K. 41
Prce, M. 56
Prijedor 24, 121, 124–25, 134; impact of return 146–47; refugee return 137–39, 140, 183; UNHCR policy 138–39

Raguz, V. M. 56
Rees, M. 116
refugees and displaced persons 12; and constituent peoples' case 60–61; Croat and Serb opposition to return

127–28; forced repatriation 131–34; impact of return 144–47, 183; right to return 59, 125–27; obstacles to return 127–31; successful return 139–44; sustainability of return 147–49; and voting rights 90–91 *see also* UNHCR
Rehn, O. 154
Reilly, B. 79
RRTF (Regional Return Task Force) 139
RS (*Republika Srpska*)132, 136, 140, 147, 162, 163, 169, 181, 182; anthem 71; constitutional structure 48–49; constituent peoples in 53; constituent peoples' case 60, 63–66, 69–70; economic viability 98; minority return 132, 136, 138–39, 144; police reform 157; poverty 106; property laws 141, 148; NGO legislation 113–15; unemployment 148;
Rumsfeld, D. 151

SAA (Stabilisation and Association Agreement) 153
Sali-Terzić, S. 114
Sanski Most 124–25, 134
SAP (Stabilisation and Association Process) 153
Sarajevo 128, 135–36
Sarajevo canton 92
Šarović, M. 64, 92, 93
SBiH (Party for Bosnia) 2, 76, 85, 86; and constitutional reform 55, 166
SCC (Serb Civic Council) 58–59, 61, 119, 176.
Schwarz-Schilling, C. 25, 39, 153, 186n
SDA (Party for Democratic Action) 55, 64, 76, 85, 90, 92, 147
SDP (Social Democratic Party) 54, 64, 81, 85, 86, 92, 167
SDS (Serb Democratic Party) 86, 93, 128, 146, 147; and 2000 elections 83, 85; and 2002 elections 92
Serbia 18, 25, 119, 120, 139, 154, 156, 157, 162; democratisation 35–36; and RS 64, 104; refugees from BiH 126
Ševo, N. 146
SFOR (Stabilisation Force) 23, 93, 96, 137, 154, 175 *see also* NATO
shared sovereignty institutions 6, 32, 62, 66, 169, 173, 178, 181
Silajdžić, H. 55, 76, 167; and constitutional reform 166

Smillie, I. 110, 111
Smith, L. 138
SNS (Serb People's Alliance) 86
SNSD (Party of Independent Social
    Democrats) 2, 77, 86, 92, 146
Sokolović, D. 30
Solana, J. 25,
SPRS (Socialist Party of the RS) 86
Stability Pact for South East Europe
    52, 120, 159, 189n10
Stakić, M. 137
Stateness problem 17–18, 33–34, 95,
    109, 166
Stepan, A. 17
Stokes, G. 34
strong interventionists 3, 28, 29–30;
    author's criticism of 30–33
South Africa 148; consociationalism in
    49–50

Tadić, M. 51
Tanović, D. 159
TI (Transparency International) 102
Tihić, S. 92, 182
Tito, J. B. 118
Todorović, B. 110, 117
Trebinje 145
Truth and Reconciliation Commission
    120–21, 122
Tudman, F. 48, 156, 163
Tuzla canton 92

Udovički, J. 98
Udreženja gradjana 118
UNHCR (United Nations High
    Commissioner for Refugees) 140;
    housing reconstruction 133; minority
    return policy 13–16, 141, 143, 149;
    and repatriation 131–33, 149; and
    return to Prijedor 138, 147; statistics
    on minority returns of 142

United States 40, 62, 156, 186n2; aid
    conditionality 100; Alliance for
    Change 85–86; BiH election 74–75,
    85; constitutional reform 164–66;
    'contact hypothesis' 145;
    disengagement from BiH 151–52;
    and the DPA 16–17, 176; and
    international deployment 20–23;
    peace enforcement 137–38; and PIC
    22, 184; policy towards Prijedor 137,
    147; reconstruction 133; SFOR
    mandate 96, 154; 'Vietmalia
    syndrome' 20; 'war on terror' 115–
    17, 151–52; and weapons 170
United States Institute of Peace 120, 164
USAID (United States Agency for
    International Development) 104

Varshney, A. 184
Vehabović, M. 70
Venice Commission 87, 88, 161, 163;
    opinion on constitutional reform
    165–66; opinion on electoral reform
    166–68 *see also* Council of Europe
VOPP (Vance-Owen Peace Plan) 34

Zenica 130
Zubak, K. 76

Wahabism 2,
Walter, B. 33,
Waters, T. 34
Westendorp, C. 24, 59, 186n5
Wilsonianism 15, 26–27,
Woodward, S. 107, 128, 144
World Bank 112, 118, 133; aid policy
    100; privatisation policy 102–3, 105,
    107

Yugoslavia 18–20, 27, 31;
    consociationalism in 69